HAMMOND®

Family Reference
WORLD ATLAS

DOUBLEDAY & COMPANY, INC.

GARDEN CITY   NEW YORK

Contents

GAZETTEER-INDEX OF THE WORLD

ABBREVIATIONS

Aust.	—Australian	I.	—Island	Rep. —Republic	U.K. —United Kingdom
Br.	—British	Is.	—Islands	S. —South	U.S.A. —United States of
Cond.	—Condominium	It.	—Italian or Italy	S. Afr.—South Africa	America
Den.	—Danish or Denmark	N.	—North	Sp. —Spain or Spanish	U.S.S.R. —Union of Soviet
E.	—East	Neth.—Netherlands		sq. mi. —square miles	Socialist Republics
Eq. Guin. —Equatorial Guinea		N.Z. —New Zealand		S.S.R.—Soviet Socialist Republic	W. —West
Fr.	—France or French	pen. —peninsula		Terr. —Territory	
Fr. Poly. —French Polynesia		Port. —Portugal or Portuguese		Trust. —Trust Territory	

Country	Area (Square Miles)	Population	Index Ref.	Plate No.
Afghanistan	250,775	19,280,000	A 2	48
Africa	11,707,000	431,900,000	......	62–65
Alabama, U.S.A.	51,609	3,665,000	......	104–105
Alaska, U.S.A.	586,412	382,000	......	106–107
Albania	11,100	2,482,000	E 5	35
Alberta, Canada	255,285	1,838,037	......	96-97
Algeria	919,591	16,776,000	G 5	62
American Samoa	76	30,000	K 7	56
Andorra	188	26,558	G 1	27
Angola	481,351	6,761,000	K14	64
Antarctica	5,500,000	....	......	11
Antigua and Dependencies (Br.)	171	73,000	G 3	77
Argentina	1,072,070	23,983,000	......	70
Arizona, U.S.A.	113,909	2,270,000	......	108–109
Arkansas, U.S.A.	53,104	2,109,000	......	110–111
Armenian S.S.R., U.S.S.R.	11,506	2,491,900	F 6	37
Ascension I., St. Helena..	34	1,146	D13	64
Asia	17,128,500	2,535,333,000	......	42–43
Australia	2,967,909	13,684,900	......	58–59
Australian Capital Terr.	939	204,200	H 7	59
Austria	32,375	7,540,000	B 3	32
Azerbaidzhan S.S.R., U.S.S.R.	33,436	5,117,100	G 6	37
Azores, Portugal	902	275,900	B 4	62
Bahamas	5,382	197,000	C 1	76
Bahrain	240	300,000	F 4	44
Balearic Islands, Spain	1,936	558,287	H 3	27
Bangladesh	55,126	82,900,000	G 4	48
Barbados	166	253,620	G 4	77
Belgium	11,781	9,813,000	C 6	20
Belize	8,867	122,000	B 1	78
Benin	43,483	3,200,000	G10	62
Bermuda (Br.)	21	52,000	G 2	77
Bhutan	18,147	1,200,000	G 3	48
Bismarck Arch., Papua New Guinea	18,976	209,051	E 6	56
Bolivia	424,163	4,804,000	G 7	68
Bophuthatswana, S. Africa	15,571	1,174,200	M17	65
Botswana	224,764	700,000	L16	65
Brazil	3,284,426	90,840,000	......	69,71
British Columbia, Canada....	366,255	2,466,608	......	98–99
British Indian Ocean Terr.	29	600	L10	43
Brunei	2,226	155,000	E 4	54
Bulgaria	42,823	8,800,000	G 4	34
Burma	261,789	31,240,000	A 2	53
Burundi	10,747	4,100,000	N12	65
California, U.S.A.	158,693	21,520,000	......	112–113
Cambodia	69,898	8,110,000	D 4	53
Cameroon	183,568	6,600,000	J10	62
Canada	3,851,809	22,992,604	......	84–85
Canal Zone (U.S.A.)	647	44,650	E 3	79
Canary Islands, Spain..	2,808	1,170,224	B 4	26
Cape of Good Hope, South Africa	261,705	2,794,873	L18	65
Cape Verde	1,557	302,000	N 5	9
Caroline Is., Terr. of the Pacific Islands......	463	54,563	E 5	56
Cayman Is. (Br.)	100	10,652	B 3	76
Celebes, Indonesia	72,986	7,665,000	G 6	55
Central African Empire	236,293	1,800,000	K10	63
Central America	197,575	19,800,000	......	78–79
Ceylon (Sri Lanka)	25,332	14,000,000	E 7	49
Chad	495,752	4,178,000	K 8	63
Channel Is. (Br.)	74	128,000	E 6	17
Chatham Is., N. Z.	372	716	J10	56
Chile	292,257	8,834,820	......	70
China (mainland)	3,691,000	853,000,000	......	50–51
China (Taiwan)	13,971	16,426,386	K 7	51
Christmas I., Aust.	52	3,032	O11	43
Cocos Is., Aust.	5.4	604	N11	43
Colombia	439,513	21,117,000	F 3	68
Colorado, U.S.A.	104,247	2,583,000	......	114–115
Comoros	719	266,000	P14	65
Congo	132,046	1,400,000	J12	64
Connecticut, U.S.A.	5,009	3,117,000	......	116–117
Cook Is. (N.Z.)	91	17,046	K 7	56
Corsica, France	3,352	269,831	A 6	25
Costa Rica	19,575	1,800,000	E 5	79
Crete, Greece	3,218	483,075	G 8	35
Cuba	44,206	8,589,000	B 2	76
Curaçao, Netherlands Antilles	182	196,170	E 4	77
Cyprus	3,473	640,000	E 5	46
Czechoslovakia	49,373	14,900,000	D 2	32
Daito Is., Japan	17	2,359	M 6	51
Delaware, U.S.A.	2,057	582,000	......	139
Denmark	16,629	5,065,313	E 9	19
District of Columbia, U.S.A.	67	702,000	B 5	138
Djibouti	8,880	250,000	P 9	63
Dominica	290	70,302	G 4	77
Dominican Republic	18,704	4,188,000	D 3	77
Ecuador	109,483	6,194,000	E 4	68
Egypt	386,650	37,900,000	M 6	63
El Salvador	8,260	3,480,000	C 4	78
England, U.K.	50,516	46,417,600	......	17
Equatorial Guinea	10,831	320,000	H11	62,64
Estonian S.S.R., U.S.S.R.	17,413	1,357,000	C 3	36
Ethiopia	471,776	27,946,000	O 9	63
Europe	4,057,000	666,116,000	......	14–15
Faerøe Is., Den.	540	39,000	D 2	14
Falkland Is. & Dependencies (Br.)	6,198	1,905	H14	71
Fiji	7,055	569,468	H 7	56
Finland	130,128	4,729,000	O 5	18
Florida, U.S.A.	58,560	8,421,000	......	118–119
France	210,038	53,300,000	......	24–25
French Guiana	35,135	51,000	K 3	69
French Polynesia	1,544	135,000	M 7	56

Country	Area (Square Miles)	Population	Index Ref.	Plate No.
Gabon	103,346	526,000	J12	64
Gambia	4,127	524,000	C 9	62
Georgia, U.S.A.	58,876	4,970,000	......	120-121
Georgian S.S.R., U.S.S.R.	26,911	4,688,000	F 6	37
Germany, East (German Democratic Republic)	41,768	16,850,000		22-23
Germany, West (Federal Republic of)	95,985	61,846,000	......	22-23
Ghana	92,099	9,900,000	F10	62
Gibraltar (Br.)	2	30,000	D 4	26
Gilbert Islands (Br.)	354	47,711	H 6	56
Great Britain & Northern Ireland (United Kingdom)	94,399	56,076,000	......	16-17
Greece	50,944	9,046,000	F 6	35
Greenland (Den.)	840,000	54,000	B12	10
Grenada	133	96,000	G 6	77
Guadeloupe and Dependencies (Fr.)	687	332,000	F 3	77
Guam (U.S.A.)	212	111,000	E 4	56
Guatemala	42,042	5,348,000	B 3	78
Guinea	94,925	4,500,000	D 9	62
Guinea-Bissau	13,948	517,000	C 9	62
Guyana	83,000	763,000	J 2	69
Haiti	10,694	4,969,000	D 3	76
Hawaii, U.S.A.	6,450	887,000	......	122
Holland (Netherlands)	15,892	13,800,000	E 4	20
Honduras	43,277	2,751,000	D 3	78
Hong Kong (Br.)	403	4,400,000	J 7	51
Hungary	35,919	10,590,000	E 3	33
Iceland	39,768	220,000	C 2	14
Idaho, U.S.A.	83,557	831,000	......	123
Illinois, U.S.A.	56,400	11,229,000	......	124-125
India	1,269,339	605,614,000	......	48-49
Indiana, U.S.A.	36,291	5,302,000	......	126-127
Indonesia	788,430	131,255,000	......	54-55
Iowa, U.S.A.	56,290	2,870,000	......	128-129
Iran	636,293	32,900,000	F 3	45
Iraq	172,476	11,400,000	D 3	44
Ireland	27,136	3,109,000	B 4	17
Israel	7,847	3,459,000	......	47
Italy	116,303	56,110,000	......	28-29
Ivory Coast	127,520	6,673,013	E10	62
Jamaica	4,411	1,989,000	C 3	76
Japan	145,730	112,200,000	......	52
Java, Indonesia	48,842	69,323,000	K 2	55
Jordan	37,737	2,700,000	......	47
Kalâtdlit-Nunât (Greenland)	840,000	54,000	B12	10
Kampuchea (Cambodia)	69,898	8,110,000	D 4	53
Kansas, U.S.A.	82,264	2,310,000	......	130-131
Kazakh S.S.R., U.S.S.R. ...	1,048,300	14,185,000	G 5	38
Kentucky, U.S.A.	40,395	3,428,000	......	132-133
Kenya	224,960	13,300,000	O11	65
Kirgiz S.S.R., U.S.S.R. ..	76,641	2,933,000	H 5	38
Korea, North	46,540	17,000,000	C 2	52
Korea, South	38,175	34,688,079	C 3	52
Kuwait	6,532	1,100,000	E 4	44
Laos	91,428	3,500,000	D 3	53
Latvian S.S.R., U.S.S.R. ..	24,595	2,365,000	B 3	36
Lebanon	4,015	3,207,000	F 6	46
Lesotho	11,720	1,100,000	M17	65
Liberia	43,000	1,600,000	E10	62
Libya	679,358	2,500,000	K 6	62-63
Liechtenstein	61	25,000	J 3	31
Lithuanian S.S.R., U.S.S.R.	25,174	3,129,000	B 3	36
Louisiana, U.S.A.	48,523	3,841,000	......	134-135
Luxembourg	999	358,000	H 8	20
Macao (Port.)	6.2	300,000	H 7	51
Madagascar	226,657	7,700,000	R15	65
Madeira Is., Portugal	307	249,300	A 2	26
Maine, U.S.A.	33,215	1,070,000	......	136-137
Malawi	45,747	5,100,000	N14	65
Malaya, Malaysia	50,806	9,000,000	C 7	53
Malaysia	128,308	12,368,000	C-F 4	54
Maldives	115	136,000	L 9	43
Mali	464,873	5,800,000	E 9	62
Malta	122	319,000	E 7	29
Man, Isle of (Br.)	227	59,000	D 3	17
Manitoba, Canada	251,000	1,021,506	......	92-93
Mariana Is., Terr. of the Pacific Islands	182	11,827	E 4	56
Marquesas Is., Fr. Poly.	492	5,174	N 6	56
Marshall Is., Terr. Pac. Is.	69	19,328	H 4	56
Martinique (Fr.)	425	341,000	G 4	77
Maryland, U.S.A.	10,577	4,144,000	......	138-139
Massachusetts, U.S.A.	8,257	5,809,000	......	140-141
Mauritania	452,702	1,318,000	D 8	62
Mauritius	790	899,000	S19	65
Mayotte (Fr.)	144	40,000	P14	65
Mexico	761,601	50,900,000	......	80-81
Michigan, U.S.A.	58,216	9,104,000	......	142-143
Midway Is. (U.S.A.)	2	2,220	H 3	56
Minnesota, U.S.A.	84,068	3,965,000	......	144-145
Mississippi, U.S.A.	47,716	2,354,000	......	146-147
Missouri, U.S.A.	69,686	4,778,000	......	148-149
Moldavian S.S.R., U.S.S.R.	13,012	3,823,000	C 5	37
Monaco	368 acres	23,610	G 6	25
Mongolia	606,163	1,500,000	E-H 2	50-51
Montana, U.S.A.	147,138	753,000	......	150-151
Montserrat (Br.)	40	12,302	G 3	77
Morocco	241,224	18,000,000	E 5	62
Mozambique	308,641	9,300,000	O15	65
Namibia (South-West Africa)	317,827	883,000	K16	64-65
Natal, S. Afr.	33,578	4,315,847	N17	65
Nauru	7.7	8,000	G 6	56
Nebraska, U.S.A.	77,227	1,553,000	......	152-153
Nepal	54,663	12,900,000	E-F 3	49
Netherlands	15,892	13,800,000	E 4	20
Netherlands Antilles	390	223,558	E 4	77
Nevada, U.S.A.	110,540	610,000	......	154
New Britain, Papua New Guinea	14,098	138,689	F 6	56
New Brunswick, Canada	28,354	677,250	C 3	86
New Caledonia & Dependencies (Fr.)	7,335	136,000	G 8	56
Newfoundland, Canada	156,185	557,725	J 4	86
New Hampshire, U.S.A.	9,304	822,000	......	155
New Hebrides (Br.-Fr. Cond.)	5,700	97,468	G 7	56
New Jersey, U.S.A.	7,836	7,336,000	......	156-157
New Mexico, U.S.A.	121,666	1,168,000	......	158-159
New South Wales, Aust.	309,433	4,847,800	H 6	59
New York, U.S.A.	49,576	18,084,000	......	160-161
New Zealand	103,736	3,121,904	M 7	59
Nicaragua	45,698	1,984,000	E 4	78
Niger	489,189	4,634,000	H 8	62
Nigeria	379,628	83,800,000	H10	62
Niue (N. Z.)	100	2,992	K 7	56
Norfolk I., Aust.	13.3	1,870	G 8	56
North America	9,363,000	314,000,000	......	74-75
North Carolina, U.S.A.	52,586	5,469,000	......	162-163
North Dakota, U.S.A.	70,665	643,000	......	164-165
Northern Ireland, U.K.	5,452	1,537,200	G 3	17
Northern Territory, Aust.	520,280	98,400	E 3	58
Northwest Territories, Canada	1,304,903	42,609	E-J 3	84-85
Norway	125,053	4,027,000	F 6	18
Nova Scotia, Canada	21,425	828,571	......	86-87
Oceania	3,292,000	21,500,000	......	56
Ohio, U.S.A.	41,222	10,690,000	......	166-167
Oklahoma, U.S.A.	69,919	2,766,000.	......	168-169
Oman	120,000	800,000	G 5	45
Ontario, Canada	412,582	8,264,465	......	90-91
Orange Free State, S. Afr.	49,866	1,744,798	M17	65
Oregon, U.S.A.	96,981	2,329,000	......	170-171
Orkney Is., Scotland	376	17,675	E 1	16
Pacific Is., Terr. of the (U.S. Trust)	707	120,000	D-G 5	56
Pakistan	310,403	72,370,000	B 3	48
Palau Is., Terr. Pac. Is.	184	12,291	D 5	56
Panama	29,209	1,444,000	G 6	79
Papua New Guinea	183,540	2,800,000	B 7	54
Paraguay	157,047	2,340,000	J 8	69,71
Pennsylvania, U.S.A.	45,333	11,862,000	......	172-173
Persia (Iran)	636,293	32,900,000	F 3	45
Peru	496,222	13,586,300	E 5	68
Philippines	115,707	43,751,000	H 4	55
Pitcairn Is. (Br.)	18	67	O 8	56
Poland	120,725	34,364,000	......	21
Portugal	35,549	8,825,000	B 3	26
Prince Edward I., Canada..	2,184	118,229	F 3	87
Puerto Rico	3,435	2,712,033	G 2	77

Country	Area (Square Miles)	Population	Index Ref.	Plate No.
Qatar	4,247	150,000	F 4	45
Québec, Canada	594,860	6,234,445		88–89
Queensland, Aust.	666,991	2,015,300	G 4	59
Réunion (Fr.)	969	475,700	R20	65
Rhode Island, U.S.A.	1,214	927,000		141
Rhodesia (Zimbabwe Rhodesia)	150,803	6,600,000	M15	65
Rumania	91,699	21,500,000	G 3	34
Russian S.F.S.R., U.S.S.R.	6,592,812	133,913,000	D–R 4	38–39
Rwanda	10,169	4,241,000	N12	65
Sabah, Malaysia	28,460	633,000	F 4-5	54–55
St. Christopher-Nevis-Anguilla (Br.)	138	62,000	F 3	77
St. Helena & Dependencies (Br.)	162	6,438	E15	64
St. Lucia	238	101,100	G 4	77
St-Pierre & Miquelon (Fr.)	93.5	6,000	H 6	87
St. Vincent & Dependencies (Br.)	150	89,129	G 4	77
Sakhalin, U.S.S.R.	29,500	600,000	P 4	39
San Marino	23.4	19,000	D 2	28
São Tomé e Príncipe	372	80,000	H11	64
Sarawak, Malaysia	48,050	950,000	E 5	54
Sardinia, Italy	9,301	1,473,800	B 4	29
Saskatchewan, Canada	251,700	921,323		94–95
Saudi Arabia	829,995	7,200,000	D 4	44
Scotland, U.K.	30,414	5,261,000	D 2	16
Senegal	75,954	5,085,388	D 9	62
Seychelles	145	60,000	T 6	9
Shetland Is., Scotland	552	18,494	G 1	16
Siam (Thailand)	198,455	42,700,000	C 3	53
Sicily, Italy	9,926	4,680,715	D 6	29
Sierra Leone	27,925	3,100,000	D10	62
Singapore	226	2,300,000	E 6	53
Society Is., Fr. Poly.	677	81,487	L 7	56
Solomon Is.	11,500	196,708	G 6	56
Somalia	246,200	3,170,000	R11	63,65
South Africa	458,179	24,400,000	L18	65
South America	6,875,000	186,000,000		68–71
South Australia, Aust.	380,070	1,247,100	E 5	58
South Carolina, U.S.A.	31,055	2,848,000		174–175
South Dakota, U.S.A.	77,047	686,000		176–177
South-West Africa	317,827	883,000	K16	64–65
Spain	194,881	36,000,000		26–27
Sri Lanka	25,332	14,000,000	E 7	49
Sudan	967,494	18,347,000	M 9	63
Sumatra, Indonesia	164,000	17,345,000	C 6	54
Suriname	55,144	389,000	J 3	69
Svalbard, Norway	23,957	2,808	C 2	18
Swaziland	6,705	500,000	N17	65
Sweden	173,665	8,236,461	J 6	19
Switzerland	15,943	6,489,000		30–31
Syria	71,498	7,585,000	G 5	46
Tadzhik S.S.R., U.S.S.R.	55,251	2,900,000	G 6	38
Tahiti, Fr. Poly.	402	61,519	M 7	56
Tanzania	363,708	15,506,000	N13	65
Tasmania, Aust.	26,383	410,800	J 8	59
Tennessee, U.S.A.	42,244	4,214,000		178–179
Texas, U.S.A.	267,339	12,487,000		180–181

Country	Area (Square Miles)	Population	Index Ref.	Plate No.
Thailand	198,455	42,700,000	C 3	53
Tibet, China	471,660	1,270,000	C 5	50
Togo	21,622	2,300,000	G10	62
Tokelau (N.Z.)	3.9	1,603	J 6	56
Tonga	270	102,000	J 7	56
Transvaal, S. Afr.	109,621	10,971,521	N17	65
Trinidad & Tobago	1,980	1,040,000	G 5	77
Tristan da Cunha, St. Helena	38	292	O 7	9
Tuamotu Arch., French Polynesia	341	6,148	M 7	56
Tunisia	63,170	5,776,000	H 5	62
Turkey	300,946	40,284,000		46
Turkmen S.S.R., U.S.S.R.	188,455	2,158,000	F 6	38
Turks & Caicos Is. (Br.)	166	6,000	D 2	76
Tuvalu	10	5,887	H 6	56
Uganda	91,076	11,400,000	N11	65
Ukrainian S.S.R., U.S.S.R.	233,089	49,438,000	D 5	37
Union of Soviet Socialist Republics	8,649,490	258,402,000		36–39
United Arab Emirates	32,278	240,000	F 5	45
United Kingdom	94,399	56,076,000		16–17
United States of America	land 3,536,855			
	land and water 3,615,123	216,237,000		102–103
Upper Volta	105,869	6,144,013	F 9	62
Uruguay	72,172	2,909,000	J10	71
Utah, U.S.A.	84,916	1,228,000		182
Uzbek S.S.R., U.S.S.R.	173,591	11,963,000	G 5	38
Vatican City	116 acres	704	B 6	29
Venezuela	352,143	10,572,000	G 2	68
Vermont, U.S.A.	9,609	476,000		183
Victoria, Aust.	87,884	3,713,200	G 7	59
Vietnam	128,405	46,600,000	D 3	53
Virginia, U.S.A.	40,817	5,032,000		184–185
Virgin Is. (Br.)	59	10,484	H 1	77
Virgin Is. (U.S.A.)	133	62,468	H 1	77
Wake I. (U.S.A.)	2.5	437	G 4	56
Wales, U.K.	8,017	2,778,000	E 4	17
Wallis & Futuna (Fr.)	106	9,000	H–J 7	56
Washington, U.S.A.	68,192	3,612,000		186–187
Western Australia, Aust.	975,920	1,148,100	C 4	58
Western Samoa	1,133	159,000	J 7	56
West Virginia, U.S.A.	24,181	1,821,000		188–189
White Russian S.S.R., U.S.S.R.	80,154	9,522,000	C 4	37
Wisconsin, U.S.A.	56,154	4,609,000		190–191
World	57,970,000	4,240,700,000		8–9
Wyoming, U.S.A.	97,914	390,000		192
Yemen Arab Republic	77,220	5,600,000	D 7	44
Yemen, Peoples Democratic Republic of	111,101	1,700,000	E 7	44
Yugoslavia	98,766	21,520,000	C 3	34
Yukon Territory, Canada	207,076	21,836	C 3	84
Zaire	918,962	25,600,000	L12	65
Zambia	290,586	4,936,000	M14	65
Zimbabwe Rhodesia	150,803	6,600,000	M15	65

THE SOLAR SYSTEM

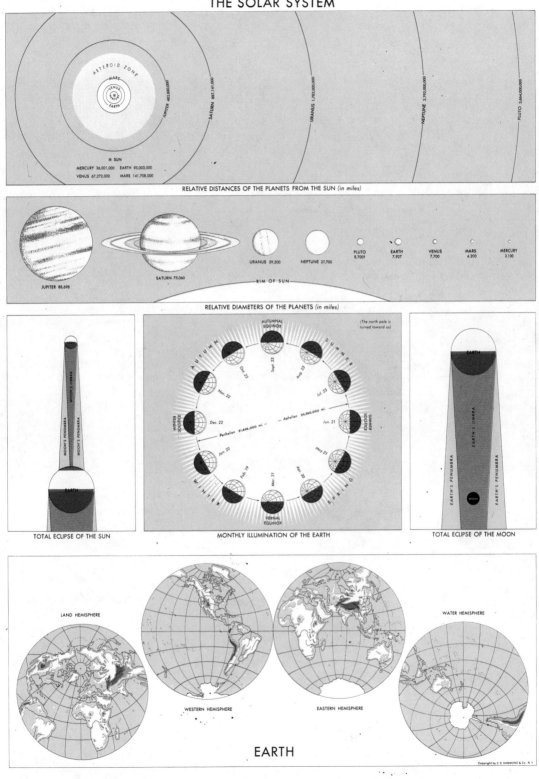

RELATIVE DISTANCES OF THE PLANETS FROM THE SUN (in miles)

RELATIVE DIAMETERS OF THE PLANETS (in miles)

TOTAL ECLIPSE OF THE SUN

MONTHLY ILLUMINATION OF THE EARTH

TOTAL ECLIPSE OF THE MOON

EARTH

THE WORLD

MERCATOR PROJECTION

EQUATORIAL SCALES

MILES

0   500   1000   1500   2000   2500

KILOMETRES

0   500   1000   1500   2000   2500

Capitals of Countries ....●

© C.S. HAMMOND & Co., Maplewood, N.J.

8

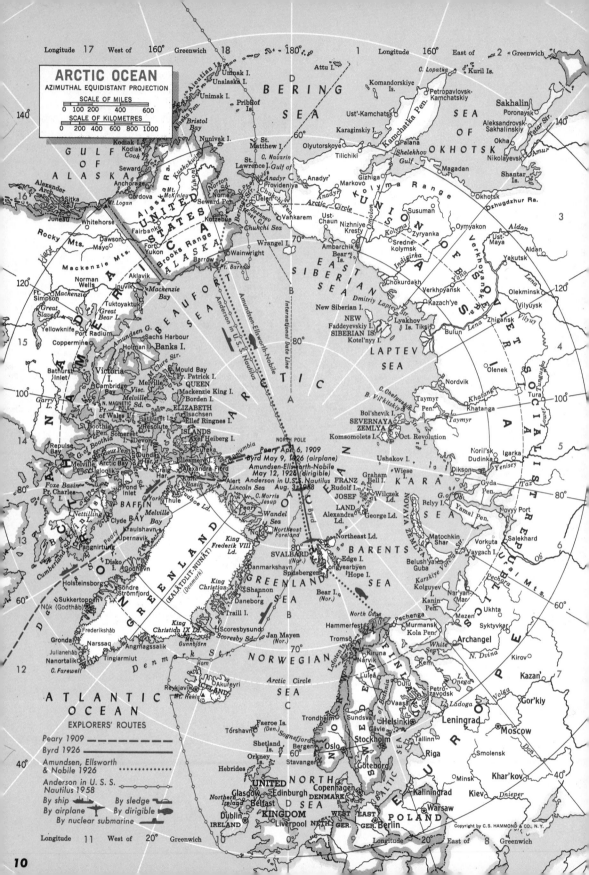

ARCTIC OCEAN — Azimuthal Equidistant Projection

EXPLORERS' ROUTES

- Peary 1909
- Byrd 1926
- Amundsen, Ellsworth & Nobile 1926
- Anderson in U.S.S. Nautilus 1958
- By ship   By sledge
- By airplane   By dirigible
- By nuclear submarine

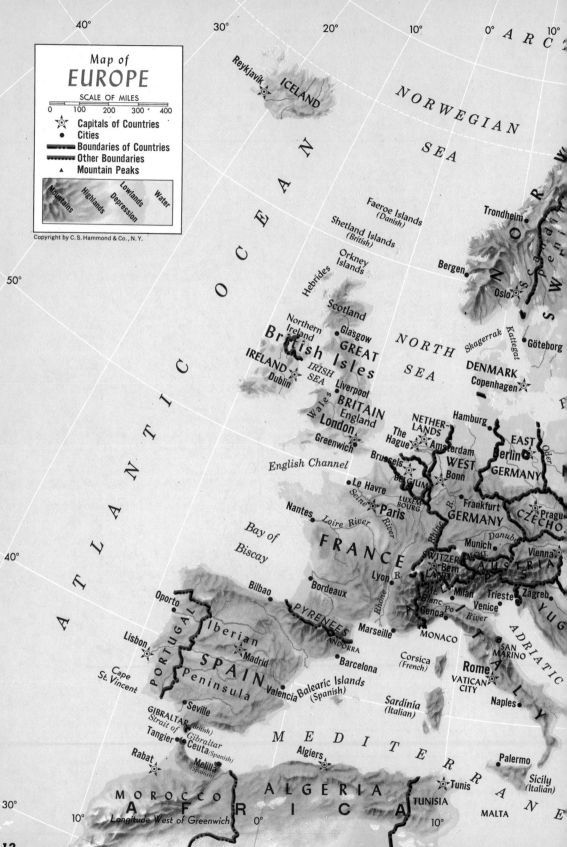

Map of
EUROPE
SCALE OF MILES
0   100   200   300   400

⛤ Capitals of Countries
● Cities
▬▬ Boundaries of Countries
▬▬▬ Other Boundaries
▲ Mountain Peaks

Mountains Highlands Lowlands Depression Water

ARCTIC

NORWEGIAN
SEA

Reykjavik ICELAND

Faeroe Islands
(Danish)

Shetland Islands
(British)

Trondheim

Bergen

Orkney
Islands

Hebrides

Scotland

Oslo

NORWAY

Skagerrak Kattegat Göteborg

Northern
Ireland Glasgow GREAT

NORTH
SEA

DENMARK

British Isles BRITAIN

IRELAND IRISH
SEA Liverpool

Dublin

Wales England

London

Greenwich

Copenhagen

Hamburg

NETHER-
LANDS

The
Hague Amsterdam

EAST
Berlin

English Channel

Brussels
BELGIUM Bonn

WEST
GERMANY

Oder R.

Le Havre

LUXEM-
BOURG

Nantes Seine River Paris

Loire River

Frankfurt
GERMANY

Prague
CZECHO.

Bay of
Biscay

FRANCE

Rhine R.

Munich Danube

SWITZER-
LAND Bern

LIECHT.

Vienna

AUSTRIA

Oporto

Bilbao

PYRENEES

Bordeaux

Lyon R.

Rhône

Mt.
Blanc Milan Trieste Zagreb

Genoa Po Venice

River

YUG

Lisbon

PORTUGAL

Iberian

SPAIN Madrid

Peninsula

ANDORRA

Marseille

MONACO

ITALY

ADRIATIC

Cape
St. Vincent

Valencia Barcelona

Balearic Islands
(Spanish)

Corsica
(French)

SAN
MARINO

Rome

VATICAN
CITY

Sardinia
(Italian)

Naples

Seville

GIBRALTAR
(British)
Strait of
Gibraltar

Tangier Ceuta
(Spanish)

MEDITERRANE

Rabat

Melilla
(Spanish)

Algiers

Palermo

Sicily
(Italian)

MOROCCO

ALGERIA

Tunis

Longitude West of Greenwich

A F R I C A

TUNISIA

MALTA

ATLANTIC OCEAN

NORTH SEA

C   O   C   E   A   N   BARENTS
20°   30°   40°   50°   60°   70°   80°
North Cape   SEA   60°
                                                              Arctic Circle
romsö   • Murmansk   Ob River   Irtysh River

              White
              Sea   • Archangel   • Sverdlovsk
       • Luleå
              Northern Dvina R.   URAL MOUNTAINS
  • Oulu

                    Lake
                    Onega
                    Lake
                    Ladoga   UNION OF SOVIET
  • Helsinki
• Stockholm   Gulf of Finland   Volga River   50°
       • Tallinn   • Leningrad   Gor'kiy Kazan   SOCIALIST REPUBLICS
       Estonia
                              • Moscow   (RUSSIA)
  • Riga   • Kuybyshev
  Latvia   Western Dvina R.   Saratov   Ural River
  Lithuania   •
                                        Don   Volga   Aral
  nzig   • Minsk   Sea
       White   River   River
  • Warsaw   Russia
  Vistula   Dnieper   Volga
OLAND   R.   • Kiev   Khar'kov •   Volgograd
  • Cracow   L'vov U k r a i n e River (Stalingrad)   CASPIAN
CARPATHIAN   • Dniester River   • Astrakhan
OVAKIA   • Rostov   SEA
  • Budapest   Sea of
R. MOUNTAINS   Azov   40°
  • Cluj
  RUMANIA   • Odessa   Crimea   CAUCASUS MOUNTAINS
                                        Mt.
  Bucharest River   BLACK SEA   El'brus • Tbilisi   • Baku
• Belgrade   Danube
  Balkan   SEA
  • Sofia
  BULGARIA
  Tiranë Peninsula   Istanbul Bosporus
ALBANIA GREECE   Salonika Dardanelles   • Ankara   T U R K E Y   • Tehran
                    AEGEAN   IRAN
  • Athens SEA   Tigris R.
  Crete   Euphrates River
  (Greek)   CYPRUS   SYRIA   • Baghdad
A 20°N   30°   LEBANON   40° I R A Q   Longitude East of Greenwich 50°

13

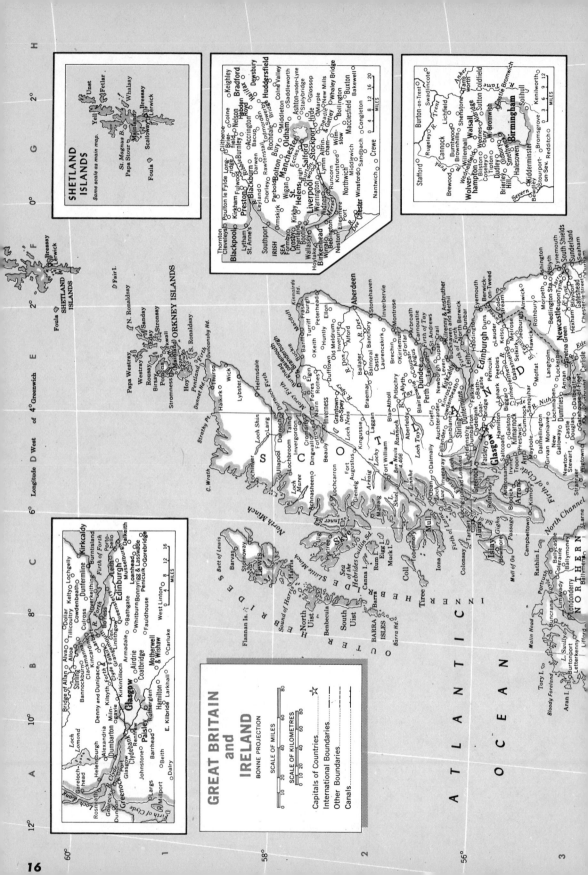

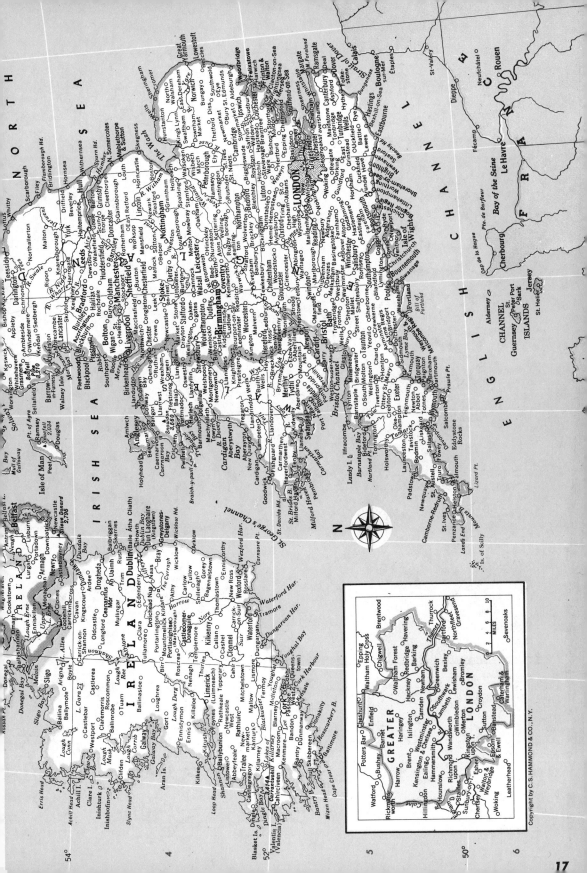

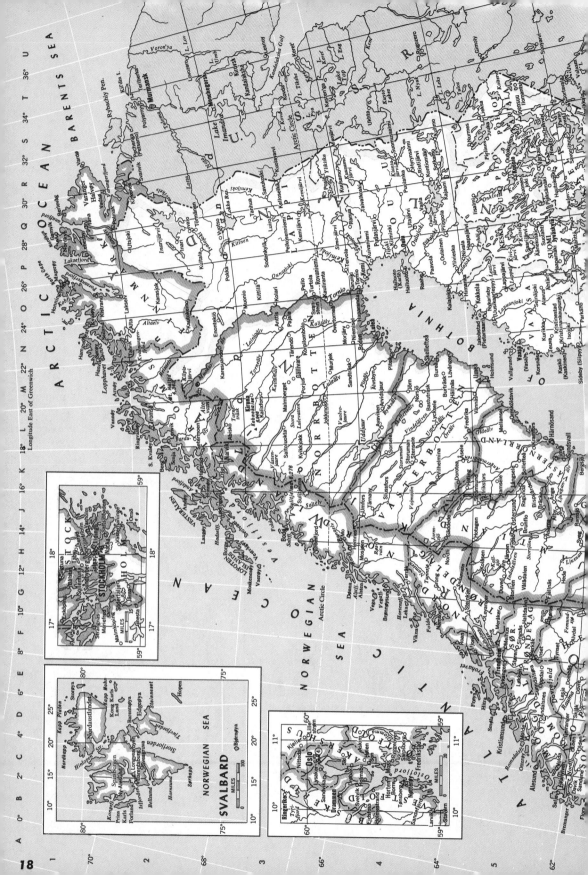

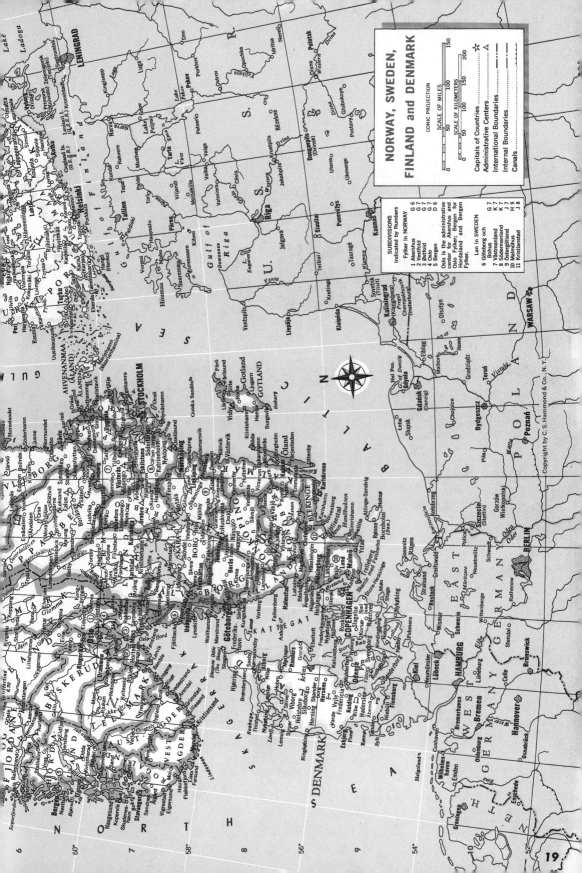

NORWAY, SWEDEN, FINLAND and DENMARK

CONIC PROJECTION

SCALE OF MILES
0   50   100   150

SCALE OF KILOMETERS
0   50   100   150   200

☆ Capitals of Countries ....
△ Administrative Centers ....
International Boundaries ....
Internal Boundaries ....
Canals ....

SUBDIVISIONS
Indicated by Numbers
Fylker in NORWAY

1 Akershus   G 6
2 Vestfold   G 7
3 Østfold   G 7
4 Oslo   D 6
5 Bergen

Oslo is the administrative
center for Akershus and
Østfold Fylker. Bergen for
Hordaland and Bergen
Fylker.

Län in SWEDEN

6 Göteborg och   G 7
   Bohus
7 Västmanland   K 7
8 Södermanland   J 7
9 Östergötland   H 9
10 Malmöhus   J 8
11 Kristianstad

Copyright by C. S. Hammond & Co., N.Y.

19

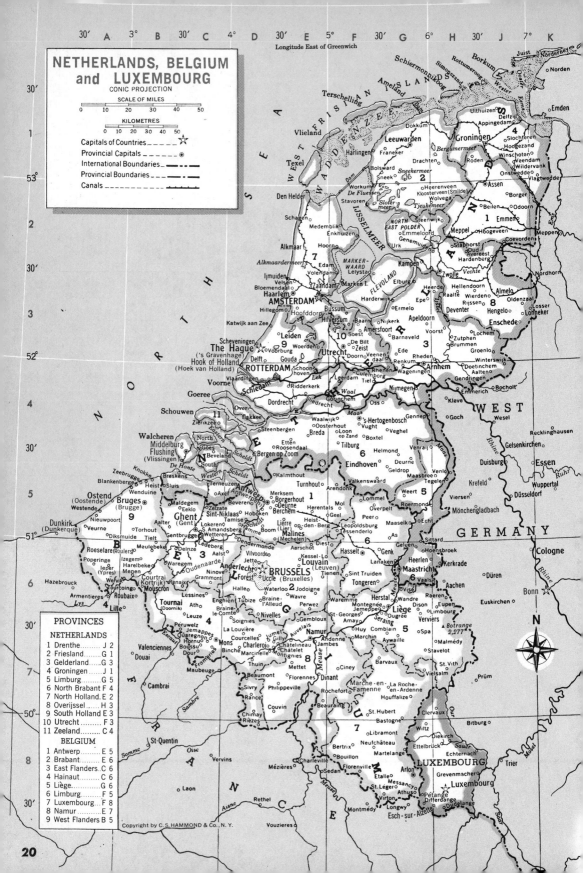

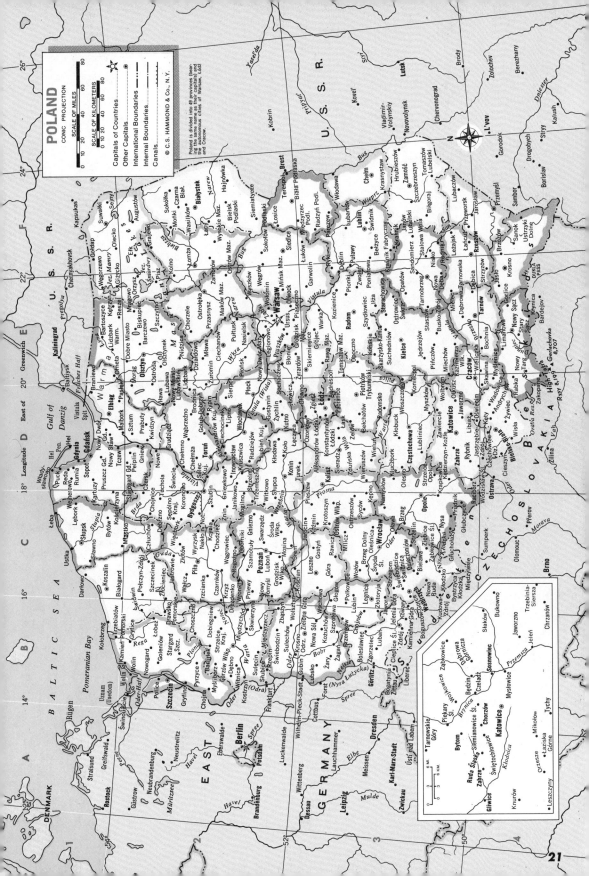

POLAND

CONIC PROJECTION

SCALE OF MILES

0 10 20 40 60 80

SCALE OF KILOMETERS

0 20 40 60 80

Capitals of Countries ⊛
Other Capitals ⊙
International Boundaries — · — · —
Internal Boundaries - - - - - -
Canals ═══════

© C.S. HAMMOND & Co., N.Y.

Poland is divided into 49 provinces, bearing the same names as their capitals and the autonomous cities of Warsaw, Łódź and Cracow.

21

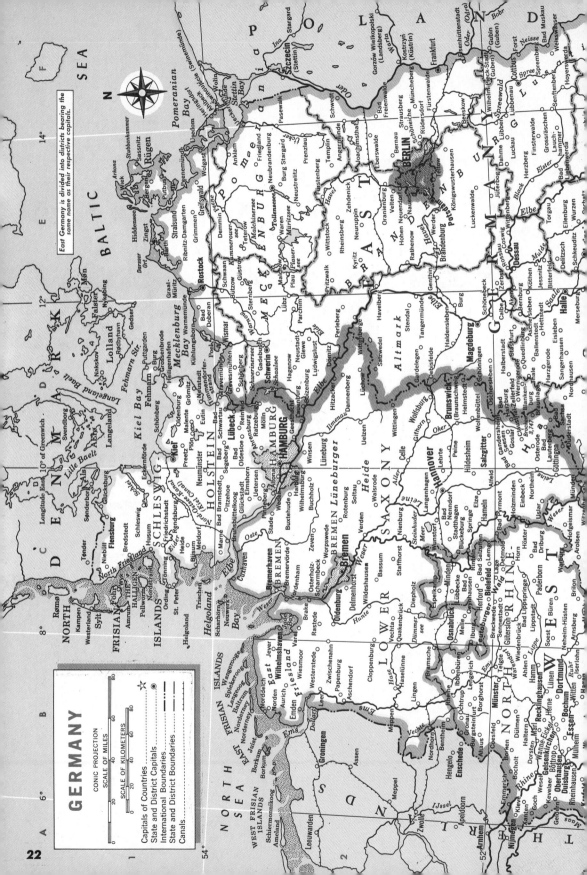

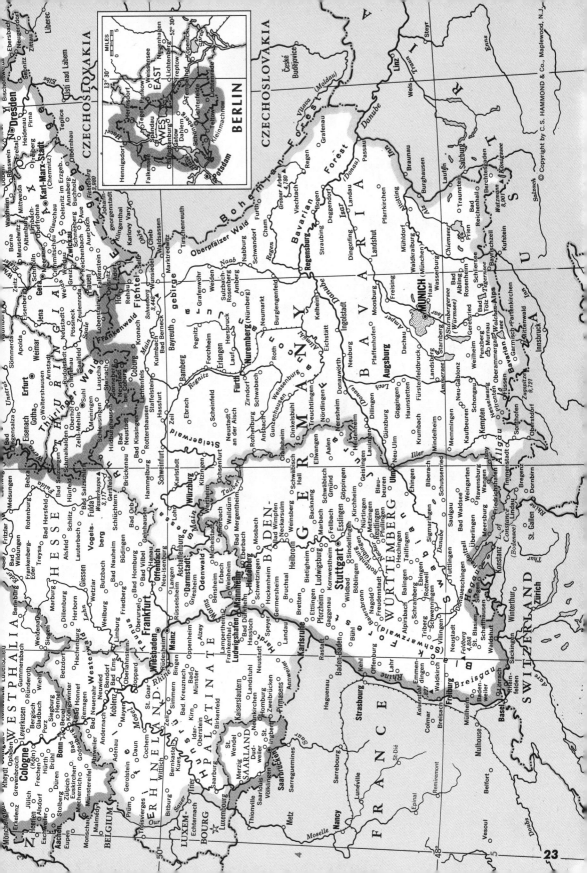

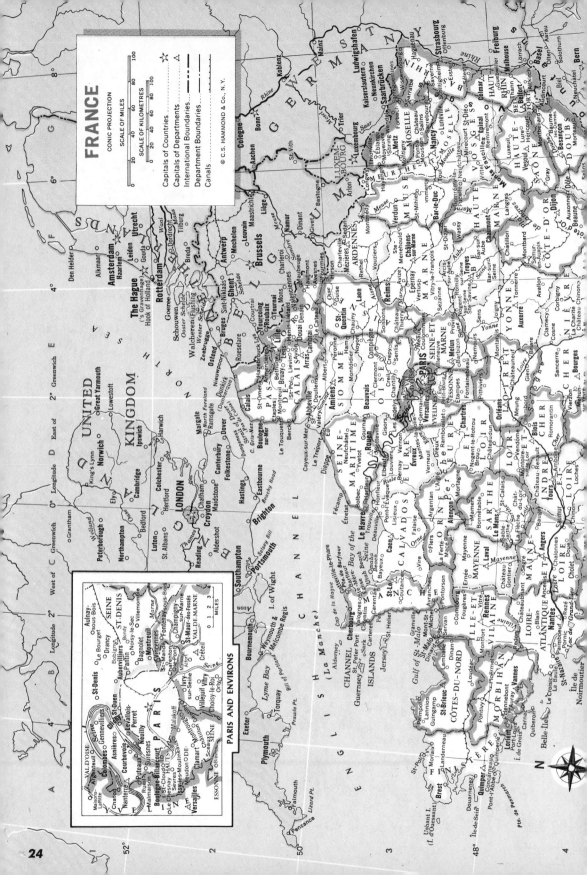

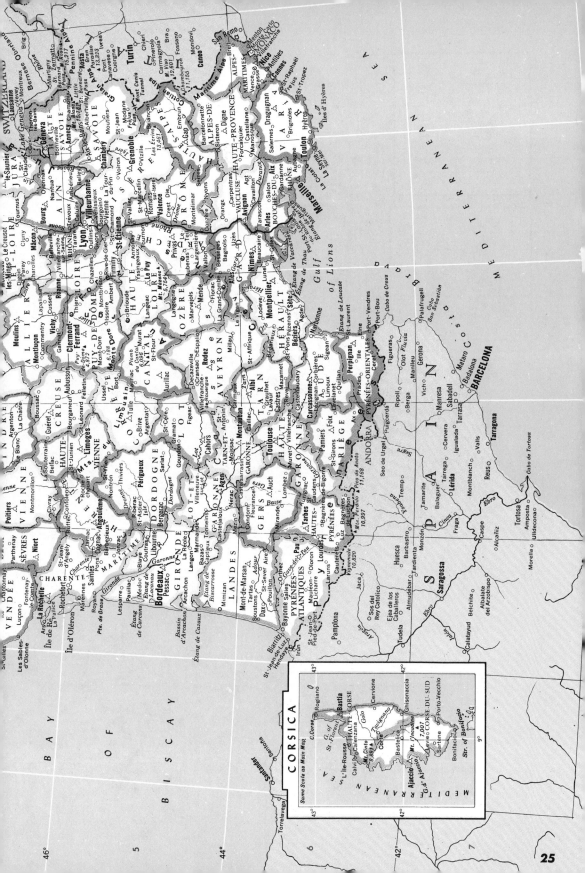

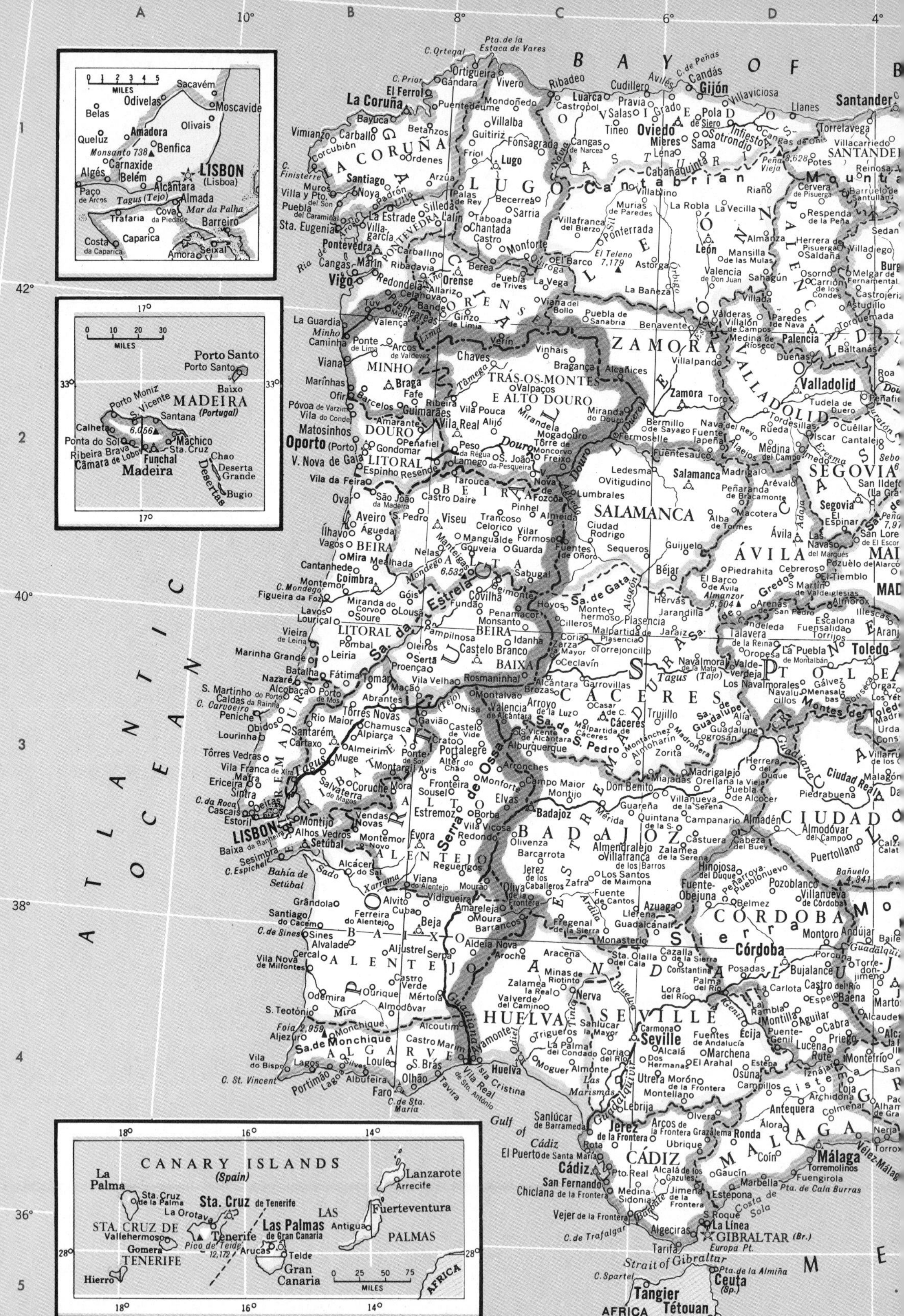

BAY OF B
ATLANTIC OCEAN
CANARY ISLANDS
(Spain)
La Palma
Sta. Cruz de la Palma
Sta. Cruz de Tenerife
La Orotava
Las Palmas de Gran Canaria
LAS PALMAS
STA. CRUZ DE TENERIFE
Lanzarote
Arrecife
Fuerteventura
Tenerife
Gomera
Hierro
Gran Canaria
AFRICA
MADEIRA
(Portugal)
Porto Santo
Funchal
Desertas
LISBON
(Lisboa)
La Coruña
El Ferrol
Santiago
Pontevedra
Vigo
Lugo
Orense
Oviedo
Gijón
Santander
León
Zamora
Valladolid
Salamanca
Segovia
Ávila
Toledo
Cáceres
Badajoz
Ciudad Real
Córdoba
Seville
Huelva
Cádiz
Málaga
Granada
Jerez de la Frontera
Oporto (Porto)
Braga
Coimbra
Aveiro
Viseu
Guarda
Castelo Branco
Portalegre
Évora
Setúbal
Beja
Faro
MINHO
TRÁS-OS-MONTES E ALTO DOURO
DOURO LITORAL
BEIRA LITORAL
BEIRA ALTA
BEIRA BAIXA
ESTREMADURA
RIBATEJO
ALTO ALENTEJO
BAIXO ALENTEJO
ALGARVE
Cantabrian Mountains
Sierra Morena
Sa. da Estrela
Sa. de Gata
Sa. de Guadalupe
Sa. de S. Pedro
Serra de Ossa
Sa. de Monchique
Tagus (Tejo)
Douro
Guadiana
Guadalquivir
Gulf of Cádiz
Strait of Gibraltar
GIBRALTAR (Br.)
La Línea
Tangier
Tétouan
Ceuta (Sp.)
AFRICA
MOROCCO
C. St. Vincent
C. de Trafalgar
C. Finisterre
C. Ortegal

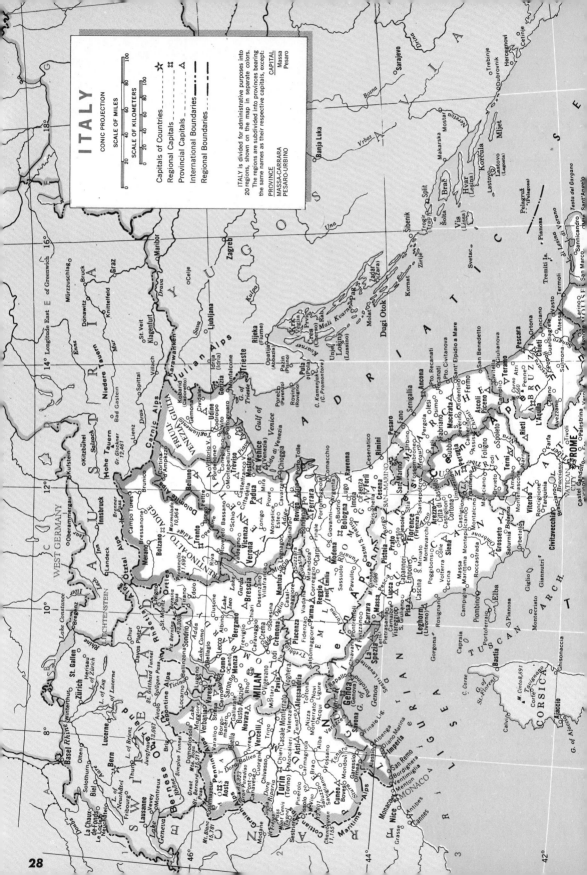

ITALY

CONIC PROJECTION

SCALE OF MILES

SCALE OF KILOMETERS

Capitals of Countries .... ✪
Regional Capitals .... ⌘
Provincial Capitals .... △
International Boundaries .... ▬▬▬
Regional Boundaries .... ▬ ▪ ▬

ITALY is divided for administrative purposes into
20 regions, shown on the map in separate colors.
The regions are subdivided into provinces bearing
the same names as their respective capitals, except:

PROVINCE	CAPITAL
MASSA-CARRARA	Massa
PESARO-URBINO	Pesaro

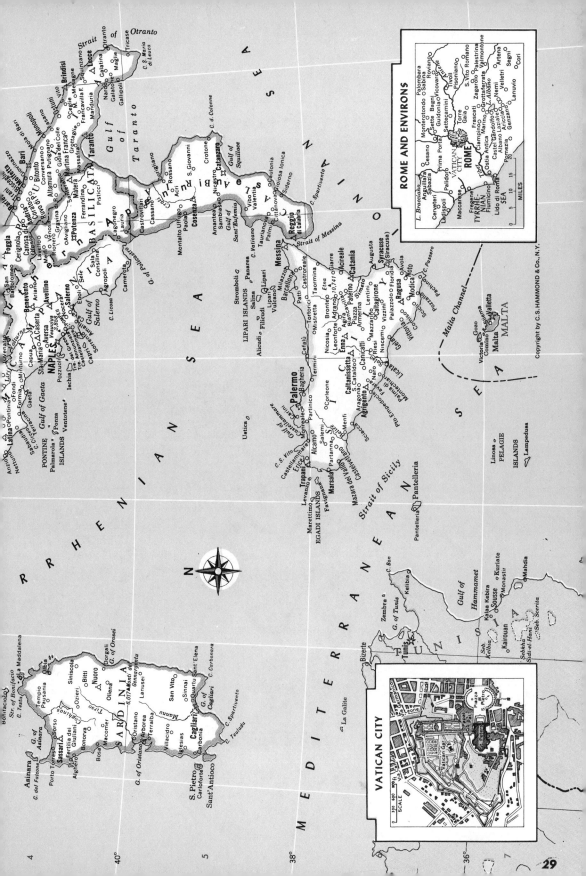

SWITZERLAND
and
LIECHTENSTEIN
CONIC PROJECTION

SCALE OF MILES

0   5   10   20   30

SCALE OF KILOMETRES

0 5 10   20   30   40   50

Capitals of Countries .... ☆
Capitals of Cantons .... ◉
International Boundaries .... ▄▄▄▄
Canals ....

® Copyright HAMMOND INCORPORATED, Maplewood, N. J.

31

© C. S. HAMMOND & Co., N. Y.

THE
BALKAN STATES

CONIC PROJECTION

SCALE OF MILES

0   25   50   75   100   125   150   175

SCALE OF KILOMETRES

0   25   50   75   100   125   150   175

Capitals of Countries ---------- ✵

Administrative Centers --------- ⬡

International Boundaries --------

Major Internal Boundaries ------

Minor Internal Boundaries ·······

Canals ------------------------

BULGARIA and GREECE are divided into counties and departments, respectively. Because of the scale no attempt has been made to delimit and name these subdivisions; their administrative centers have, however, been designated. The larger divisions named in Greece are well-known geographical regions, without administrative function.
RUMANIA consists of thirty-nine counties and three cities of regional status, Bucharest, Constanța and Petroșeni. Scale does not permit delimiting these counties.
ALBANIA is divided into twenty-seven districts. Scale does not permit the delimitation of these divisions.
YUGOSLAVIA is a federation of six republics. The Serbian republic includes an autonomous province (Voyvodina), and an autonomous region (Kosovo-Mitohiyan).

35

UNION OF SOVIET SOCIALIST REPUBLICS
European Part

CONIC PROJECTION

SCALE OF MILES

50   100   200   300

SCALE OF KILOMETRES

0   50 100   200   300

National Capitals............................☆
Capitals of Union Republics...............⊠
Administrative Centers......................△
International boundaries....................
Union Republic boundaries.................
A.S.S.R., Oblast, Kray boundaries......
Autonomous Oblast boundaries..........
National Okrug boundaries................
Canals..

The government of the United States has not recognized the incorporation of Estonia, Latvia and Lithuania into the Soviet Union, nor does it recognize as final the de facto western limit of Polish administration in Germany (the Oder-Neisse line).

Longitude East of Greenwich

36

GULF OF OB'
KARA SEA
Novaya Zemlya
NORWAY
SWEDEN
FINLAND
WHITE SEA
GULF OF BOTHNIA
Kola Pen.
Murmansk
Archangel (Arkhangel'sk)
Severodvinsk (Molotovsk)
Timan Ridge
Ural Mts.
Northern Ural Mts.
Central Ural Mts.
Pechora
Sverdlovsk
Chelyabinsk
Perm' (Molotov)
Kirov
Izhevsk
Kazan'
LENINGRAD
Leningrad
Kronshtadt
Helsinki
Stockholm
Uppsala
Tallinn (Reval)
ESTONIAN S.S.R.
LATVIAN S.S.R.
Riga
LITHUANIAN S.S.R.
Vilnius
R.S.F.S.R.
Pskov
Novgorod
Yaroslavl'
Ivanovo
Kostroma
Vologda
Rybinsk
Cherepovets
Kalinin
Petrozavodsk
L. Onega
L. Ladoga
Arctic Circle

UNION OF SOVIET
SOCIALIST REPUBLICS

CONIC PROJECTION

SCALE OF MILES

0 100 200 300 400 500 600

SCALE OF KILOMETERS

0 100 200 300 400 500 600

Capitals   Boundaries

⊛ National ....
☆ Union Republic ....
◉ A.S.S.R. ....
◎ Autonomous Oblast ....
◦ National Okrug ....

38

Map of
ASIA

SCALE OF MILES
0 200 400 600 800 1000

Capitals of Countries ✦
Cities •
Boundaries of Countries
Other Boundaries
Mountain Peaks ▲
Canals

Water
Lowlands
Depression
Highlands
Mountains

Copyright by C.S. Hammond & Co., N.Y.

41

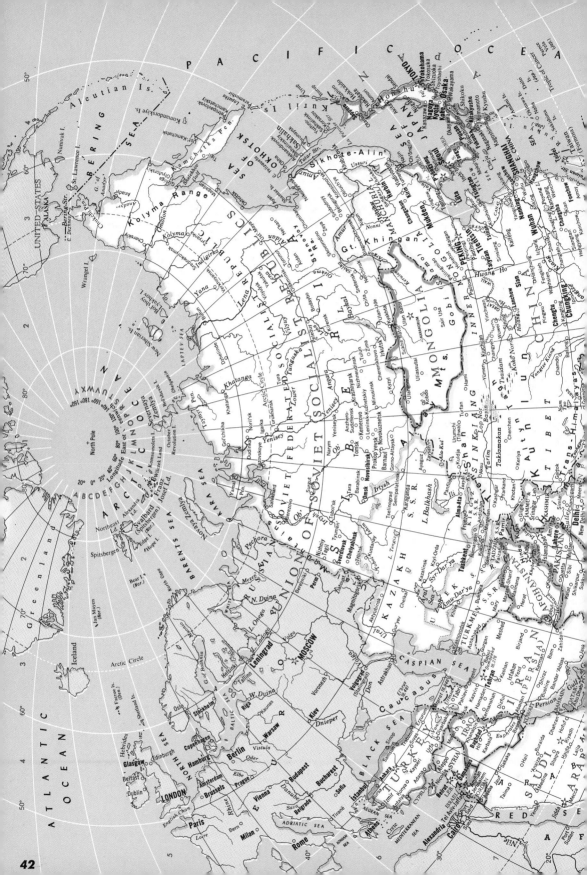

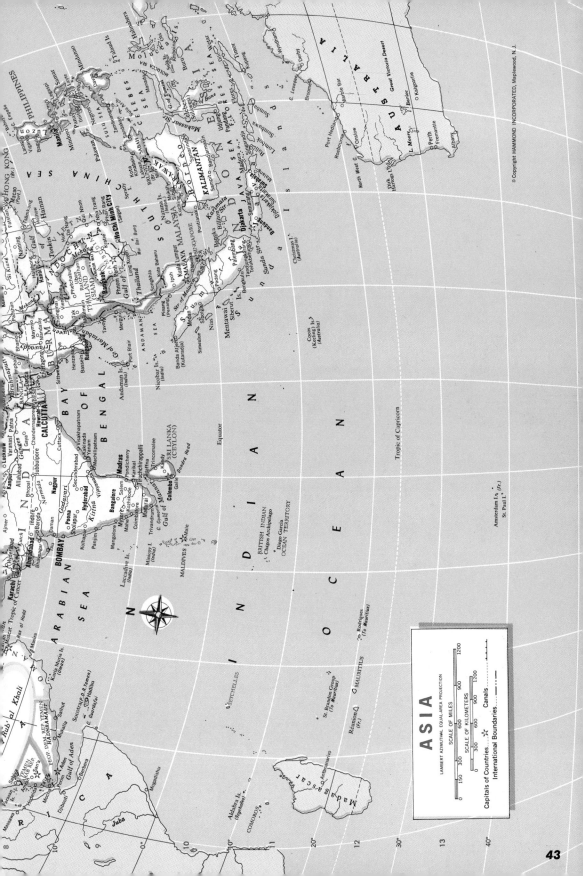

ASIA

LAMBERT AZIMUTHAL EQUAL-AREA PROJECTION

SCALE OF MILES

0   150   300   600   900   1200

SCALE OF KILOMETERS

0   150 300   600   900   1200

Capitals of Countries..........☆   Canals..............
International Boundaries..........

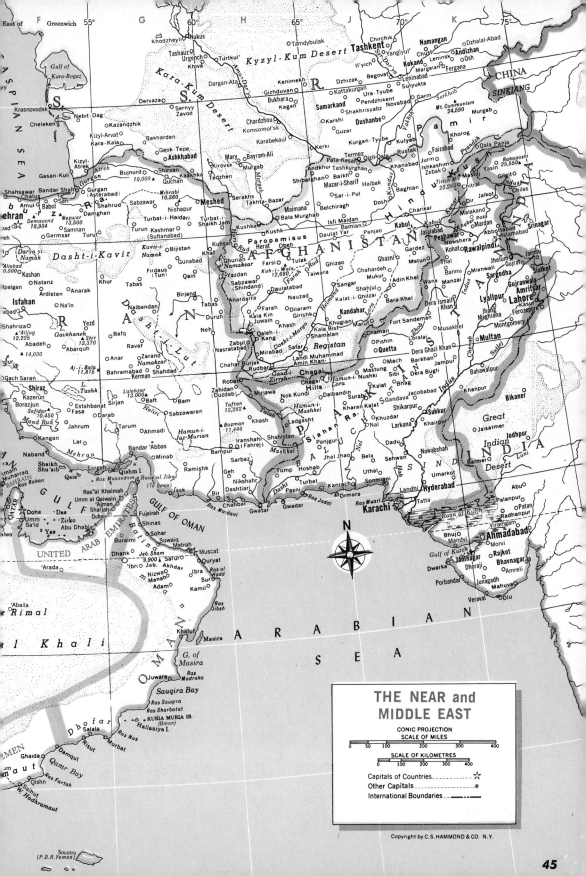

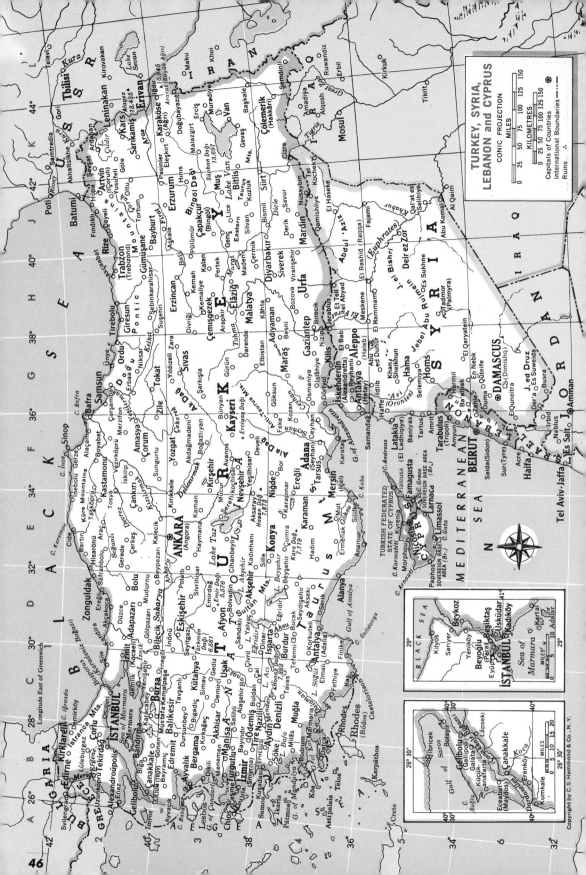

TURKEY, SYRIA,
LEBANON and CYPRUS

CONIC PROJECTION

MILES

KILOMETRES

Capitals of Countries ⊛
International Boundaries ---
Ruins ∴

46

ISRAEL and JORDAN

CYLINDRICAL PROJECTION

Copyright by C.S. HAMMOND & CO., N.Y.

SCALE OF MILES

0 5 10 15 20 25 30

SCALE OF KILOMETRES

0 5 10 15 20 25 30

Capitals of Countries .... ★
Other Capitals .... ⊙
International Boundaries ____
Internal Boundaries ----
Demilitarized Zone Boundaries ·····
Neutral Zone Boundaries ----

47

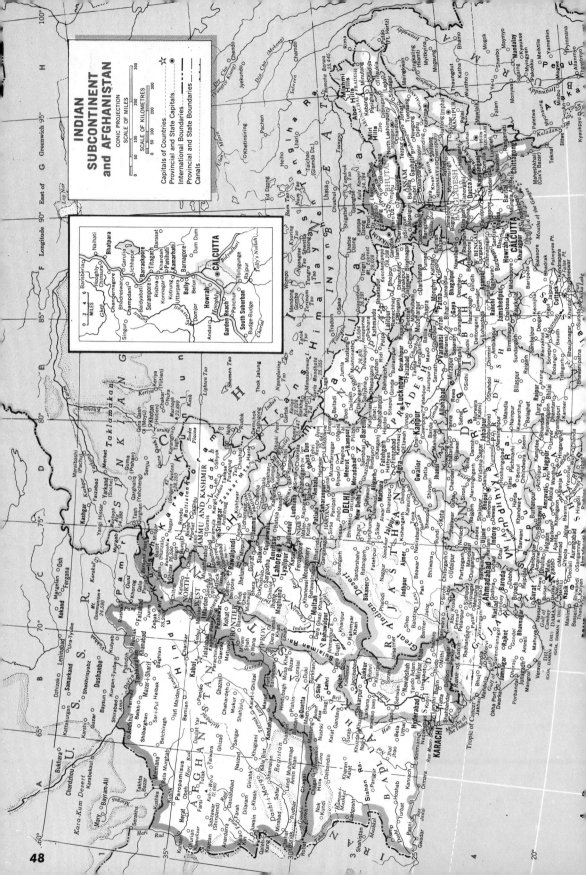

TOKYO

YOKOHAMA

YOKOSUKA

NAMPO-SHOTO

BONIN ISLANDS
(OGASAWARA GUNTO)

VOLCANO ISLANDS
(KAZAN-RETTO)

Same scale as main map

SAKISHIMA ISLANDS

Tropic of Cancer

KYOTO

OSAKA

KOBE

SAKAI

HOKKAIDO

HONSHU

E A S T   C H I N A   S E A

P A C I F I C   O C E A N

S E A   O F   J A P A N

U. S. S. R.

C H I N A

NORTH KOREA

SOUTH KOREA

Pyongyang

Seoul

Vladivostok

Changchun

KYUSHU

SHIKOKU

YELLOW SEA

EAST CHINA SEA

Kaohsiung
Taitung
TAIWAN
(Formosa)
(China)

Batan Is.

Babuyan Is.

Banguis
Laoag
Aparri
Tuguegarao
Bangued
Vigan
Bontoc
Ilagan
Baguio
Bayombong
Lingayen
Cabanatuan
Luzon
Tarlac
Malolos
Iba
Polillo I.

MANILA
Cavite

Lubang Is.
Batangas
Daet
Catanduanes I.
Calapan
Lucena
Naga
Legaspi
Sibuyan
San Jose
Mindoro
Sea
Sibuyan
Sorsogon
C. Espiritu Santo
Mohdragon
Busuanga I.
CALAMIAN
GROUP
Masbate
Samar
Roxas
Visayan
Catbalogan
Panay
Iloilo
Sea
Tacloban
Leyte
Bacolod
Cebu
Dinagat I.

Palawan
Negros
Bohol
Siargao I.
Puerto Princesa
Dumaguete
Mindanao
Butuan
Cagayan Is.
Sea
Cagayan
de Oro
Bislig

PHILIPPINES

© Copyright HAMMOND INCORPORATED, Maplewood, N.J.

JAVA
MILES
0 25 50

J A V A   S E A

DJAKARTA
(Batavia)
Tandjungpriok
Serang
St. Nicholas Pt.
Merak
Karimundjawa Is.
Bawean
Bangkalan
Pandeglang
Tangerang
Bekasi
Krawang
Indramaju Pt.
Indramaju
Rembang
Labuan
Rangkas-
bitung
Purwakarta
Subang
Madjalengka
Tjirebon
Pekalongan
Semarang
Kudus
Kragan
Tuban
Bogor
Tjiandjur
Tjimahi
Tjiawi
Brebes
Tegal
Batang
Pemalang
Kendal
Demak
Blora
Gresik
Lamongan
Sumenep
Mt. Gede
9,705
Sukabumi
Bandung
Garut
Kuningan
Bumiaju
Purwokerto
Purwodadi
Bodjonegoro
Lamongan
Madura
Pamekasan
Mt. Ditung
6,296
Pelabuhan
Ratu
Bay
Tasikmalaja
Mt. Slamet
11,247
Purworedjo
Wonosobo
Temanggung
Sragen
Ngawi
Surabaja
Sampang
Madura Strait
Pameungpeuk
Tjidjulang
Mt. Sumbing
11,060
Magelang
Salatiga
Madiun
Modjokerto
Sidoardjo
Situbondo
Tjilatjap
Kebumen
Klaten
Magetan
Kediri
Pasuruan
Probolinggo
Panarukan
Surakarta
Ponorogo
Mt.
Kawi
8,651
Turen
Bondowoso
DJOKJAKARTA
Patjitan
Trenggalek
Tulungagung
Blitar
Malang
Djember
Banjuwangi
Mt. Semeru
12,060
Nusa
Barung
Mt. Raung
10,932

I N D I A N   O C E A N

SOUTHEAST ASIA
LAMBERT AZIMUTHAL EQUAL-AREA PROJECTION

SCALE OF MILES
0 100 200 400 600

SCALE OF KILOMETRES
0 100 200 400 600

Capitals of Countries_____☆
Administrative Center_____◉
International Boundaries_____
Other Boundaries_____

P H I L I P P I N E   S E A

Cagayan Sulu
PANGUTARAN
GROUP
SULU
ARCHIPELAGO
Jolo
TAPUL GROUP
TAWITAWI GROUP

Zamboanga
Basilan
Marawi
Cateel
Siokun
Cotabato
Mindanao
Davao
Moro
Gulf
Mt. Matutum
7,623
Glan
C. San Agustin
Sarangani Is.
Tinaca Pt.

C E L E B E S
S E A

Kawio Is.
Beo
Karakelong
TALAUD IS.
Tahuna
Sangihe
SANGIHE
ISLANDS
Siau
Tahulandang

P A C I F I C

Palau Is.

TERRITORY OF THE

Sonsorol

PACIFIC ISLANDS
(U. S. Trusteeship)

Pulo Anna
Merir

Tobi

O C E A N

C. Torawitan
Manado
Bitung
Amurang
Tondano
Djailolo
Ternate
Kau
Tobelo
Palaleh
Isimu
Kotamobagu
Soasiu
Tidore
Weda
Halmahera
Asia Is.
Pegun
Mapia Is.

C. Sopi
Wajabula
Morotai
Gorontalo
Galela
Buli

Gulf of Tomini
TOGIAN IS.

M O L U C C A
Gebe
Waigeo
Cape of Good Hope
SCHOUTEN
ISLANDS

BATJAN
IS.
Gani
Labuha
Dampier Str.
Sorong
Manokwari
Numfoor
Biak
Supiori
Japen
Wakde
Demta

Donggala
C. Sisi
Ampana
Luwuk
Peleng
Banggai
RADJA
AMPAT
GR.
Salawati
Deberai (Vogelkop)
Pen.
Ranski
Sarmi
Djajapura
(Hollandia)

Pasangkaju
Mamudju
Palu
Toli
Toli
Gulf of
Tolo
BANGGAI
ARCHIPELAGO
Taliabu
Mangole
Lekitobi
Obi
Misool
C. Sabra
Berau Bay
Wasior
(Geelvink)
Bay
Waren
Serui
Djajawidjaja
Moffin B.
C. Perham

Karosa
Kolonodale
Lake Towuti
SULA
IS.
Sanana
Boano
C. Fatagar
Tuting
Nabire
Wamena
Enarotali
Sudirman Ra.
Puntjak Djaja
16,400
Idenburg R.

Masamba
Palopo
Mt. Rantekombola
11,335
Salabangka Is.
Manui
Piru
Wahai
C E R A M   S E A
Amahai
Bula
Babo
C. van den
Bosch
Kokonao

Pinrang
Parepare
Sengkang
Kendari
BURU
SEA
Buru
Namlea
Leksula
Ceram
Piru
Geser
Gorong
Adi
Agats

C. Mandar
Madjene
Wowoni
Amboina
(Ambon)
Bandanaira
Gorong
Watubela Is.
Nuhutjut
Wokam
Kobroor
ARU
IS.
Workai
Tanahmeran
Kepio
Digul

Watampone
Sindjai
Muna
Butung
Wangiwangi
TUKANGBESI
IS.
Penju Is.
(Turtle Is.)
Banda Sea
EWAB
(KAI)
IS.
Kur
Tual
Nuhurowa
Trangan
Muli Str.
Mindiptana

ung Pandang
(Makassar)
Bulu Kumba
Kabaena
Serua
Nila
Larat
Jamdena
TANIMBAR
IS.
Muting
Okaba
Merauke

Rewata
Benteng
Bonthain
Salajar
(Kabia)
Matjan
(Tiger) I.
Binongko
Gunungapi
Damar
(Romang)
Babar
Sera
Tepa
Adaut
Saumlaki
Selaru
Komoran
C. Vals

F L O R E S
Kalao
Kalaotoa
Roma
Wetar
Wonreli
Moa
Masela
Dolak
(Frederik Hendrik)
I.

S A V U   S E A
Komodo
Ruteng
Flores
Larantuka
Adonara
Lomblen
Alor
Kalabahi
Vila
Kisar
LETI IS.
Sermata

Sangeang
Dompu
Endeh
Solor
Pantar
Ombai Str.
Dili
Lifuqueue
Lakor

Waikabubako
Maumere
Vila Salazar
Vila Armindo Monteiro
Timor

Sumba
(Sandalwood)
Waingapu
Sawu
Soë
Atambua
Baa
Kupang
Roti

T I M O R
S E A

A R A F U R A   S E A

Melville I.
Bathurst I.
C. Croker
Croker I.
C. Wessel
Wessel Is.

A U S T R A L I A

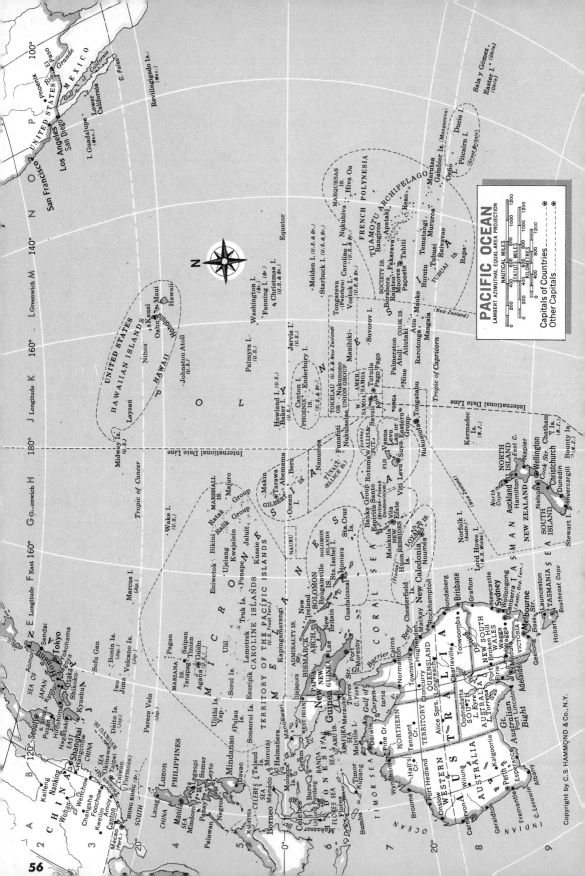

PACIFIC OCEAN
LAMBERT AZIMUTHAL EQUAL-AREA PROJECTION

NAUTICAL MILES

STATUTE MILES

KILOMETERS

Capitals of Countries ⊛
Other Capitals ⊙

56

Copyright by C.S. HAMMOND & Co., N.Y.

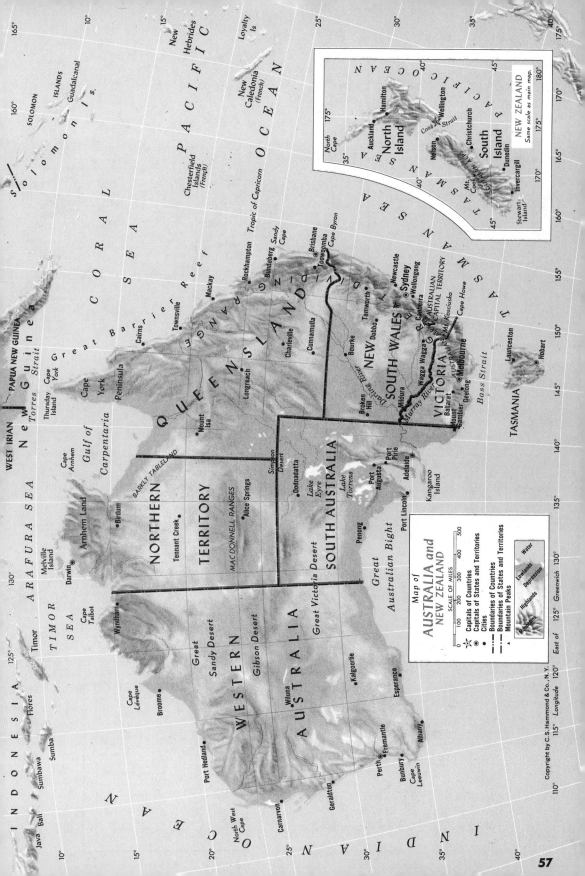

Map of
AUSTRALIA and
NEW ZEALAND

SCALE OF MILES

Capitals of Countries
Capitals of States and Territories
Cities
Boundaries of Countries
Boundaries of States and Territories
Mountain Peaks

Water
Lowlands
Depression
Highlands
Mountains

NEW ZEALAND
Same scale as main map.

57

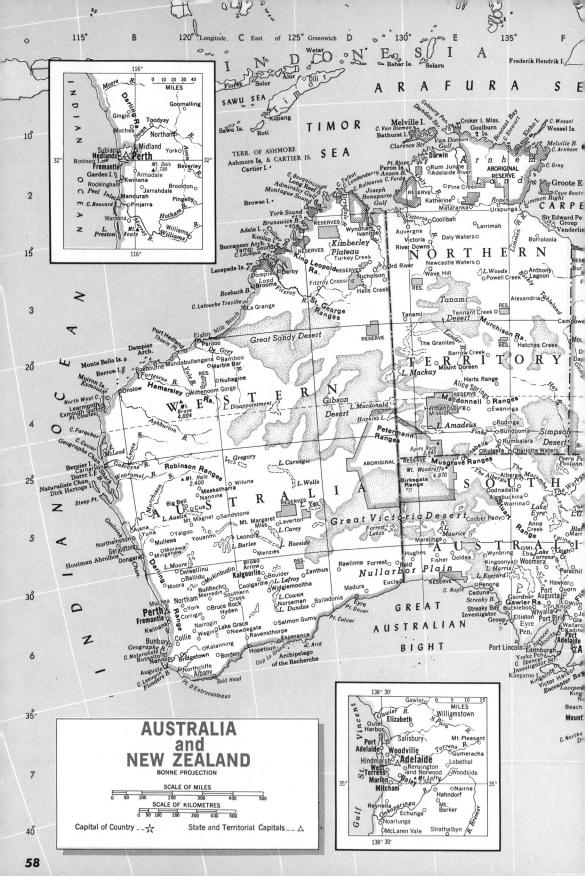

AUSTRALIA and NEW ZEALAND
BONNE PROJECTION

SCALE OF MILES

0   50   100   200   300   400   500

SCALE OF KILOMETRES

0 50 100   200   300   400   500

Capital of Country ___ ☆   State and Territorial Capitals ___ ⌂

PAPUA NEW GUINEA

Gulf of Papua

Torres Str.

CORAL SEA

QUEENSLAND

CORAL SEA ISLANDS TERRITORY

NEW SOUTH WALES

VICTORIA

TASMANIA

MELBOURNE

MELBOURNE inset — 145°, 38°, PORT PHILLIP BAY, Geelong

SYDNEY inset — 151°, 34°, Parramatta, Bankstown, Liverpool, Botany Bay, Wollongong, TASMAN SEA

NORTH ISLAND

Auckland

SOUTH ISLAND

NEW ZEALAND
Same scale as main map

TASMAN SEA

PACIFIC OCEAN

Longitude 170° East of 175° Greenwich 180°

UNION OF SOVIET SOCIALIST REPUBLICS
(RUSSIA)

Aral
Sea

CASPIAN SEA

IRAN

Persian Gulf

KUWAIT
QATAR
UN. ARAB EMIR.

SAUDI ARABIA

YEMEN ARAB REP.
PEOP. DEM. REP. YEMEN

Gulf of Aden
Cape Guardafui

SOMALIA

Mogadishu

Harghessa
DJIBOUTI

ETHIOPIA

KENYA

Lake Turkana

RED SEA

Asmara
Addis Ababa

IRAQ

SYRIA

JORDAN

LEBANON
ISRAEL

CYPRUS

TURKEY

BLACK SEA

AEGEAN SEA

Port Said
Suez Canal

Cairo
Alexandria

EGYPT

Port Sudan

Khartoum

Blue Nile

White Nile

SUDAN

Aswān

Lake Nasser

Nile

River

El Fasher

Mongalla

Lake

Mt.

CENTRAL AFRICAN EMPIRE

Bangui

Ubangi River

River

P

E

POLAND
EAST GER.
WEST GERMANY
CZECHOSLOVAKIA
AUSTRIA
HUNGARY
SWITZ.
YUGOSLAVIA
RUMANIA
BULGARIA
GREECE
ALBANIA
ITALY
ADRIATIC SEA
NETH.
BELG.
FRANCE

GREAT BRITAIN

Bay of Biscay

ATLANTIC

OCEAN

SPAIN

PORTUGAL

Strait of Gibraltar
Tangier
Casablanca
Rabat

MOROCCO
ATLAS MOUNTAINS

Madeira
(Portuguese)

Canary Islands
(Spanish)

Azores
(Portuguese)

Cape Verde

Dakar
SENEGAL

Senegal River

MAURITANIA

Nouakchott

GAMBIA
GUINEA-BISSAU

GUINEA

Freetown
SIERRA LEONE

Conakry

Monrovia
LIBERIA

Cape Palmas

IVORY COAST

Abidjan

MALI

Timbuktu

Niger River

Bamako
Ouagadougou
UPPER VOLTA

GHANA

Accra

L. Volta

TOGO
BENIN

Lomé
Porto-Novo

Lagos
Ibadan

NIGERIA

Niamey

NIGER

Kano

N'Djamena
Lake Chad

CHAD

TIBESTI MTS.

Fezzan
Murzuk

LIBYA

Tripoli
Tripolitania
Benghazi
Cyrenaica

Libyan Desert

Tropic of Cancer

SAHARA DESERT

AHAGGAR MTS.

ALGERIA

Aïn Salah

Béchar

Oran
Algiers

TUNISIA
Tunis

MALTA

Sicily

MEDITERRANEAN SEA

Corsica
Sardinia

Crete

Kano

CAMEROON

Yaoundé

EQUATORIAL GUINEA
Macías Nguema Biyogo

Gulf

60

Map of
AFRICA
SCALE OF MILES

Capitals of Countries
Cities
Boundaries of Countries
Other Boundaries
Mountain Peaks
Canals
Falls

Water
Lowlands
Depression
Highlands
Mountains

Copyright by C. S. Hammond & Co., N.Y.

10°   20°   30°   40°

Tamatave
Antananarivo
COMOROS
MADAGASCAR
Tuléar
Cape
Ste-Marie

Mombasa
Zanzibar
Dar es
Salaam
Nairobi
Mt.
Kilimanjaro
Lake
Victoria
RWANDA
BURUNDI
Bukavu
Lake
Tanganyika
TANZANIA
Lake
Nyasa
MALAWI
Lilongwe
Beira
Blantyre
MOZAMBIQUE
Mozambique Channel

INDIAN

OCEAN

ZAIRE
Kinshasa
Brazzaville
Pointe-Noire
Cabinda
(Angola)
GABON
CONGO
Luanda
Benguela
Huambo
ANGOLA
Lubumbashi
Kasai
River
Congo
River
Zambezi River

Kabwe
Lusaka
ZAMBIA
Kabwe
Victoria
Falls
Salisbury
ZIMBABWE
RHODESIA
BOTSWANA
Kalahari Desert
SOUTH-
WEST
AFRICA
(NAMIBIA)
(to South Africa)
Windhoek
Walvis Bay
(to South Africa)
Limpopo R.
Pretoria
Johannes-
burg
Kimberley
Orange River
SOUTH AFRICA
Maputo
WAZILAND
LESOTHO
Durban
East London
Port Elizabeth
Cape Town
Cape of
Good Hope

St. Helena
(British)

Ascension
(British)

ATLANTIC

OCEAN

Tropic of Capricorn

of
Guinea

30° 20° 10° Greenwich 0° Longitude 10° East of 20° Greenwich 30° 40°

West of Longitude

10°

20°

30°

40°

61

MAP CONTINUED ON

AFRICA
NORTHERN PART

LAMBERT AZIMUTHAL EQUAL-AREA PROJECTION

SCALE OF MILES
0   100 200   400   600

SCALE OF KILOMETRES
0   100 200   400   600

Capitals of Countries ----------- ☆
Other Capitals ----------------- ◉
International Boundaries -----·---
Internal Boundaries ------------
Canals ----- Wells ----- ○

© Copyright HAMMOND INCORPORATED, Maplewood, N.J.

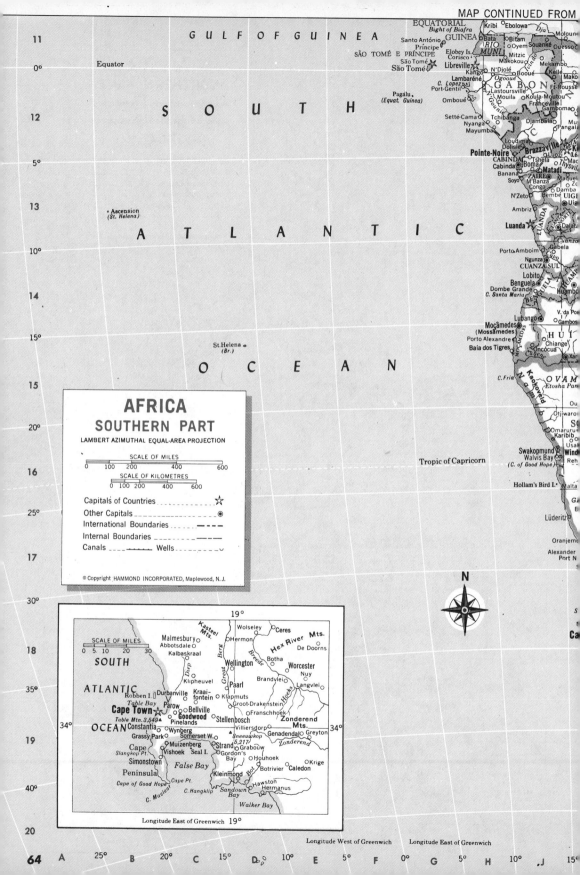

AFRICA
SOUTHERN PART
LAMBERT AZIMUTHAL EQUAL-AREA PROJECTION

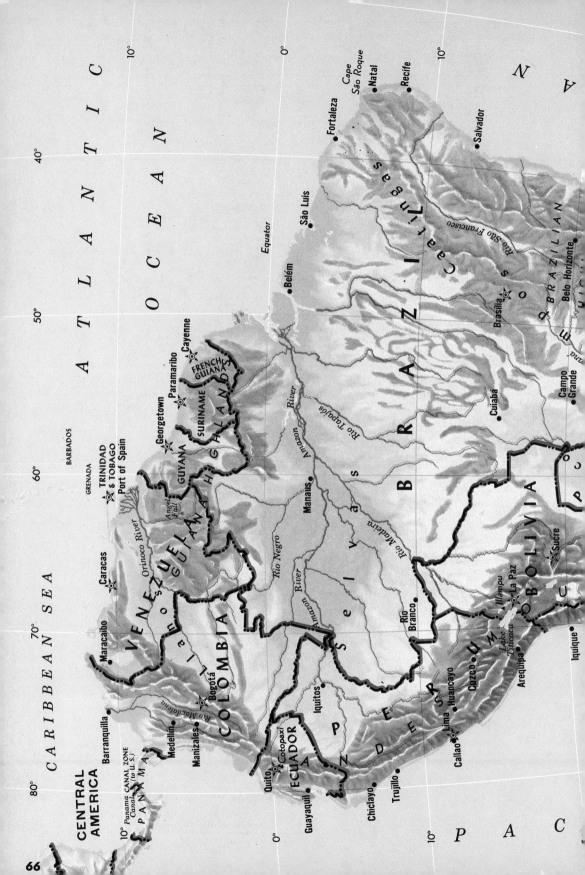

CENTRAL
AMERICA

CARIBBEAN SEA

ATLANTIC OCEAN

Equator

Cape São Roque
Natal
Recife

Fortaleza

Salvador

São Luis

Belém

C a a t i n g a s

BARBADOS

GRENADA

TRINIDAD
& TOBAGO
Port of Spain

Cayenne

Paramaribo

FRENCH
GUIANA

Georgetown

SURINAME

GUYANA

B R A Z I L I A N

Rio São Francisco

Brasília

Belo Horizonte

Cuiabá

Campo
Grande

Barranquilla

Panama CANAL ZONE
Canal (to U. S.)

PANAMA

Maracaibo

Caracas

Medellín

Manizales

Bogotá

COLOMBIA

VENEZUELA

Orinoco River

Angel
Fall

G U I A N A   H I G H L A N D S

Rio Magdalena

Amazon River

Rio Negro

Manaus

Rio Branco

Rio Madeira

S e l v a s

Rio Tapajós

B R A Z I L

Quito

Cotopaxi

ECUADOR

Guayaquil

Iquitos

P E R U

Amazon River

Chiclayo

Trujillo

A N D E S

Lima

Callao

Huancayo

Cuzco

Arequipa

Lake
Titicaca

Illampu

La Paz

BOLIVIA

Sucre

Iquique

P A C I F I C

66

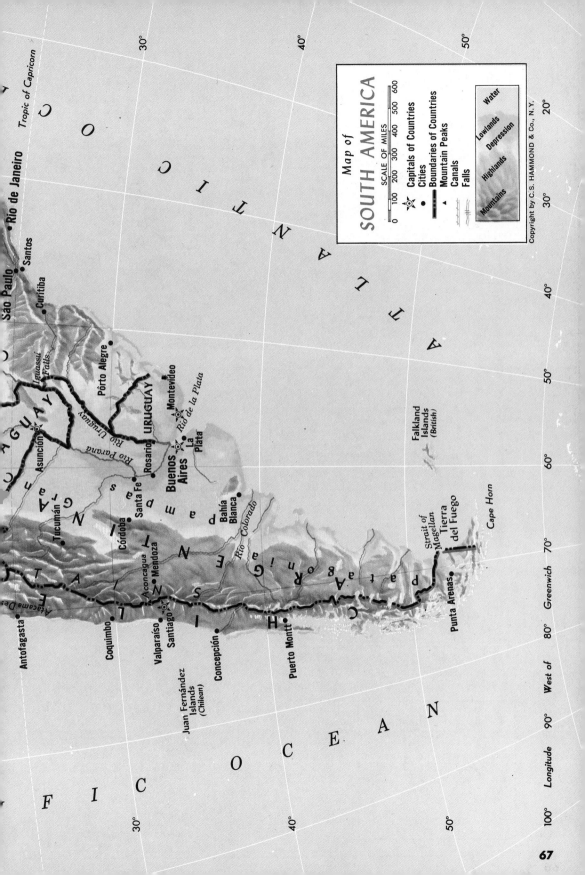

Map of
SOUTH AMERICA

SCALE OF MILES

0   100   200   300   400   500   600

Capitals of Countries
Cities
Boundaries of Countries
Mountain Peaks
Canals
Falls

Water
Lowlands
Depression
Highlands
Mountains

Tropic of Capricorn

Rio de Janeiro

São Paulo

Santos

Curitiba

A T L Á N T I C O

Pôrto Alegre

Iguassu Falls

P A R A G U A Y

Asunción

Rio Paraná

Rio Uruguay

URUGUAY

Montevideo

Rio de la Plata

Rosario

Santa Fe

Buenos Aires

La Plata

A R G E N T I N A

Tucumán

Córdoba

Mendoza

Aconcagua

Bahía Blanca

Rio Colorado

Falkland Islands (British)

Strait of Magellan

Tierra del Fuego

Cape Horn

Atacama Des.

Antofagasta

Coquimbo

Valparaíso

Santiago

Concepción

C H I L E

P A T A G O N I A

Puerto Montt

Punta Arenas

Juan Fernández Islands (Chilean)

West of   Greenwich

Longitude   90°   80°   70°   60°   50°

P A C I F I C   O C E A N

67

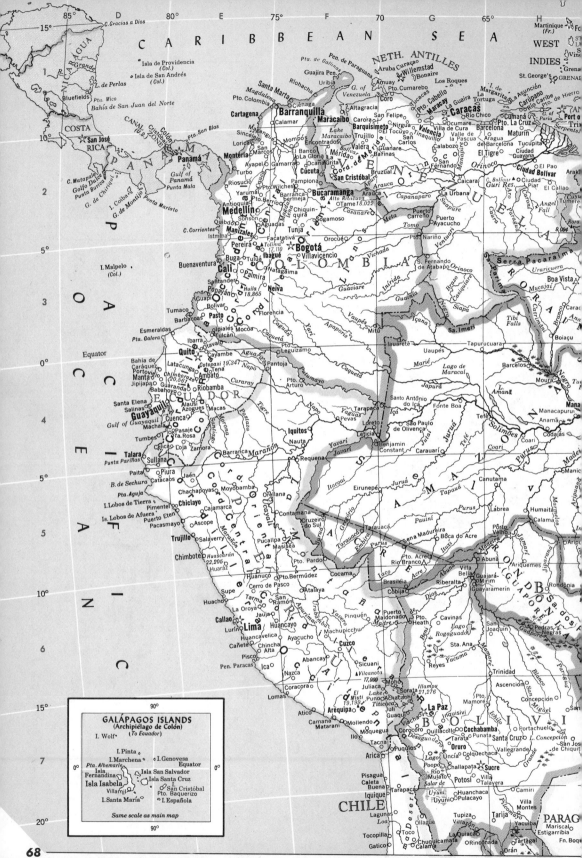

MAP CONTINUED ON

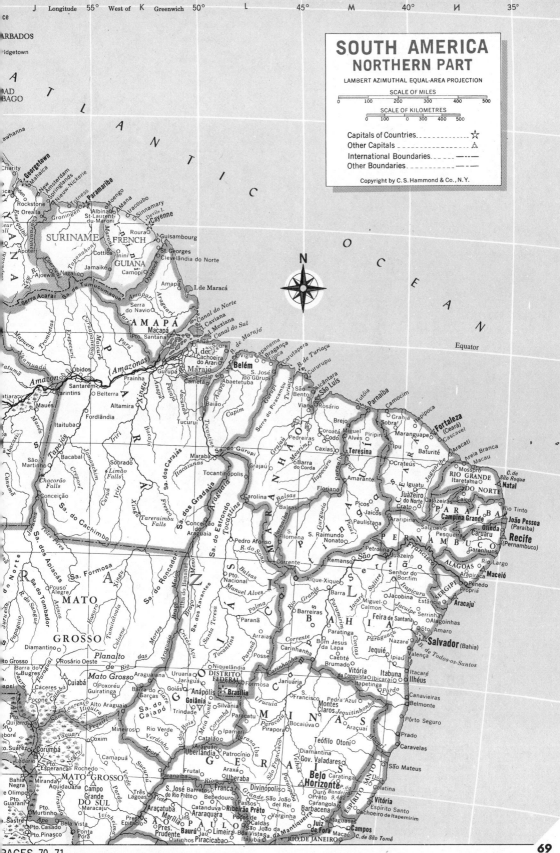

8 — Tropic of Capricorn

25°

9

30°

I. de San Félix · · I.San Ambrosio
(Chile)   (Chile)

10

JUAN FERNÁNDEZ IS.
(Chile)
I. Alejandro   I. Robinson
Selkirk   Crusoe
          I. Santa Clara

P A C I F I C   O C E A N

35°

40°

45°

50°

55°

SOUTH AMERICA
SOUTHERN PART
LAMBERT AZIMUTHAL EQUAL-AREA PROJECTION

SCALE OF MILES
0   100   200   300   400   500

SCALE OF KILOMETRES
0   100   200   300   400   500

Capitals of Countries ------------ ☆
Other Capitals ---------------- Δ
International Boundaries --- — · —
Other Boundaries --------- — · —

© Copyright HAMMOND INCORPORATED, Maplewood, N.J.

DRAKE PAS

70   A   95°   B   90°   C   85°   D   80°   E   75°   F   70° Longitude   65° West of

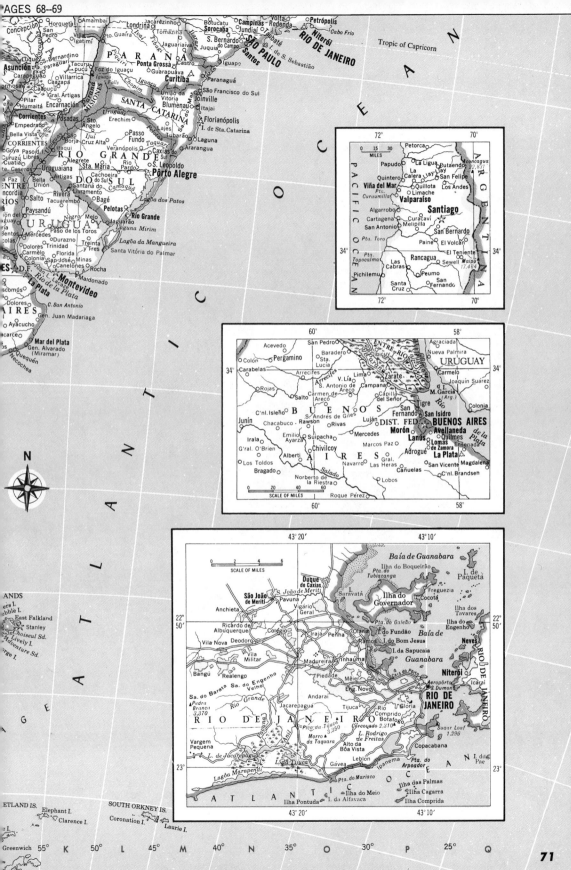

Tropic of Capricorn

O C E A N

PACIFIC OCEAN

Santiago inset (72°–70°, 34°)

Petorca
Papudo
La Ligua   Putaendo   Aconcagua 22,831
La Calera   Calle Llay   San Felipe   Los Andes
Quintero   Quillota   Limache
Viña del Mar   Pta. Curaumilla
Valparaíso   Algarrobo   Santiago
Cartagena   Curacaví   Melipilla
San Antonio   Pta. Toro   San Bernardo
Pta. Topocalma   Paine   El Volcán   El Teniente
Pichilemu   Las Cabras   Rancagua   Sewell   Maipú 17,484
Santa Cruz   Peumo   San Fernando

ARGENTINA

MILES 0 15 30

Buenos Aires inset (60°–58°, 34°)

Acevedo   San Pedro   Ibicuy   ENTRE RÍOS   Agraciada   Nueva Palmira   URUGUAY
Colon   Baradero   Sta. Lucía   Carmelo   Joaquín Suárez
Carabelas   Arrecifes   V. Lía   Lima   Zárate   M. García (Arg.)   Colonia
Rojas   Arrecifes   S. Antonio de Areco   Campana   Capilla del Señor   Tigre
Salto   Carmen de Areco   San Fernando   San Isidro
Junín   C'nl. Isleño   B U E N O S   Luján   San BUENOS AIRES   de la
Chacabuco · Rawson   S. Andrés de Giles   Morón   Avellaneda   Plata
Irala   Emilio Ayarza   Suipacha   Rivas   Lanús   Quilmes   Ensenada
G'ral. O'Brien   Alberti   Chivilcoy   Mercedes   Lomas de Zamora   La Plata   Magdalena
Los Toldos   A I R E S   Marcos Paz   Adrogué   San Vicente
Bragado   Navarro   Las Heras   Cañuelas   C'nl. Brandsen
Norberto de la Riestra   Salado   Gral.   Lobos
Roque Pérez

SCALE OF MILES   0 20 40 60

Rio de Janeiro inset (43°20′–43°10′, 22°50′–23°)

Baía de Guanabara
Ilha do Boqueirão   Pta. do Tubiacanga   I. de Paquetá
Duque de Caxias   S. João de Meriti   Saravatá   Freguezia   Cocotá
São João de Meriti   Pavuna   Ilha do Governador   Ilha dos Tavares
Anchieta   Vigário Geral   Pta. do Galeão   Ilha do Engenho
Ricardo de Albuquerque   Colégio   Olaria   I. do Fundão   Baía de   Neves
Vila Nova   Deodoro   Iraja   Penha   Ramos   I. do Bom Jesus   Niterói
Bangú   Vila Militar   Madureira   Inhaúma   I. da Sapucaia   Guanabara   Icaraí
Realengo   Piedade   Méier   Eng. Novo   Aeropôrto S. Dumont   RIO DE JANEIRO
Sa. do Barata   Sa. do Engenho Velho   Andaraí   Gloria   Botafogo
Pedra Branca 3,370   Rio Grande   Jacarepaguá   Tijuca   Rio Comprido   Sugar Loaf 1,296
R I O   D E   J A N E I R O   Pico da Tijuca 3,350   Corcovado 2,310
Vargem Pequena   Morro da Taquara   Alto da Bôa Vista   L. Rodrigo de Freitas   Copacabana
I. de Jacarepaguá   I. da Tijuca   Leblon   Ipanema   Pta. do Arpoador   I. do Pae
Lagoa Marapendi   Gávea   Pta. do Marisco   Ilha das Palmas
Pta. do Pontuda   I. da Alfavaca   Ilha do Meio   Ilha Cagarra
A T L A N T I C   O C E A N   Ilha Comprida

SCALE OF MILES   0 2 4 6

Main map

Concepción   Horqueta   Amambai   Jacarèzinho   Londrina   Botucatu   Volta Redonda   Petrópolis
San Pedro   Villa Ygatimí   to. Guaíra   Ivaí   Tômazina   Jaguariaíva   Castro   Sorocaba   Jundiaí   Tiuité   Niterói   RIO DE JANEIRO   Cabo Frio
S. Bernardino   P A R A N Á   Ponta Grossa   Campinas   S. Bernardo do Campo   SÃO PAULO   I. de S. Sebastião
Asunción   Paraguarí   Foz do Iguaçu   Curitiba   Juquiá   Santos
Carapeguá   Villarrica   Iguaçu   Paranaguá   Iguapé
Caacupú   Caazapá   Falls   Chopim   São Francisco do Sul
Pilar   Gral. Artigas   M I S I O N E S   União da Vitoria   Joinville
Humaitá   Encarnación   SANTA   Blumenau   Itajaí
Posadas   CATARINA   Florianópolis
Corrientes   Ijuí   Erechim   Uruguaí   I. de Sta. Catarina
Goya   Paso de los Libres   Sto. Angelo   Lajes   Laguna
Curuzú Cuatiá   Cruz Alta   R I O   G R A N D E   Araranguá
La Paz   Bella Unión   Alegrete   Passo Fundo   Veranópolis   Caxias do Sul
Concordia   Artigas   Sta. María   Cachoeira do Sul   S. Leopoldo
ENTRE   Rivera   Livramento   Camaquã   Pôrto Alegre
Paysandú   Tacuarembó   Bagé   Lagôa dos Patos
U R U G U A Y   Negro Melo   Pelotas
Salto   Paso de los Toros   Jaguarão   Rio Grande
Mercedes   Durazno   Treinta y Tres   Laguna Mirim
Dolores   Trinidad   Florida   Rocha   Lagôa da Mangueira
Carmelo   San José   Canelones   Santa Vitória do Palmar
Colonia   Montevideo   Maldonado
D.F.   Río de la Plata   C. San Antonio
La Plata   Gen. Juan Madariaga   Ayacucho
Dolores   Mar del Plata   Gen. Alvarado (Miramar)
Necochea   Quequén

O C E A N

A T L A N T I C   O C E A N

N

FALKLAND ISLANDS   West Falkland   Choiseul Sd.   East Falkland   Stanley   Lively I.   Adventure Sd.

SHETLAND IS.   Elephant I.   Clarence I.   SOUTH ORKNEY IS.   Coronation I.   Laurie I.

Greenwich 55°   K   50°   L   45°   M   40°   N   35°   O   30°   P   25°   Q   **71**

ARCTIC OCEAN

ICELAND

Newfoundland

St. Pierre &
Miquelon
(French)

Nova
Scotia

Halifax

Boston

New York

Philadelphia

GREENLAND
(Danish)

Davis Strait

Labrador

Goose
Bay

St. Lawrence River

MOUNTAINS

Montréal

Ottawa

Toronto

Cleveland

Detroit

Chicago

Great Lakes

Baffin
Bay

Thule

Baffin Island

Hudson
Bay

Minneapolis

North Pole

North
Magnetic
Pole

Ellesmere Island

Arctic Circle

Churchill

Lake
Winnipeg

Winnipeg

Missouri

CANADA

80°

Victoria
Island

Great
Bear Lake

Great
Slave Lake

Grea

Mackenzie River

Edmonton

Calgary

ROCKY MOUN

80°

ARCTIC

OCEAN

Point
Barrow

UNITED STATES

Alaska

Yukon

Mt.
McKinley

Anchorage

Whitehorse

Juneau

Queen
Charlotte
Islands

Vancouver
Island

Vancouver

Seattle

Portland

CASCADE RANGE

Columbia

Great
Salt Lake or

San

ASIA

Bering Strait

70°

PACI

60°

50°

40°

72

Hatteras

Bermuda
(British)

Cape Canaveral

Jacksonville

B A H A M A S

Miami

Tropic of Cancer

20°

PUERTO
RICO
(to U.S.)

DOMINICAN
REPUBLIC

HAITI

West Indies SEA

C U B A

JAMAICA

CARIBBEAN

Havana

Gulf of Mexico

A P P A L A C H I A N S

Mt. Mitchell

Atlanta

Memphis

New
Orleans

Mississippi River

M E X I C O

Yucatán
Peninsula

BELIZE

HONDURAS

GUATEMALA

EL SALVADOR

NICARAGUA

COSTA
RICA

PANAMA

CANAL (to U.S.)
ZONE

Panama Canal

CENTRAL

AMERICA

VENEZUELA

COLOMBIA

S O U T H

A M E R I C A

BRAZIL

BOLIVIA

E C U A D O R

P E R U

70°

10°

0°

10°

80°

Greenwich

U N I T E D   S T A T E S

Dallas

Houston

P l a i n s

Rio Grande

El Paso

Monterrey

Guadalajara

Veracruz

Mexico City

Phoenix

San Diego

Los Angeles

Mt. Whitney

S I E R R A   N E V A D A

Colorado R.

Lower California

90°

100°

110°

120°

130°

Longitude

West of

Equator

Galápagos
Islands
(Ecuadoran)

P A C I F I C   O C E A N

20°

10°

0°

10°

30°

Map of
NORTH AMERICA

SCALE OF MILES

0   200   400   600   800

- ⊛ Capitals of Countries
- ● Cities
- ▬▪▬ Boundaries of Countries
- ▲ Mountain Peaks
- Canals

Water

Lowlands

Depression

Highlands

Mountains

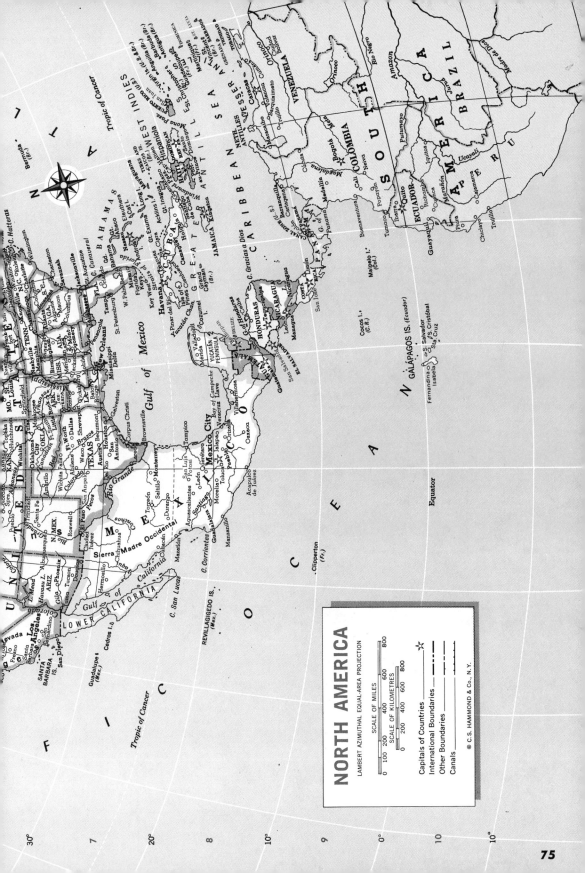

NORTH AMERICA

LAMBERT AZIMUTHAL EQUAL-AREA PROJECTION

SCALE OF MILES
0   100   200   400   600   800

SCALE OF KILOMETRES
0   200   400   600   800

Capitals of Countries .... ☆

International Boundaries ⎯ ⎯ ⎯ ⎯

Other Boundaries ⎯ ⎯ ⎯ ⎯

Canals ⎯⎯⎯⎯⎯⎯⎯

© C.S. HAMMOND & Co., N.Y.

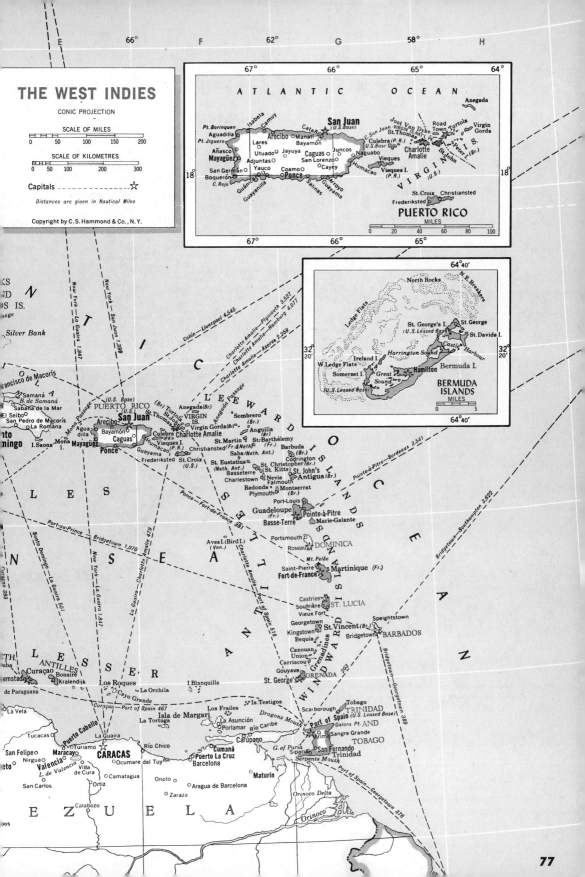

THE WEST INDIES

CONIC PROJECTION

SCALE OF MILES

0   50   100   150   200

SCALE OF KILOMETRES

0 50 100   200   300

Capitals - - - - - - - - ☆

Distances are given in Nautical Miles

Copyright by C.S. Hammond & Co., N.Y.

PUERTO RICO

ATLANTIC OCEAN

MILES

0   20   40   60   80   100

BERMUDA ISLANDS

MILES

0   5

CENTRAL AMERICA

CONIC PROJECTION

SCALE OF MILES

0 25 50   100   150

SCALE OF KILOMETRES

0 25 50   100   150

Capitals of Countries . . . . ☆
International Boundaries . . . .
Canals . . . .

© Copyright HAMMOND INCORPORATED, Maplewood, N.J.

78

MEXICO

CONIC PROJECTION

SCALE OF MILES

0   100   200

SCALE OF KILOMETRES

0   100   200   300

National Capitals..............☆   State Capitals.............⊙
International Boundaries..▪—▪▪—▪   State Boundaries .....—▪—

© C. S. HAMMOND & Co., N.Y.

States Indicated by Numbers

1	Tlaxcala	6	Querétaro
2	Morelos	7	Guanajuato
3	Distrito Federal	8	Aguascalientes
4	México	9	Nayarit
5	Hidalgo	10	Colima

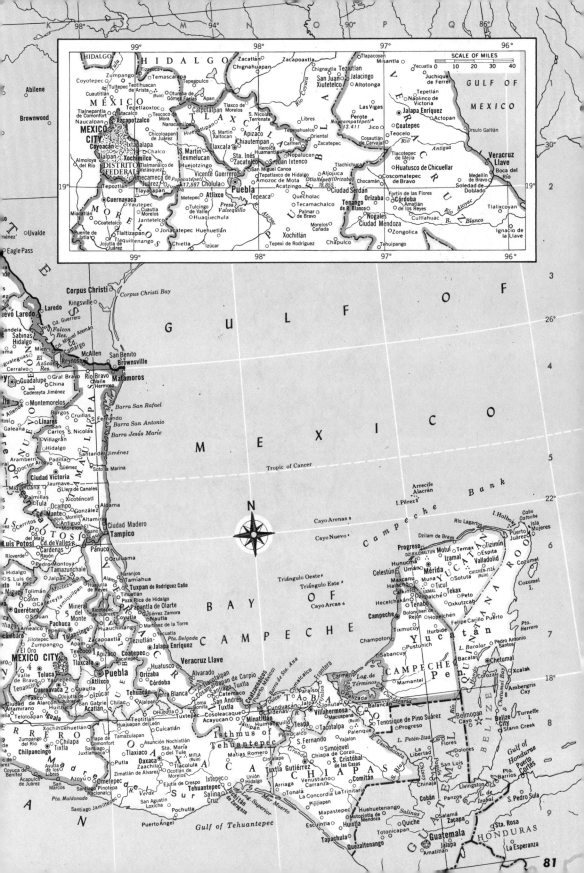

ASIA
U.S.S.R.
BERING
St. Lawrence
Island
Bering Strait
SEA
60°
70°
Nome
Yukon
UNITED STATES
ALASKA
ALASKA RANGE
Mt. McKinley
Fairbanks
BROOKS RANGE
River
Anchorage
Alaska Peninsula
Kodiak
Island
Gulf of Alaska
PACIFIC
OCEAN
50°
Alexander
Archipelago
Juneau
COAST
Prince Rupert
Hazelton
Queen
Charlotte
Islands
Kitimat
BRITISH
Prince
George
ROCKY
COLUMBIA
MOUNTAINS
River
Fraser
Vancouver
Island
Kamloops
Victoria
Vancouver
Cape
Flattery
Seattle
CASCADE RANGE
Portland
Columbia
River
40°
130°
120°
Longitude
110°
West of
100°

ARCTIC
OCEAN
180°
170°
160°
150°
140°
130° 120° 110°
80°
Point Barrow
BEAUFORT
SEA
North Magnetic Pole
Queen Eliza
M'Clure Strait
Viscount Melvi
Sound
Banks
Island
Amundsen
Gulf
Victoria
Prince
of
Wale
Islan
Island
DISTRICT
Inuvik
Coppermine
Great Bear
Lake
Port Radium
YUKON
MACKENZIE
TERRITORY
Dawson
Mt.
Logan
Whitehorse
Mackenzie
River
MACKENZIE MTS
DISTRICT
OF MACKENZIE
NORTHWEST
Fort
Providence
Yellowknife
Fort
Nelson
Fort Smith
Great Slave
Lake
Uranium City
Peace River
Lake
Athabasca
Reindee
Lake
Dawson
Creek
Peace
River
Fort
McMurray
ALBERTA
M
Flin Flo
The Pas
Edmonton
N.
Saskatchewan R.
SASKATCHEWAN
Prince
Albert
Calgary
Saskatchewan R.
Saskatoon
Medicine
Hat
S.
Saskatchewan R.
Regina
Winnip
Lethbridge
Moose Jaw
Bran
Spokane
Snake
River
Missouri
Helena
Bismarck
UNITED
STA
Boise
River
Pierre
R.

Map of
CANADA
SCALE OF MILES
0 100 200 300 400 500
⛤ Capitals of Countries
◉ Capitals of Provinces
and Territories
• Cities
▬▬ Boundaries of Countries
━━ Boundaries of Provinces
and Territories
┈┈ Boundaries of Districts
▲ Mountain Peaks

82

ICELAND

Reykjavik

90° 80° 70° 60° 50° 40° 30° 20°

80° 70°

G R E E N L A N D
(Danish)

h Islands

Ellesmere Island

Devon Island

Thule

BAFFIN

BAY

60°

FRANKLIN

Lancaster Sound

Arctic Circle

Gulf of Boothia

Baffin Island

Davis Strait

Godthåb

Cape
Farewell

STRICT

Foxe

Basin

Frobisher Bay

A T L A N T I C

OF T E R R I T O R I E S

Southampton
Island

Hudson Strait

O C E A N

EWATIN

Chesterfield
Inlet

Ungava
Peninsula

Nain

50°

HUDSON

Inoucdjouac

Fort-
Chimo

L a b r a d o r

N e w f o u n d l a n d

Battle
Harbour

Churchill

BAY

Belcher
Islands

Schefferville

Goose Bay

Grand
Falls

Newfoundland

Gander

St.
John's

Port
Nelson

River

Fort George

Anticosti
Island

Corner
Brook

ITOBA

Severn
River

James

Bay

Q U E B E C

Lake
Mistassini

Sept-Îles

Gulf of
St. Lawrence

St. Pierre &
Miquelon
(French)

peg

Moosonee

Gaspé
Peninsula

PRINCE
EDWARD
ISLAND

Charlottetown

Sydney

Cape Breton
Island

Sable Island

O N T A R I O

Lake Nipigon

Chicoutimi

NEW
BRUNSWICK

Moncton

NOVA

Kenora

Kapuskasing

Rouyn

Quebec

River

Fredericton

SCOTIA

Halifax

Lake of
the Woods

Thunder
Bay

Timmins

North
Bay

Sudbury

Montreal

St. Lawrence

Sherbrooke

Saint
John

APPALACHIAN MTS.

Yarmouth

Cape Sable

40°

Duluth

Lake Superior

Sault
Ste Marie

Ottawa

Cornwall

St. Paul

Lake
Huron

Toronto

Lake
Ontario

Boston

Minneapolis

Milwaukee

Lake Michigan

Buffalo

New York

Mississippi R.

Detroit
Windsor

Lake Erie

Greenwich

90°

80°

70°

Copyright by C. S. HAMMOND & Co. N.Y.

83

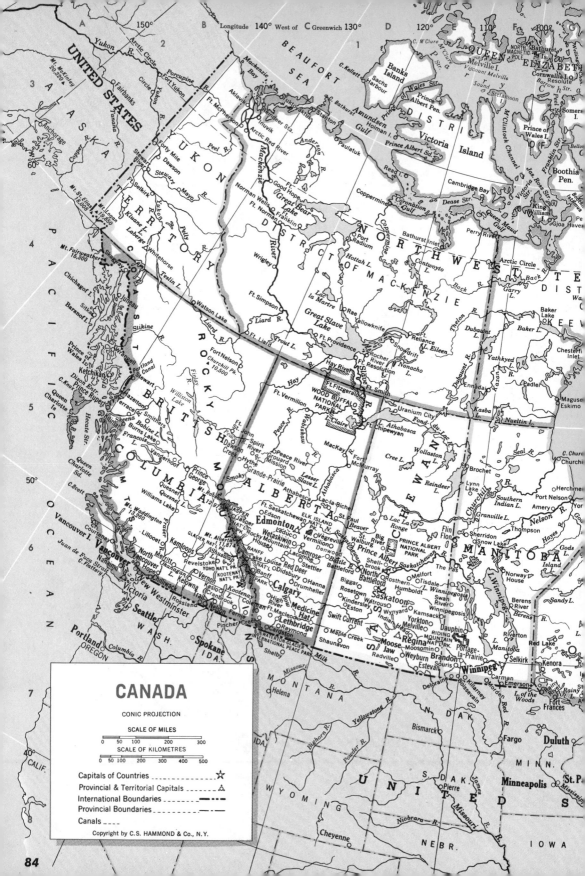

CANADA

CONIC PROJECTION

SCALE OF MILES

0 50 100 200 300

SCALE OF KILOMETRES

0 50 100 200 300 400 500

Capitals of Countries .... ☆

Provincial & Territorial Capitals ...... △

International Boundaries ---·---·---

Provincial Boundaries ----·----

Canals ----

Copyright by C.S. HAMMOND & Co., N.Y.

84

GREENLAND
BAFFIN BAY
DAVIS STRAIT
ATLANTIC OCEAN
HUDSON BAY
Hudson Str.
FOXE BASIN
BAFFIN ISLAND
Ungava Peninsula
Ungava Bay
QUEBEC
NEWFOUNDLAND
Labrador
NEW BRUNSWICK
NOVA SCOTIA
PRINCE EDWARD I.
Gulf of St. Lawrence
MAINE
VT.
N.H.
MASS.
CONN.
R.I.
N.Y.
PA.
N.J.
MICH.
ILLINOIS
QUEEN ELIZABETH ISLANDS
Scale of Miles
0 50 100 200
ARCTIC OCEAN
ELLESMERE
SVERDRUP ISLANDS
PARRY ISLANDS
Devon I.
Melville Island
Bathurst I.
Cornwallis I.
Resolute
N. MAG. POLE
Viscount Melville Sd.
Lancaster Sd.
Jones Sd.
M'Clure Str.
Banks I.
Prince Patrick I.
Eglinton
Brock I.
Borden I.
Mackenzie King I.
Ellef Ringnes I.
Amund Ringnes I.
Meighen I.
Peary Chan.
Axel Heiberg Island
Eureka
Alexandra Fiord
Grise Fiord
Cornwall I.
Graham I.
Alert
C. Columbia
Kennedy Chan.
Kane Basin
Nares Str.
Smith Sd.
Grise Fiord
Lancaster Sound
Bylot I.
Arctic Bay
Pond Inlet
Admiralty Inlet
Brodeur Pen.
Clyde
Clyde Inlet
C. Raper
Home Bay
Upernavik
Svartenhuk Pen.
Umanak Fiord
Nugssuaq Pen.
Disko I.
Godhavn
Disko Bay
Holsteinsborg
Padloping I.
C. Dyer
C. Walsingham
Cumberland Pen.
Pangnirtung
Cumberland Sound
Nettilling L.
Amadjuak L.
Hall Pen.
Frobisher Bay
Lake Harbour
Resolution I.
Amadjuak
Cape Dorset
Salisbury I.
Foxe Pen.
Bowman Bay
Prince Charles I.
Fury and Hecla Str.
Igloolik
Jens Munk I.
Committee Bay
Melville Pen.
Rae Isthmus
Repulse Bay
Frozen Str.
Foxe Chan.
Southampton I.
Coral Harbour
Roes Welcome Sound
Evans Str.
Nottingham I.
Fisher Str.
C. Low
Coats I.
Mansel I.
Ivugivik
Saglouc
Maricourt (Wakeham)
Akpatok I.
C. Chidley
Hebron
Nutak
Bellin (Payne)
Povungnituk
C. Smith
Payne L.
Port-Nouveau-Québec
Ottawa Is.
Portland Promontory
Inoucdjouac (Port-Harrison)
L. Minto
Ft.-Chimo
Koksoak R.
R. à la Baleine
Fort McKenzie
George R.
Nain
Hopedale
C. Harrison
Hamilton Inlet
Rigolet
Cartwright
Melville L.
Battle Harbour
Belle Isle
C. Bauld
Bell I.
White Bay
Fogo I.
Smallwood Res.
Goose Bay
Churchill R.
Schefferville
Kaniapiskau R.
Clearwater L.
Lac Bienville
Belcher Is.
Richmond Gulf
Poste-de-la-Baleine
Grande R. de la Baleine
C. Henrietta Maria
La Grande-Rivière
Wabush
Natashquan R.
Romaine R.
Str. of Belle Isle
Grand Falls
Gander
Bonavista
Harbour Grace
St. John's
C. Race
Stephenville
Corner Brook
Channel-Port aux Basques
ST. PIERRE & MIQUELON (Fr.)
C. Ray
Cabot Strait
C. North
Magdalen Is.
Pte. Louis XIV
James Bay
Fort-George
Opinaca R.
Eastmain R.
Pletipi L.
Gagnon
R. Moisie
Mingan
Havre-St.-Pierre
Anticosti I.
Sept-Îles Seven Is.
Port-Cartier-Ouest
Port-Menier
Gaspé
Cap-Chat
Chandler
Manicouagan R.
Betsiamites R.
Péribonca R.
Mistassibi R.
Akimiski I.
East-Main
Fort-Rupert
Charlton I.
L. Mistassini
Nottaway R.
Chibougamau
Fawn L.
Winisk R.
Ekwan R.
Attawapiskat R.
Fort Albany
Albany R.
Moosonee
Ogoki R.
Abitibi R.
Missinaibi R.
Armstrong Sta.
Nakina
Kenogami R.
Lookout
Geraldton
Hearst
Kapuskasing
Cochrane
L. Abitibi
La Sarre
Taschereau
Amos
Bell R.
Gouin Res.
L. St-Jean
Roberval
Jonquière
Chicoutimi
Tadoussac
Mont-Joli
Rimouski
Campbellton
Bathurst
Charlottetown
Inverness
Glace Bay
Sydney
Cape Breton I.
Souris
Sable I.
Rivière-du-Loup
Edmundston
Newcastle
Chatham
Moncton
Amherst
Truro
Nipigon
Marathon
Oba
Iroquois Falls
Kirkland Lake
Noranda
Rouyn
Val-d'Or
Timmins
Englehart
Baie-St-Paul
La Tuque
Québec
L. Baskatong
Shawinigan
Trois-Rivières
Woodstock
Fredericton
Saint John
St. Stephen
Bay of Fundy
Windsor
Dartmouth
Halifax
Lunenburg
Bridgewater
Yarmouth
C. Sable
Thunder Bay
White River
Chapleau
New Liskeard
Cobalt
L. Timiskaming
Gatineau R.
Mont-Laurier
MONTRÉAL
Augusta
I. Royale
Lake Superior
Sault Ste. Marie
Sault-Ste-Marie
Thessalon
Blind River
Sudbury
Sturgeon Falls
North Bay
Mattawa
Callander
Pembroke
Renfrew
Ottawa R.
Hull
Ottawa
Sherbrooke
Manitoulin I.
Georgian Bay
Parry Sound
Peterborough
Cornwall
Kingston
Montpelier
Lake Huron
Owen Sound
L. Michigan
TORONTO
Guelph
Hamilton
L. Ontario
Niagara Falls
Buffalo
Albany
BOSTON
C. Cod
Sarnia
London
Milwaukee
DETROIT
Windsor
L. Erie
Cleveland
NEW YORK
STATES

MARITIME PROVINCES

SCALE OF MILES

0 10 20 30 40 50

Provincial Capitals ⋯⋯⋯ ⊛   Provincial Boundaries ― ⋅ ―
County Seats ⋯⋯⋯⋯⋯ ⊙   County Boundaries ― ― ―
International Boundaries ― ⋅⋅ ―

Copyright by C. S. HAMMOND & CO., N.Y.

86

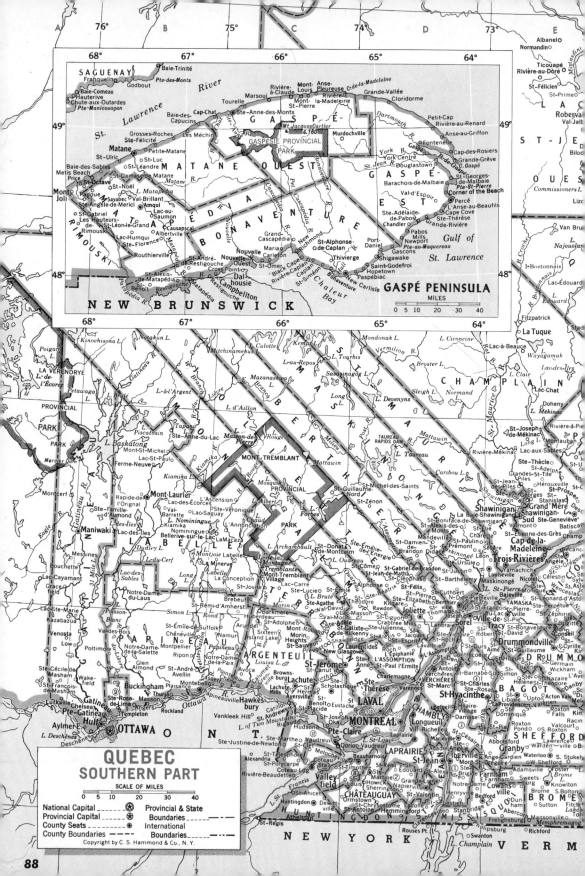

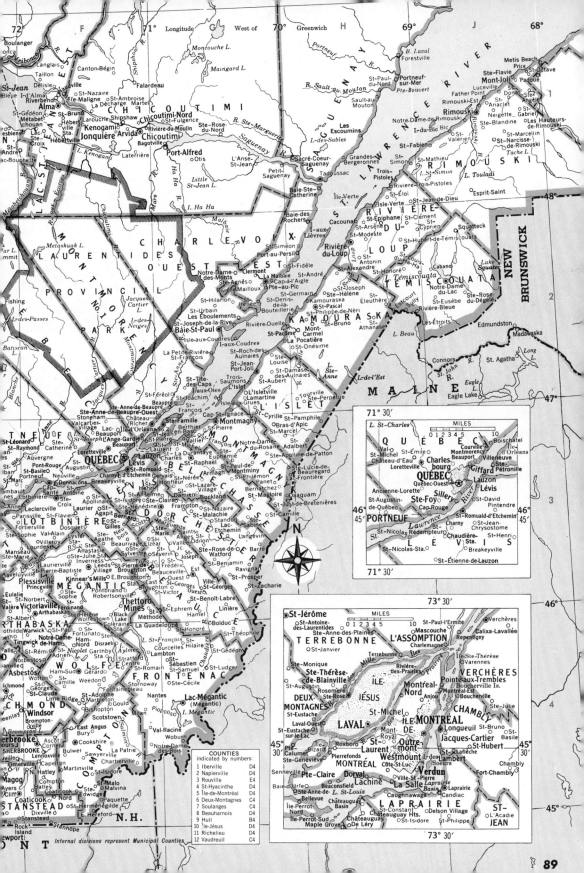

COUNTIES
indicated by numbers:

1 Iberville   D4
2 Napierville   D4
3 Rouville   E4
4 St-Hyacinthe   D4
5 Île-de-Montréal D4
6 Deux-Montagnes   C4
7 Soulanges   C4
8 Beauharnois   D4
9 Hull   B4
10 Île-Jésus   D4
11 Richelieu   D4
12 Vaudreuil   C4

Internal divisions represent Municipal Counties

ONTARIO
SOUTHERN PART

SCALE

0 10 20 30 40 50 MI.

0 10 20 30 40 50 KM.

National Capital .... ⊛
Provincial Capital .... ⊛
County Seats ....
International
Boundaries ....

Provincial & State
Boundaries ....
County Boundaries ....
Canals ....

© C.S. HAMMOND & Co., N.Y.

ONTARIO
CENTRAL PART

0 25 50 75 100 125 MI.

0 25 50 75 100 125 KM.

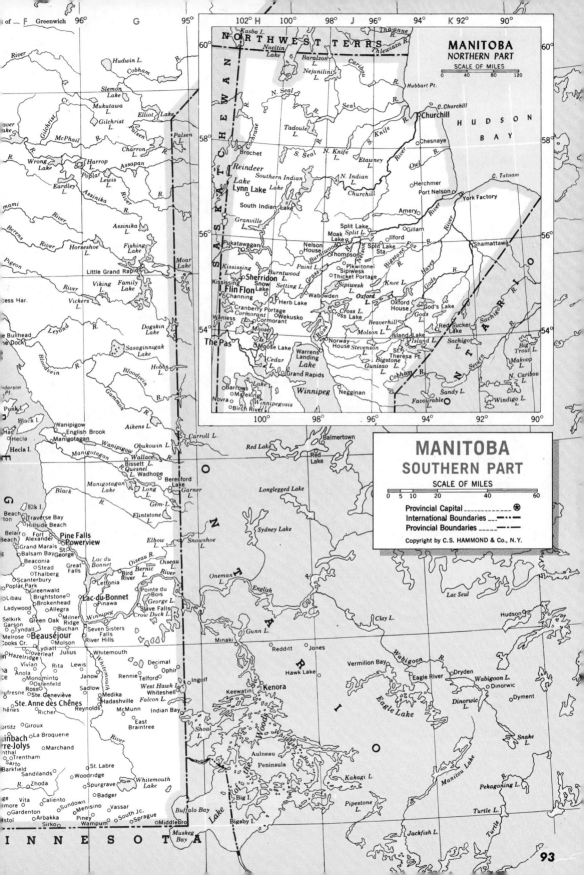

SASKATCHEWAN NORTHERN PART

N.W. TERR'S.

20 40 60 80 100 MI.
0 20 40 60 80 100 KM.

ALBERTA · MANITOBA

Camsell Portage Eldorado
Uranium City Bushell Beaverlodge L.
Fond du Lac Stony Rapids Scott Selwyn L.
L. Athabasca Black L. Charlebois L.
Riou L. Black Fond. Bickerton Lake
Cluff Lake McFarlane R. Cochrane R.
Trout R. Collins Bay
William R. Cree Wollaston L. Wollaston
Forrest L. Geikie River
Cree L. Geikie R.
Lloyd Lake Wathaman R. Highrock Lake
Clearwater R. Frobisher L. Foster R. Brabant L.
Turnor Lake Mudjatik R. Haultain R.
La Loche Peter Pond L. LAC LA RONGE PROV. PK. Sandy Bay
Buffalo Narrows Ile-à-la-Crosse Lac Ile-à-la-Crosse Pine House Churchill Pelican Narrows
Canoe L. Canoe Beauval La Ronge Lac La Ronge Amisk L.
Primrose L. MEADOW LAKE PROV. PARK Doré L. Air Ronge Deschambault WAPAWEKKA HILLS Attitti L.
Goodsoil Dore Lake Molanosa Flin Flon
Dorintosh Green Lake Montreal L. Denare Beach
Peerless Creighton
Perceland PRINCE ALBERT NAT'L. PK. Cumberland L. Sturgeon Weir

SASKATCHEWAN
SOUTHERN PART

SCALE

0 5 10 20 40 60 MI.
0 5 10 20 40 60 KM.

Provincial Capital ·········· ⊛
International Boundaries ·—·—·—
Provincial Boundaries ·—··—··—

Copyright by C. S. HAMMOND & CO., N.Y.

(Main map – Southern Part, selected labels)

Mossy R. Cumberland
Saskatchewan River The Pas
Torch R. Saskeram L.
Squaw Rapids Carrot R. Pasquia R.
Tobin Lake Turnberry
White Fox PASQUIA HILLS
Nipawin
Smokey River
Codette Carrot River Moose
Pontrilas Orange Jordan River
Carlea Aylsham Connell Creek
Ridgedale Zenon Park Arborfield
Crooksby New Osgoode Clashmoor
Tisdale Peesane Crooked Mistatim Prairie
Valparaiso Eldersley River River
Bjorkdale
Sylvania Steen Ghelan
McKague Revoy Carragana Bertwell
Algrove Beach Somme Dillabough
GREENWATER LAKE PROV. PARK Porcupine Plain Reserve
Archerwill Nora Etomami PORCUPINE HILLS
Rose Perigord
Valley Ponass Usherville
Fosston Lakes Rockford Endeavour
Kelvington Nut Mountain Swan Plain
Hendon Lintlaw Okla Hinchliffe Arabella
Paswegin Hazel Dell Ketchen Lady Lake Whitebeech
Wadena Kylemore Danbury
Kuroki Margo Invermay Tadmore Preeceville Stenen
Mozart Elfros Ramsay Dernic Hyas
Wynyard Leslie Edmore Tuffnell Sturgis Norquay
Wishart Insinger Theodore Pelly
Bankend Good Spirit L. Buchanan St. Philips
West Bend Springside
BEAVER HILLS Parkerview Gorlitz
Goodeve GOODSPIRIT PROV. PARK Ebenezer Rhein Togo
Keliher Jedburgh Orcadia Stornoway
Jasmin Willowbrook Arcola Hamton
Ituna Fonehill Tonkin Dunleath Runnymede
Hubbard Otthon Rokeby Wroxton Deepdale
Goodeve Fenwood Leech Saltcoats Dropmore
Dysart Crescent Lake MacNutt Inglis
Lipton FILE HILLS Birmingham Bredenbury
Fort San Lorlie Duff Cana Churchbridge Russell
Balcarres PHEASANT HILLS Killaly Langenburg
Abernethy Lemberg Neudorf Grayson Marchwell
Fort Katepwa Beach Hyde Atwater Yarbo
Qu'Appelle Edgeley Dubuc Esterhazy Gerald
Avonhurst Marieval West Bird Stockholm Spy Hill
Indian Head Sintaluta Hazel Cliffe Tantallon
Wolseley Summerberry Bear Creek
Vibank Broadview Rocanville
Davin Odessa Grenfell Oakshela Percival Whitewood Welwyn
Kendal Baring Glenavon Burrows Wapella
Montmartre Candiac Windthorst St. Hubert Mission
Francis Peebles Kipling Moosomin
Sedley Bemersyde Langbank Fleming
Tyvan Mutrie Vandura
Osage Corning Kennedy Kelso Doonside
Colfax Fillmore Wawota Fairlight
Cedoux Creelman Handsworth Walpole Maryfield
Yellow Grass Talmage Kenosee Park Carlyle L. Ryerson Virden
McTaggart Heward MOOSE MTN. Resort Parkman
Weyburn Griffin Stoughton Kisbey Carlyle Manor Redvers
Ralph Froude Arcola Wauchope
Halbrite Innis Forget Wordsworth Cr. Bellegarde
Goodwater Midale Willmar Antler
Colgate Macoun Benson Woodley Browning Cantal Storthoaks
Tribune Cullen Lampman Alida Fertile
Bromhead Hitchcock Steelman Alameda
Ratcliffe Ongre Frobisher Oxbow Carievale
Outram Torquay Bienfait Glen Ewen
Roche Percee Beaver Park Carnduff
North Portal Lyleton
Crosby Flaxton Sherwood Antler

ALBERTA · SASKATCHEWAN

(Eastern/Manitoba side labels)

Shoal Lake Birtle Minnedosa Neepawa Gladstone
Beulah Hamiota Rivers
Rossburn Glencairn
RIDING MOUNTAIN NATIONAL PARK
Brandon Carberry
Oak Lake SPRUCE WOODS PROV. PARK
Souris
Hartney Minto Greenway
Lauder
Whitewater L. Boissevain Killarney
Melita Deloraine Wakopa
TURTLE MTN. PROV. PARK
St. John Hansboro
Bottineau Dunseith

N O R T H   D A K O T A

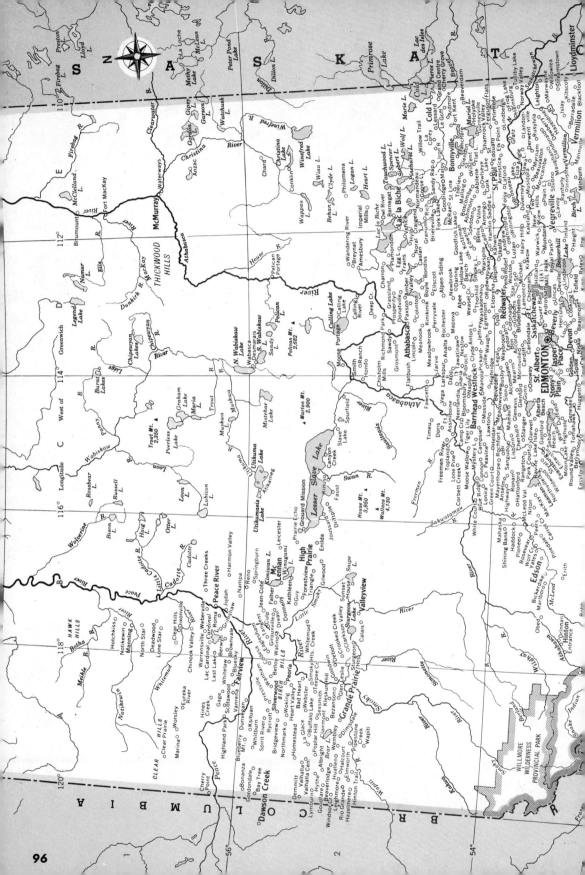

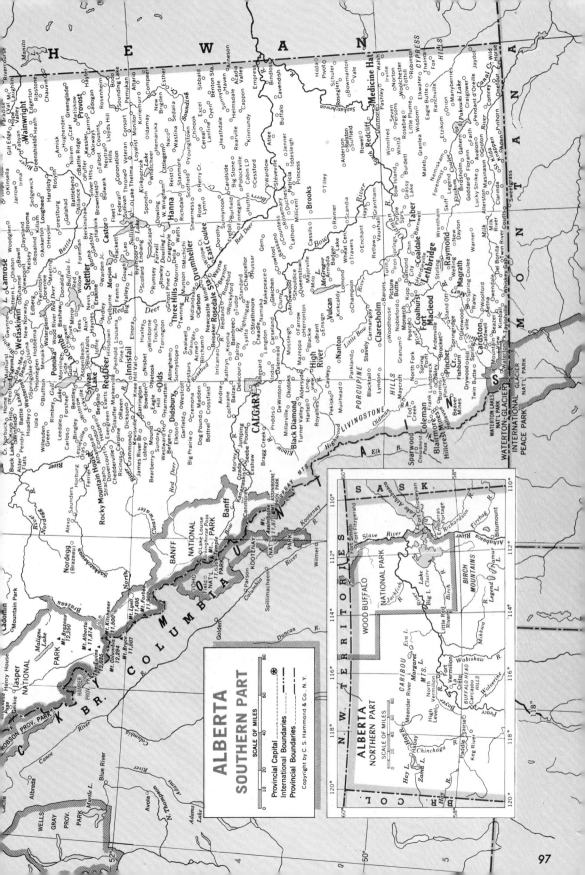

ALBERTA
SOUTHERN PART

SCALE OF MILES

Provincial Capital ⊛
International Boundaries
Provincial Boundaries

Copyright by C. S. Hammond & Co., N. Y.

ALBERTA
NORTHERN PART

SCALE OF MILES

BRITISH COLUMBIA
SOUTHERN PART

SCALE

0   15   30   60   90   120 MI.

0   15   30   60   90   120 KM.

Provincial Capital .... ⊛
State Capital .... ◉
International Boundaries .... —··—··—
Provincial Boundaries .... —·—·—·

© C.S. HAMMOND & CO., N.Y.

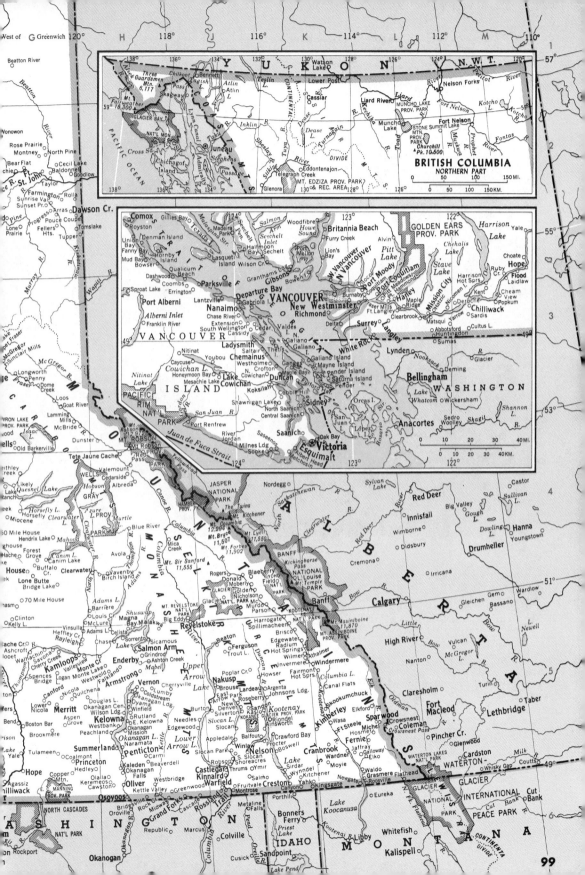

Map of
UNITED STATES
LAMBERT CONFORMAL CONIC PROJECTION
Copyright by C. S. HAMMOND & Co., N.Y.
SCALE OF MILES
0   50   100   200   300

Capitals of Countries
State and Provincial Capitals
International Boundaries
State Boundaries
Provincial Boundaries

Copyright by C. S. Hammond & Co., N.Y.

APPROXIMATE ELEVATIONS
10,000 ft.
5,000 ft.
2,000 ft.
1,000 ft.
500 ft.
Sea level
Depression

Longitude 90° West of Greenwich

UNITED STATES

POLYCONIC PROJECTION

SCALE OF MILES

0 50 100 200 300 400

SCALE OF KILOMETRES

100 200 300 400

Capitals of Countries .... ☆
State Capitals .... △
International Boundaries ....

© Copyright HAMMOND INCORPORATED, Maplewood, N.J.

103

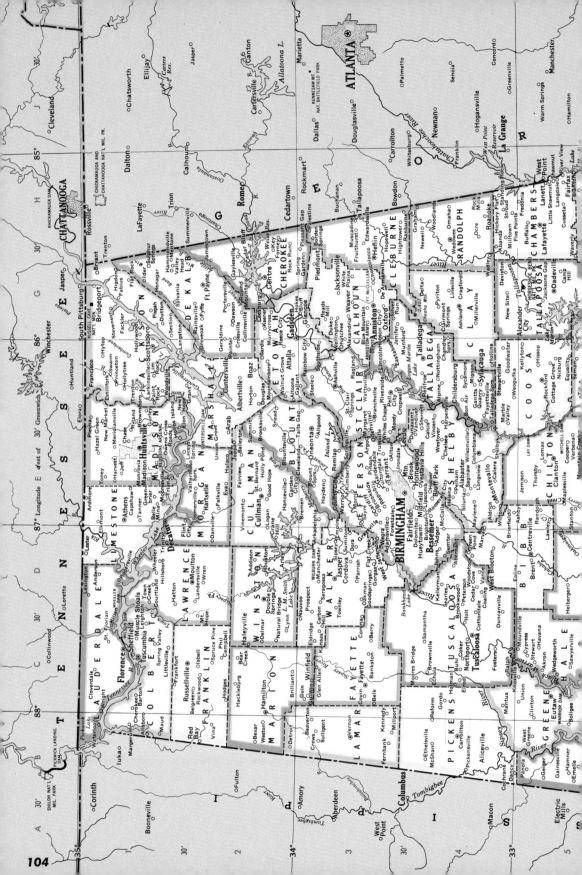

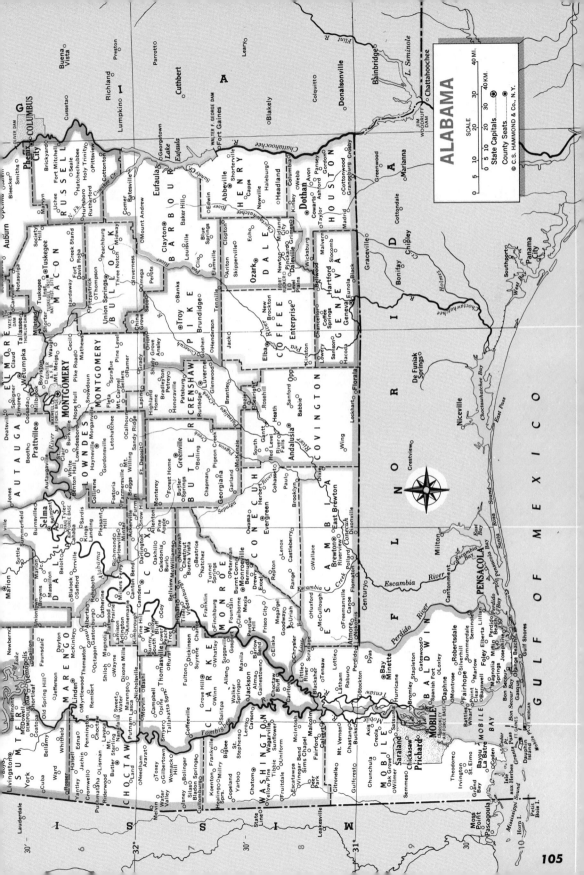

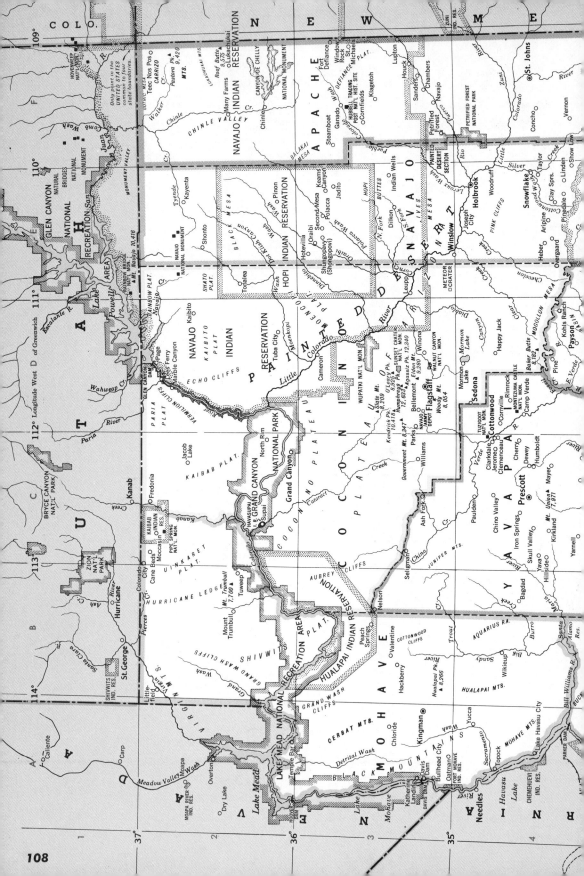

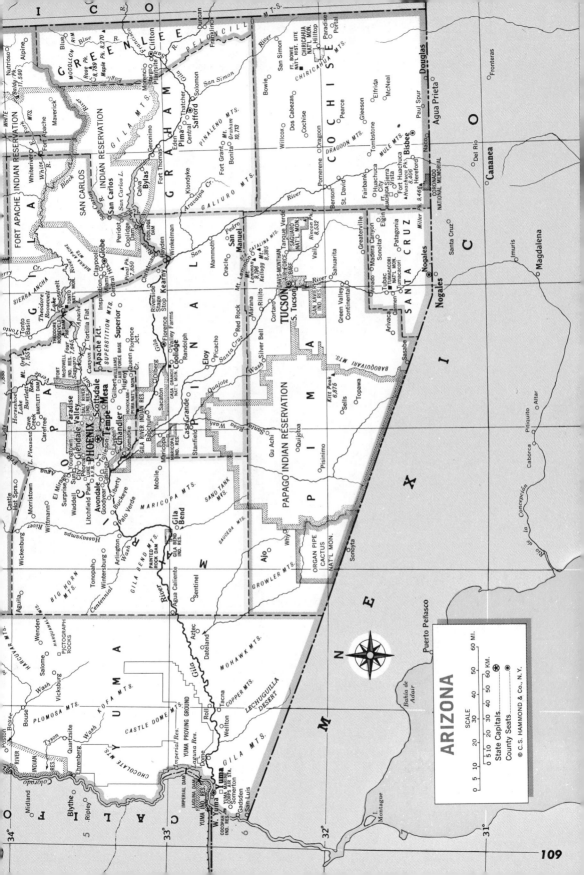

ARIZONA

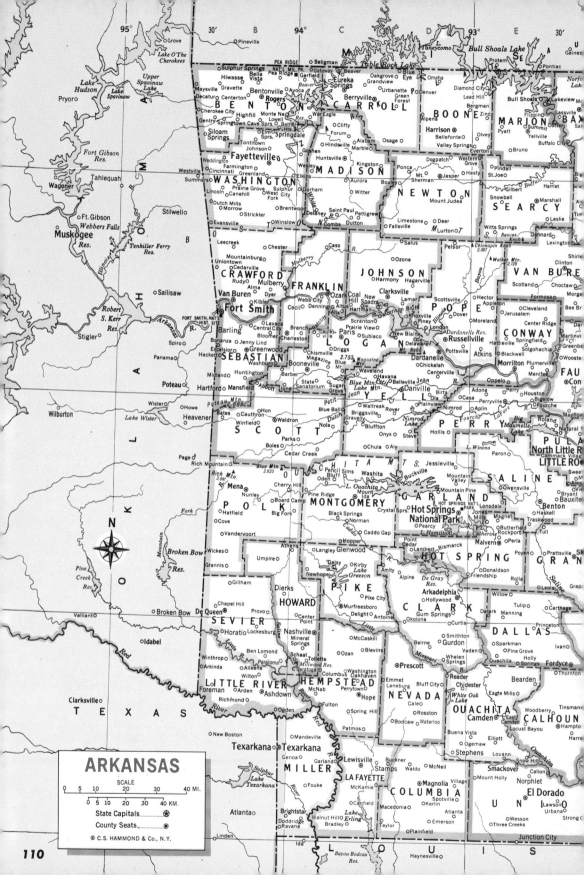

ARKANSAS

SCALE

0 5 10 20 30 40 MI.

0 5 10 20 30 40 KM.

State Capitals ⊛

County Seats ⊙

© C.S. HAMMOND & Co., N.Y.

110

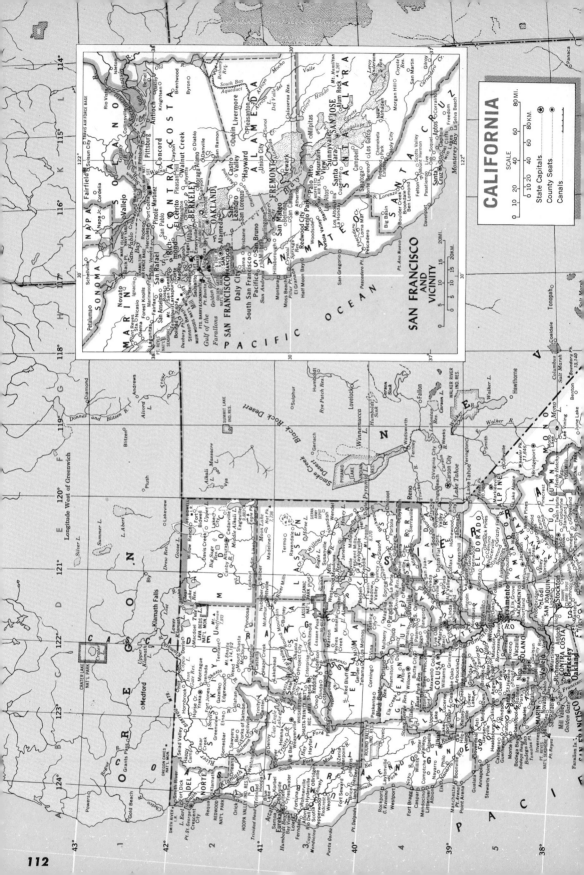

CALIFORNIA

San Francisco and Vicinity

Pacific Ocean

OREGON

NEVADA

SCALE
0 10 20 40 60 80 MI.
0 10 20 40 60 80 KM.

State Capitals
County Seats
Canals

SACRAMENTO AND VICINITY

LOS ANGELES AND VICINITY

113

COLORADO

SCALE
0 5 10 20   30   40 MI.
0 5 10 20   30   40 KM.

State Capitals........⊛ County Seats........◉

© C.S. HAMMOND & Co., N.Y.

CONNECTICUT

SCALE

State Capitals .... ⊛

© C.S. HAMMOND & Co., N.Y.

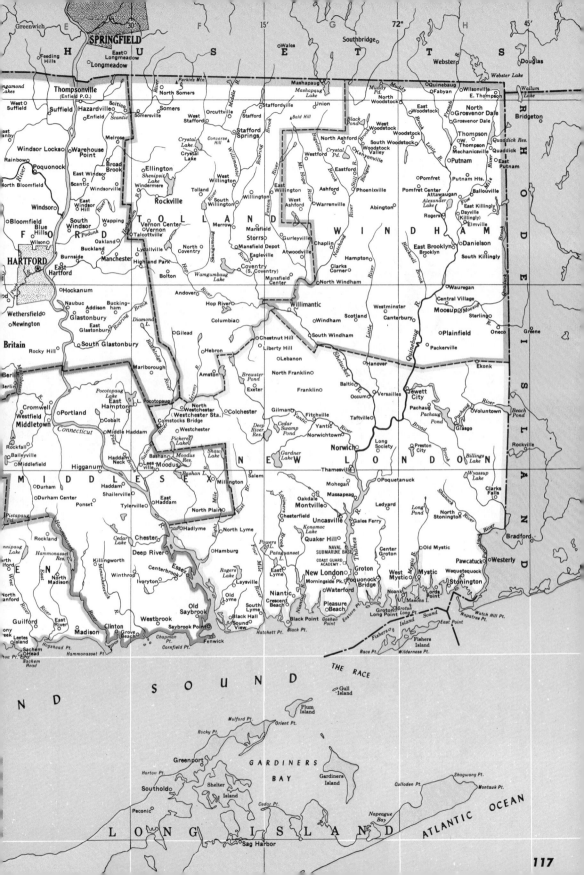

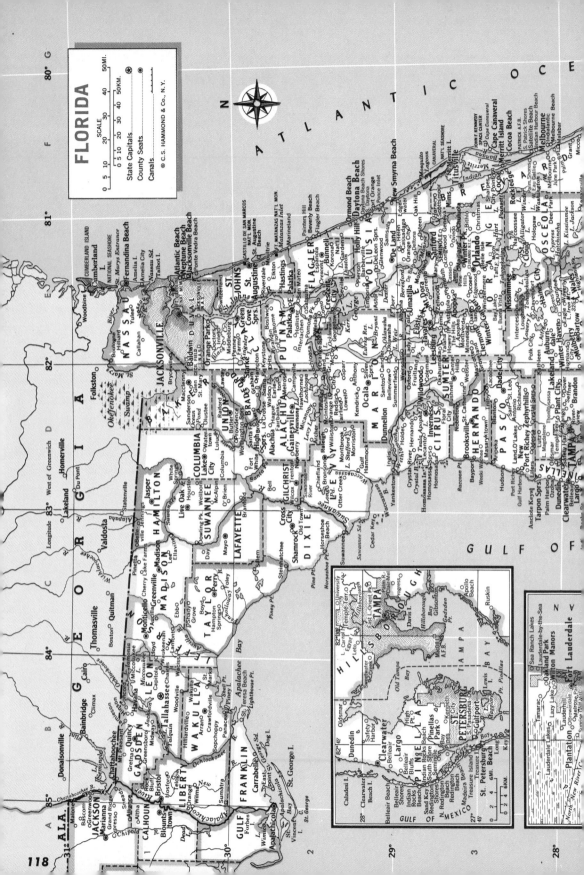

FLORIDA

SCALE
0 5 10 20 30 40 50 MI.
0 5 10 20 30 40 50 KM.

⊗ State Capitals
◉ County Seats
—— Canals

© C.S. HAMMOND & Co., N.Y.

ATLANTIC OCEAN

GULF OF MEXICO

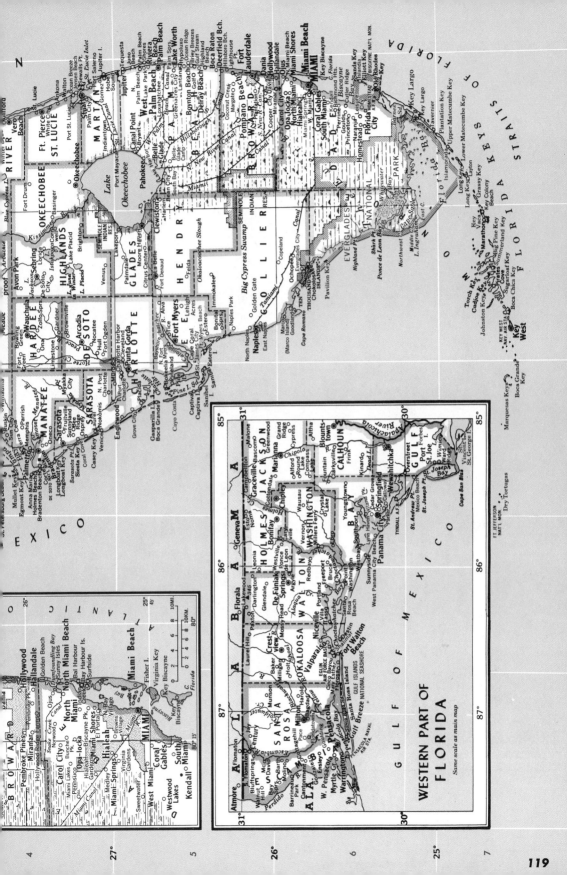

WESTERN PART OF FLORIDA

Same scale as main map

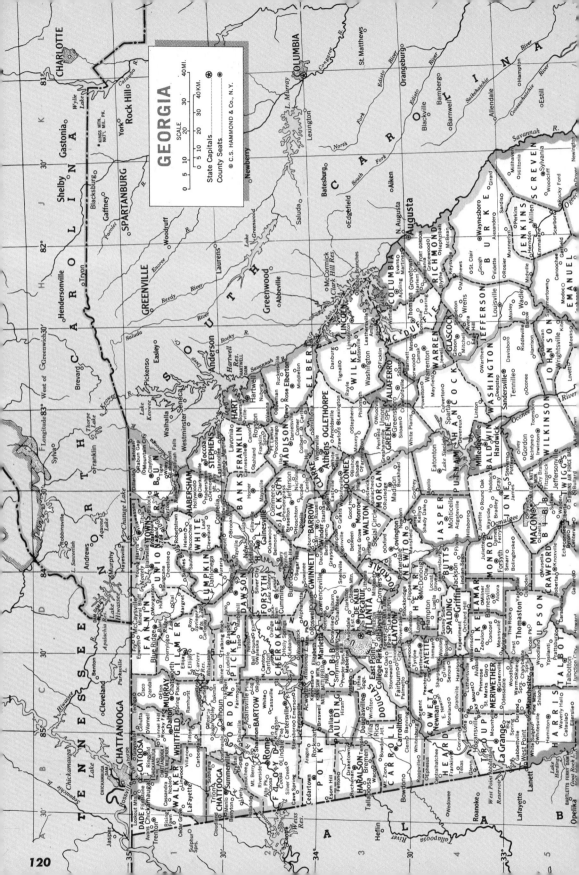

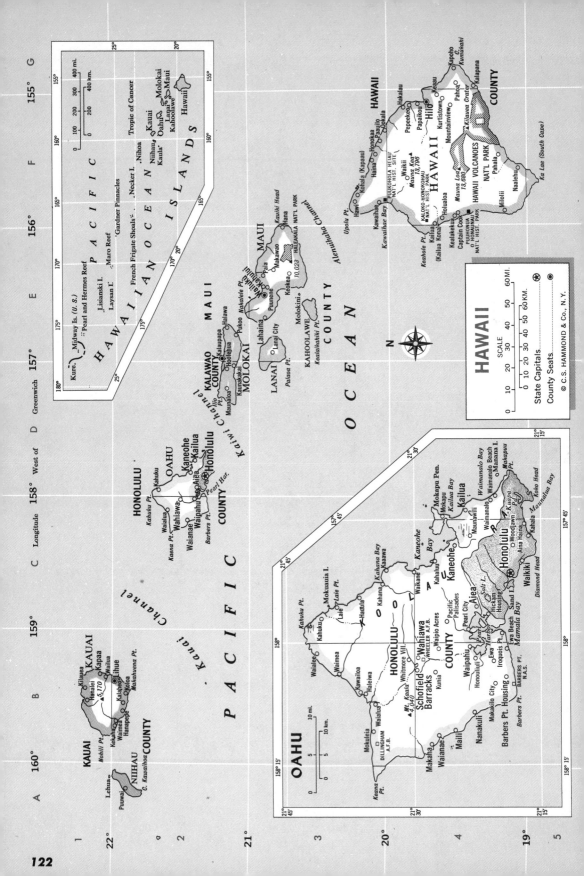

HAWAII

G 155° F 156° E 157° D Greenwich 157° Longitude 158° C West of 158° 159° B 160° A

PACIFIC OCEAN

HAWAIIAN ISLANDS

Kure · Midway Is. (U.S.)
Pearl and Hermes Reef
Lisianski I.
Laysan I.
Maro Reef
Gardner Pinnacles
French Frigate Shoals
Necker I.
Nihoa
Niihau Kaula

Tropic of Cancer

Kauai
Oahu Molokai
Lanai Maui
Kahoolawe
Hawaii

400 mi.
400 km.

HAWAII COUNTY

Kohala (Kapaau)
Haina (Kapaau)
Honokaa
Kukuihaele
Paauilo
Pepeekeo
Papaikou
Hilo
Pahoa
Kapoho
C. Kumukahi
Kalapana

Hawi
Kawaihae Bay
Waikii
Mauna Kea 13,796
Kilauea Crater
Kurtistown
Mountainview

Keahole Pt.
(Kailua Kona)
Kealakekua
Captain Cook
Honaunau
Mauna Loa 13,680
HAWAII VOLCANOES NAT'L PARK
Pahala
Milolii
Naalehu
Ka Lae (South Cape)

MAUI
Kauiki Head
Hana
HALEAKALA NAT'L PARK
Makawao 10,023
Paia
Kahului
Wailuku
Lahaina
Puunene
Keokea

KALAWAO COUNTY
MOLOKAI
Kalaupapa
Kaluaaha
Halawa
Pukoo
Kaunakakai
Maunaloa
Kualapuu
Hoolehua

LANAI
Lanai City
Molokini
Palaoa Pt.
Kealaikahiki Pt.
KAHOOLAWE

MAUI COUNTY

PACIFIC OCEAN

Kaiwi Channel
Kalohi Channel

OAHU
Kahuku
Kaneohe
Kailua
Waialua
Wahiawa
Waipahu Aiea
Honolulu
Pearl Har.
Barbers Pt.
Waianae

HONOLULU COUNTY
HONOLULU

Kaena Pt.

KAUAI
Kilauea
Hanalei
Kapaa
Kilohana 5,170
Kalaheo Lihue
Nawiliwili Pt.
Koloa
Waimea
Hanapepe
Makahuena Pt.

NIIHAU
Lehua
Puuwai
C. Kawaihoa

KAUAI COUNTY

Kauai Channel

N

SCALE
0 10 20 30 40 50 60KM.
0 10 20 30 40 50 60MI.
⊛ State Capitals
◉ County Seats
© C.S. HAMMOND & Co., N.Y.

OAHU

158° 15'
21° 45'
21° 30'
21° 15'

Kahuku Pt.
Kahuku
Mokuauia I.
Laie Pt.
Laie
Hauula
Kahana Bay
Kahana
Kaaawa
Waikane
Waialee
Waimea
Kahaluu
Haleiwa
Waialua
Kawailoa
Mokapu Pen.
Mokapu
Kailua Bay
Kailua
Manana I.
Waimanalo Bay
Waimanalo Beach
Waimanalo
Makapuu
Koolau Range
Kaneohe
Mokapa Pt.
Kaneohe Bay

Mokuleia
DILLINGHAM A.F.B.
Mt. Kaala 4,040
Schofield Barracks
WHEELER A.F.B.
Wahiawa
Whitmore Vill.
Wahiawa
Pacific Palisades
Waipio Acres
Pearl City
Aiea
Salt L.
HONOLULU
Woodlawn
Aina Haina
Kuapa Pd.
Kahala
Waikiki
Koko Head
Diamond Head
Maunalua Bay

Waianae
Maili
Nanakuli
Makaha
Lualualei
Waiahole
Waipahu
Ewa
Honouliuli
Iroquois Pt.
Ewa Beach
Barbers Pt. Housing
BARBERS PT. N.A.S.
Makakilo City
Kunia
Barbers Pt.
Pearl Harbor
Hickam Housing
Hickam A.F.B.
Sand I.
Mamala Bay

HONOLULU COUNTY

Keana Pt.

10 mi.
10 km.
5
0

158° 15'
21° 45'
21° 30'
21° 15'

157° 45'
158°
157° 30'

21° 15'
21°

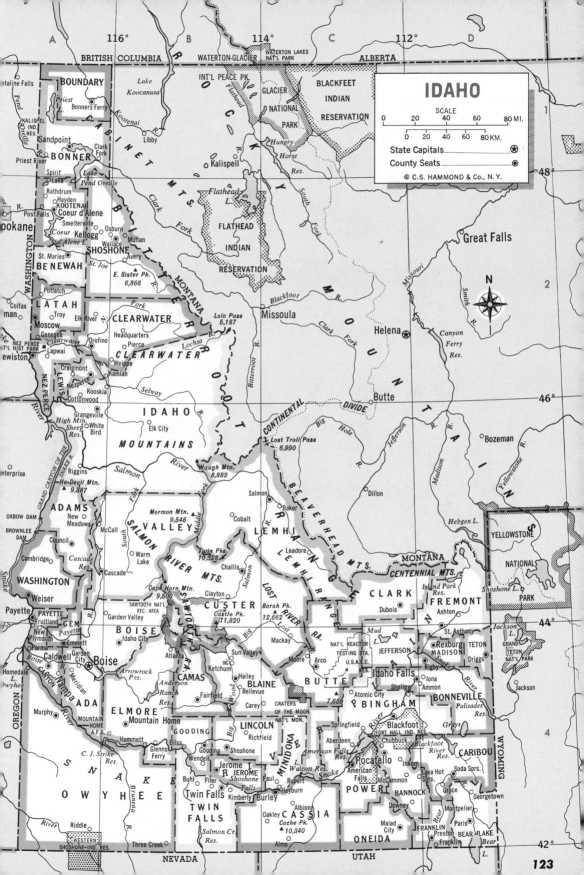

IDAHO

SCALE

0 20 40 60 80 MI.

0 20 40 60 80 KM.

State Capitals.............⊛
County Seats.............◉

© C.S. HAMMOND & Co., N.Y.

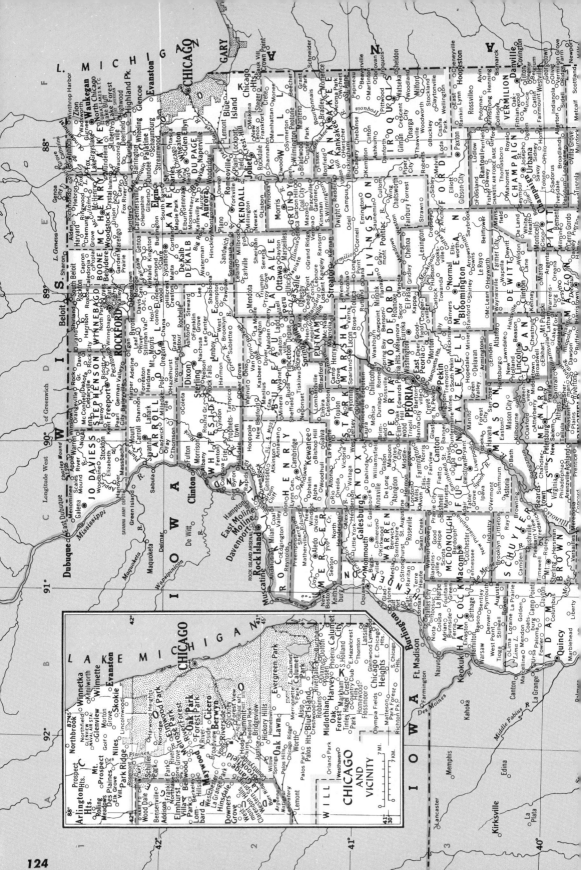

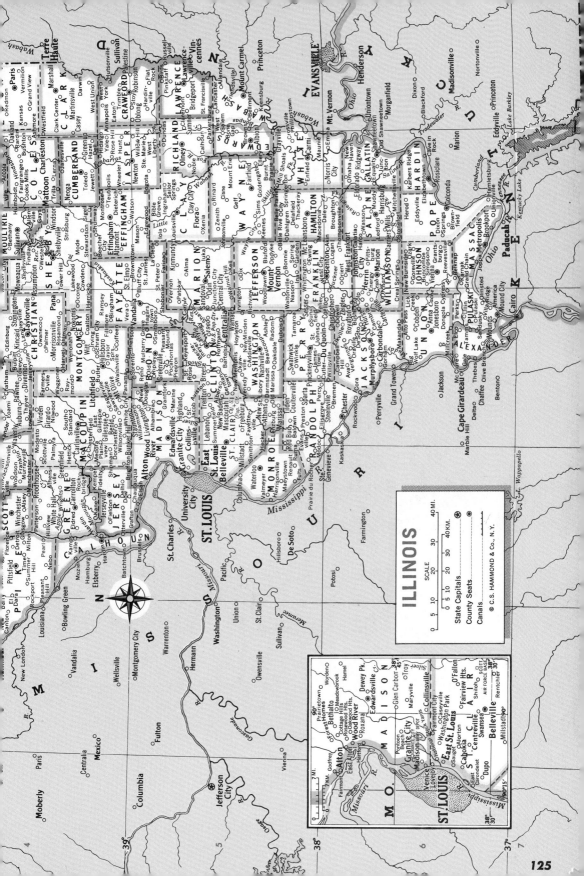

ILLINOIS

SCALE

State Capitals ⊛
County Seats ◉
Canals

© C. S. HAMMOND & CO., N.Y.

ST. LOUIS

125

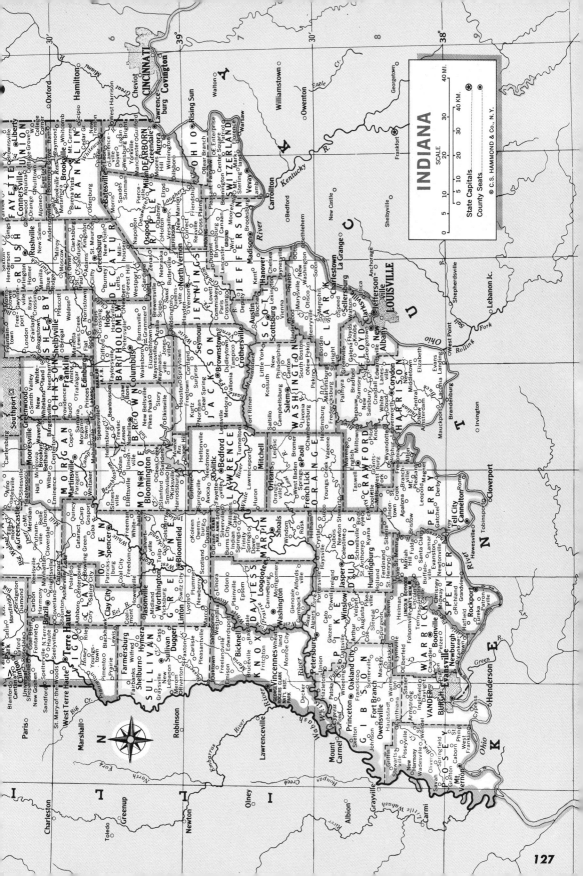

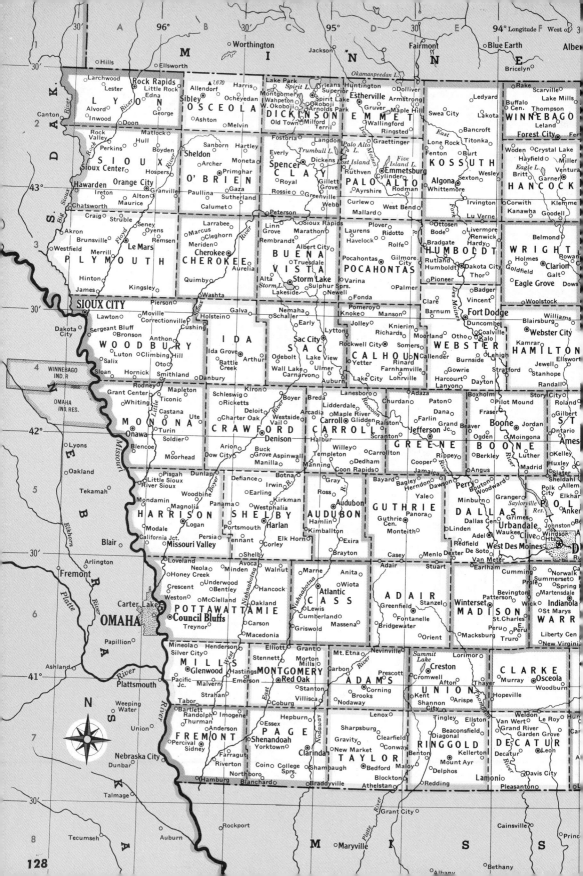

129

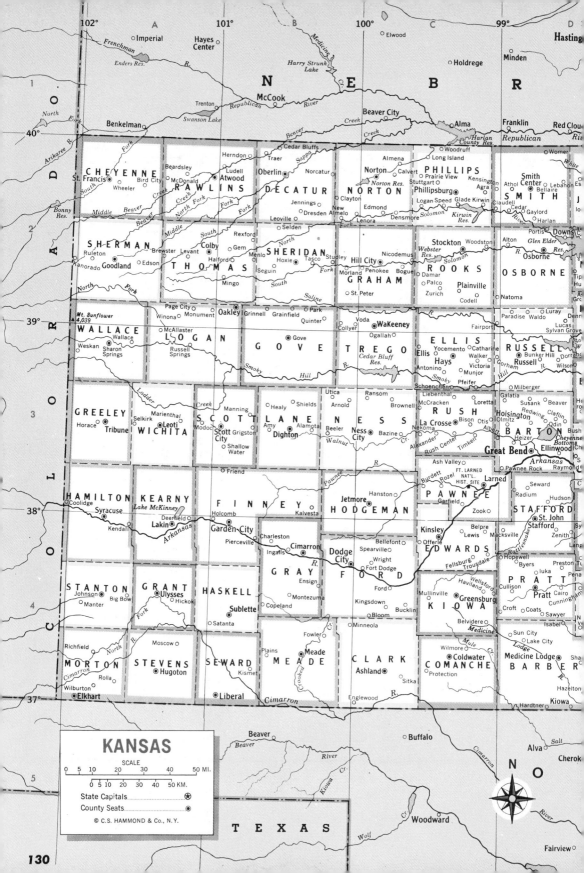

KENTUCKY

SCALE

0 5 10 20 30 40MI.

0 5 10 20 30 40 KM.

State Capitals .... ⊛

County Seats .... ◉

© C.S. HAMMOND & Co., N.Y.

LOUISIANA

SCALE

0 5 10 20 30 40 MI.

0 5 10 20 30 40 KM.

State Capitals...............⊛

Parish Seats...............◉

Canals...............

© C.S. Hammond & Co., N.Y.

134

NEW ORLEANS, BATON ROUGE AND VICINITY

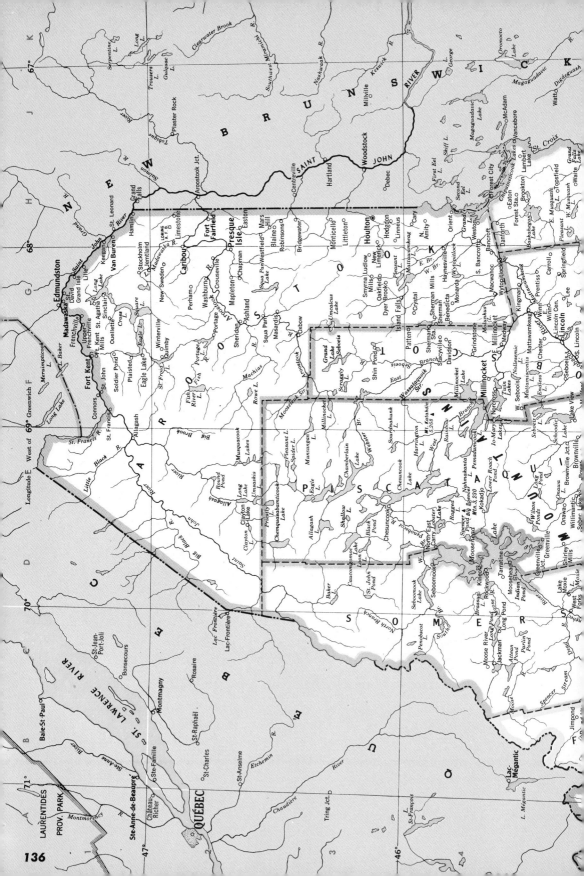

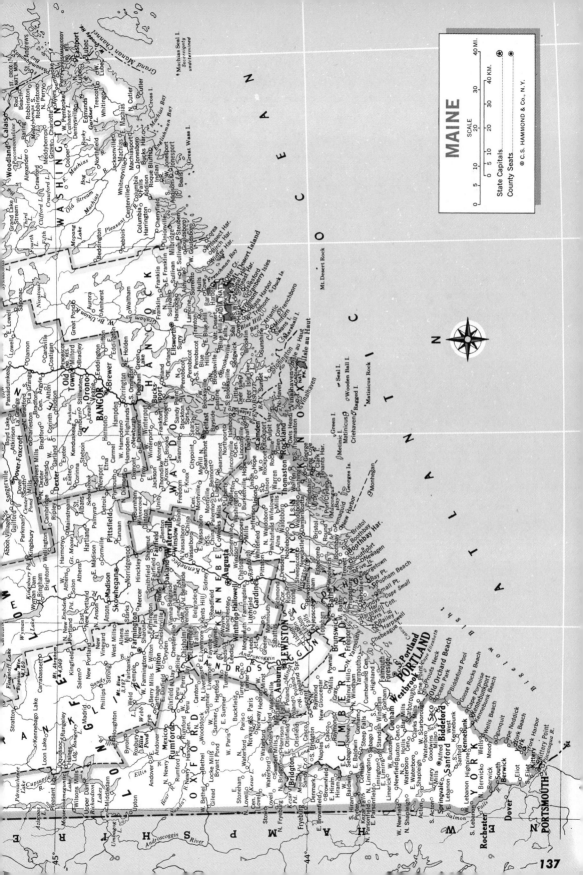

MAINE

SCALE

State Capitals ⊛
County Seats ⊙

© C.S. HAMMOND & Co., N.Y.

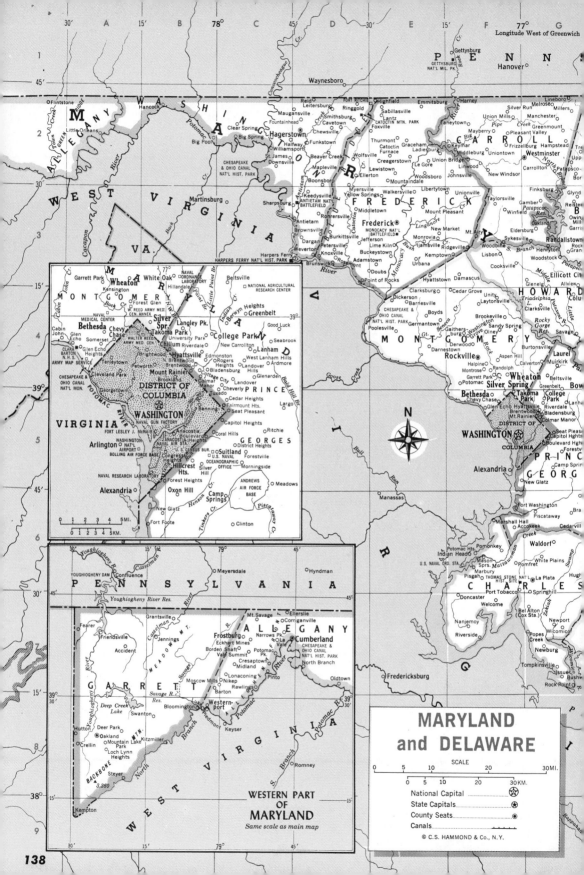

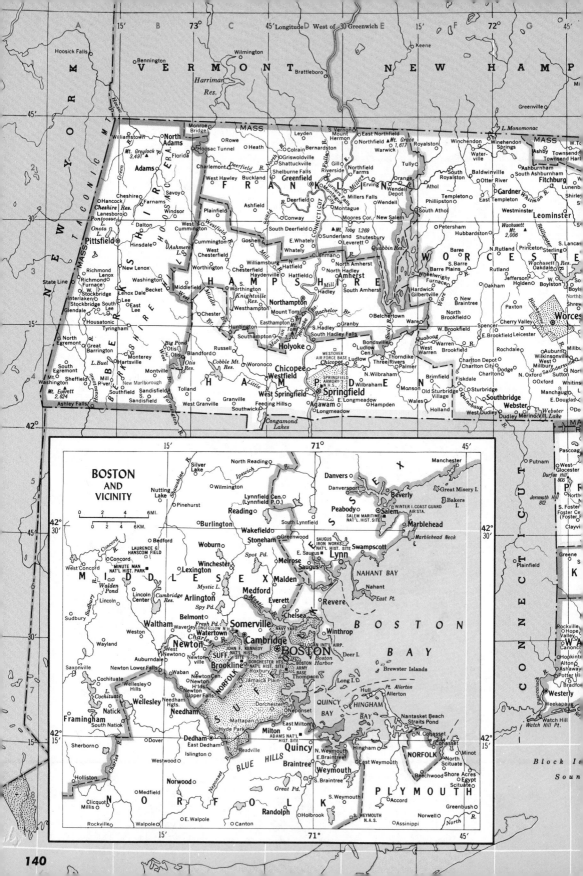

MASSACHUSETTS
and
RHODE ISLAND

SCALE
0   5   10   15   20MI.
0   5   10   15   20KM.

State Capitals............................⊛
County Seats & Courthouses........◉
Canals.................................

© C.S. HAMMOND & Co., N.Y.

141

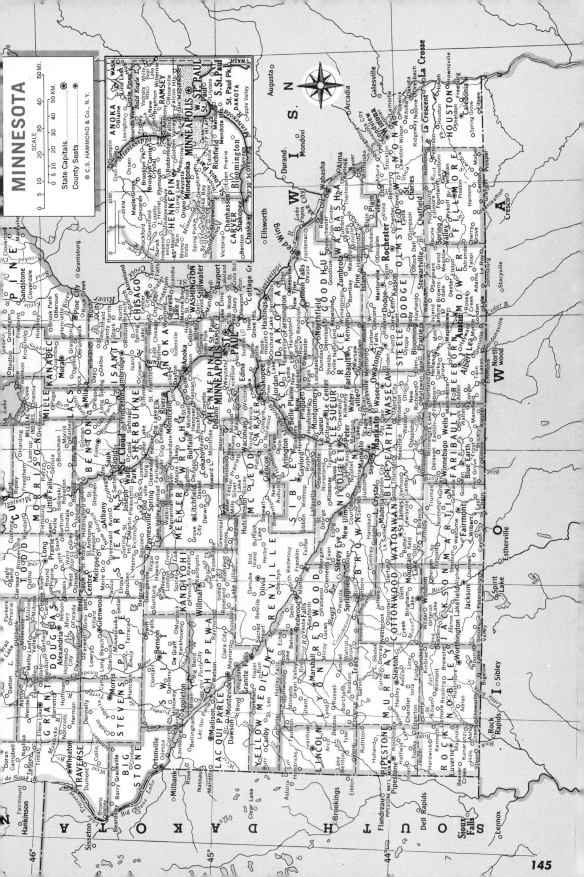

MINNESOTA

SCALE

State Capitals ⊛
County Seats ◉

© C.S. HAMMOND & Co., N.Y.

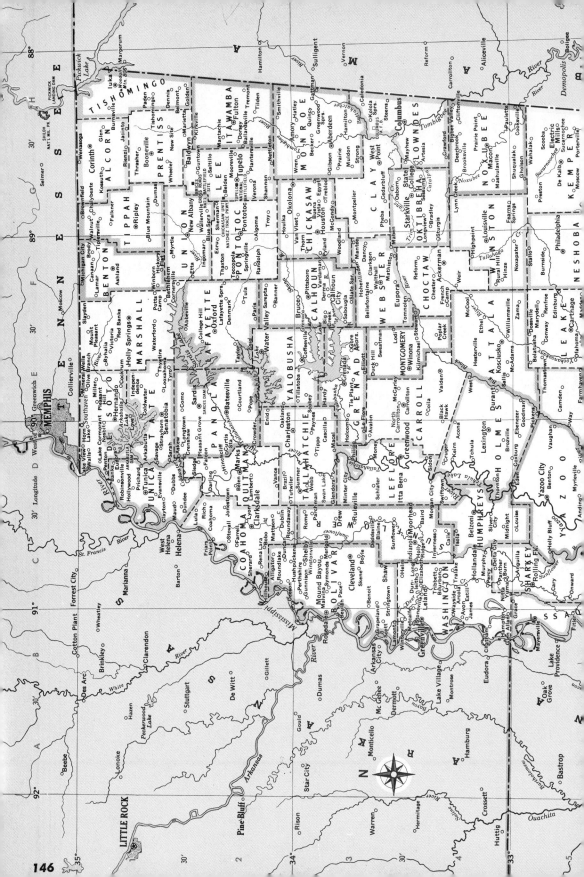

MISSISSIPPI

SCALE

State Capitals: ⊛
County Seats: ⊙

© C.S. HAMMOND & Co., N.Y.

147

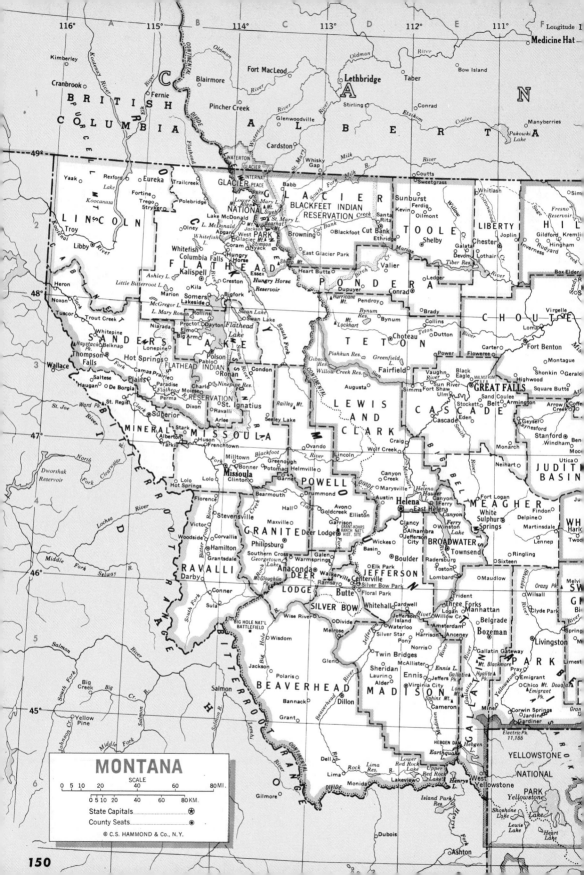

MONTANA

SCALE

| 0 | 5 | 10 | 20 | 40 | 60 | 80 MI. |

| 0 | 5 | 10 | 20 | 40 | 60 | 80 KM. |

State Capitals...............⊛

County Seats...............◉

Ⓒ C.S. HAMMOND & Co., N.Y.

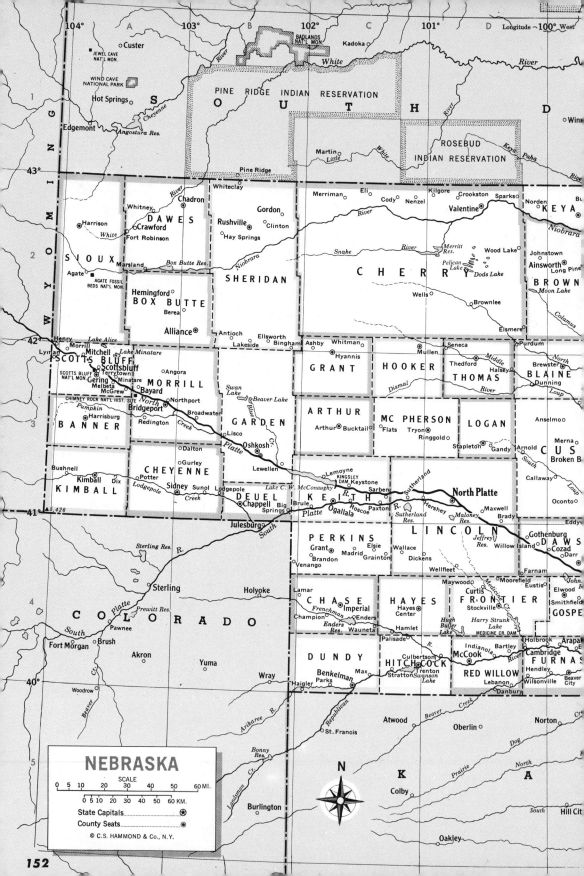

NEBRASKA

SCALE

0 5 10   20   30   40   50   60 MI.

0 5 10 20   40   60 KM.

State Capitals .... ⊛

County Seats .... ◉

© C.S. HAMMOND & Co., N.Y.

152

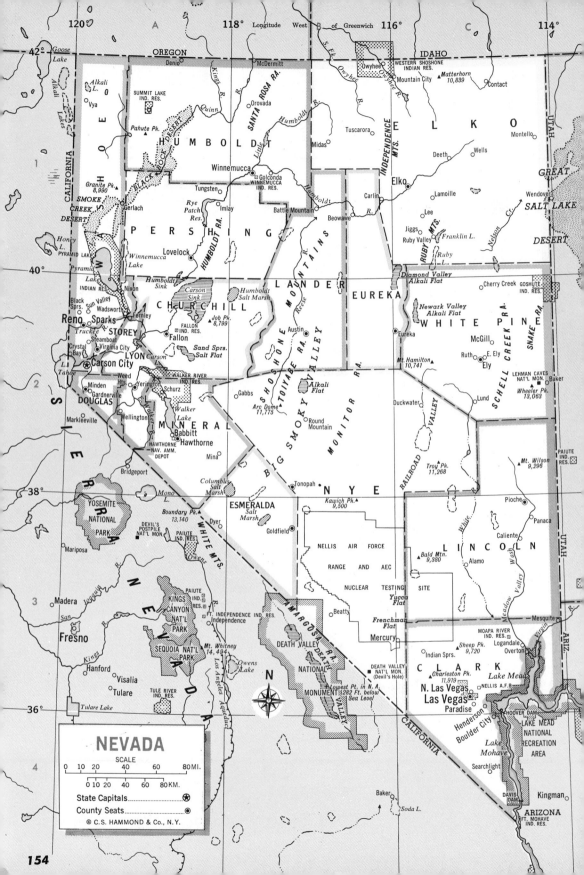

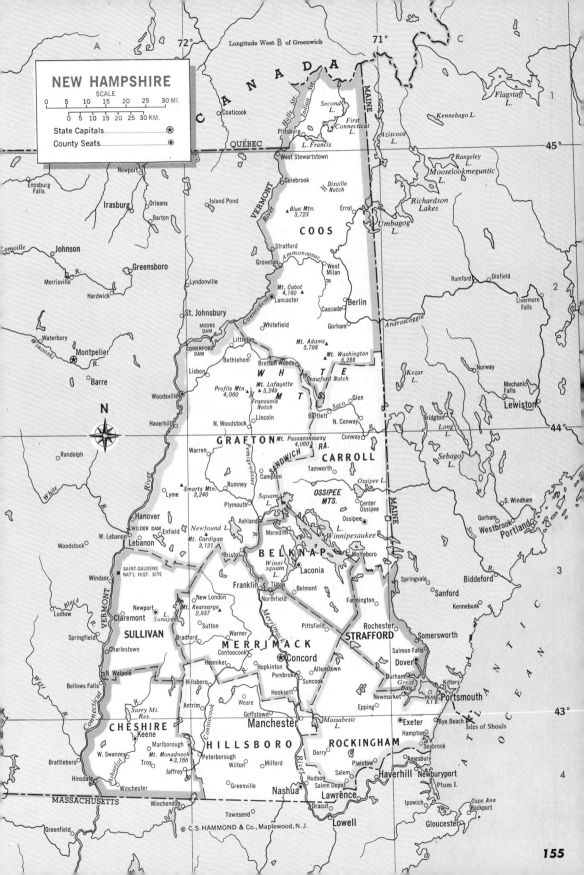

NEW HAMPSHIRE

SCALE

0 5 10 15 20 25 30 MI.

0 5 10 15 20 25 30 KM.

State Capitals..............⊛

County Seats..............◉

Longitude West B of Greenwich

CANADA

QUÉBEC

Coaticook

Pittsburg

L. Francis

Second L.

First Connecticut L.

West Stewartstown

Colebrook

Dixville Notch

Errol

Flagstaff L.

Kennebago L.

Aziscoos L.

Richardson Lakes

Mooselookmeguntic L.

Rangeley L.

45°

Enosburg Falls

Newport

Irasburg

Orleans

Barton

Island Pond

Blue Mtn. 3,723

COOS

Umbagog L.

Rumford

Dixfield

1

Johnson

Greensboro

Morrisville

Hardwick

Lyndonville

Stratford

Groveton

West Milan

Berlin

Androscoggin

Livermore Falls

Lewiston

2

Waterbury

Montpelier

Barre

St. Johnsbury

MOORE DAM

COMERFORD DAM

Whitefield

Mt. Cabot 4,160

Lancaster

Cascade

Gorham

Mt. Adams 5,798

Mt. Washington 6,288

Kezar L.

Norway

Mechanic Falls

Woodsville

Littleton

Bethlehem

Lisbon

Bretton Woods

WHITE MTS.

Crawford Notch

Glen

Bridgton

Long L.

Haverhill

Mt. Lafayette 5,249

Profile Mtn. 4,060

Franconia Notch

Lincoln

Bartlett

N. Conway

Saco

44°

Randolph

N. Woodstock

GRAFTON

Warren

Mt. Passaconaway 4,060

SANDWICH RA.

CARROLL

Tamworth

Sebago L.

Lyme

Smarts Mtn. 3,240

Rumney

Campton

OSSIPEE MTS.

Ossipee L.

Center Ossipee

S. Windham

Gorham

Westbrook

Portland

Woodstock

Hanover

W. Lebanon

WILDER DAM

Enfield

Lebanon

Newfound L.

Mt. Cardigan 3,121

Bristol

Plymouth

Ashland

Meredith

Squam L.

Ossipee

L. Winnipesaukee

Wolfeboro

3

Windsor

SAINT-GAUDENS NAT'L. HIST. SITE

BELKNAP

Winnisquam L.

Laconia

Springvale

Sanford

Biddeford

Ludlow

Black R.

Claremont

Newport

Mt. Kearsarge 2,937

New London

L. Sunapee

Sutton

Franklin

Tilton

Northfield

Belmont

Farmington

Kennebunk

Springfield

Charlestown

SULLIVAN

Bradford

Warner

MERRIMACK

Pittsfield

Rochester

Somersworth

VERMONT

N. Walpole

Bellows Falls

Henniker

Contoocook

Hopkinton

Concord

Allenstown

Suncook

Pembroke

STRAFFORD

Salmon Falls

Dover

Durham

Great Bay

Kittery

43°

Surry Mt. Res.

Hillsboro

Antrim

Weare

Goffstown

Hooksett

Newmarket

PEASE A.F.B.

Portsmouth

Epping

Exeter

Rye Beach

Isles of Shoals

CHESHIRE

Keene

Marlborough

Mt. Monadnock 3,166

Troy

Jaffrey

Peterborough

Wilton

HILLSBORO

Manchester

Massabesic L.

ROCKINGHAM

Derry

Hampton

W. Swanzey

Milford

Amesbury

Seabrook

Brattleboro

Hinsdale

Winchester

Greenville

Nashua

Hudson

Salem

Plaistow

Haverhill

Newburyport

Plum I.

4

MASSACHUSETTS

Winchendon

Townsend

Dracut

Lawrence

Lowell

Ipswich

Cape Ann

Rockport

Gloucester

Greenfield

© C.S. HAMMOND & Co., Maplewood, N.J.

VERMONT

MAINE

Connecticut River

Pemigewasset River

Merrimack River

Contoocook R.

Ashuelot R.

West R.

Winooski R.

ATLANTIC OCEAN

155

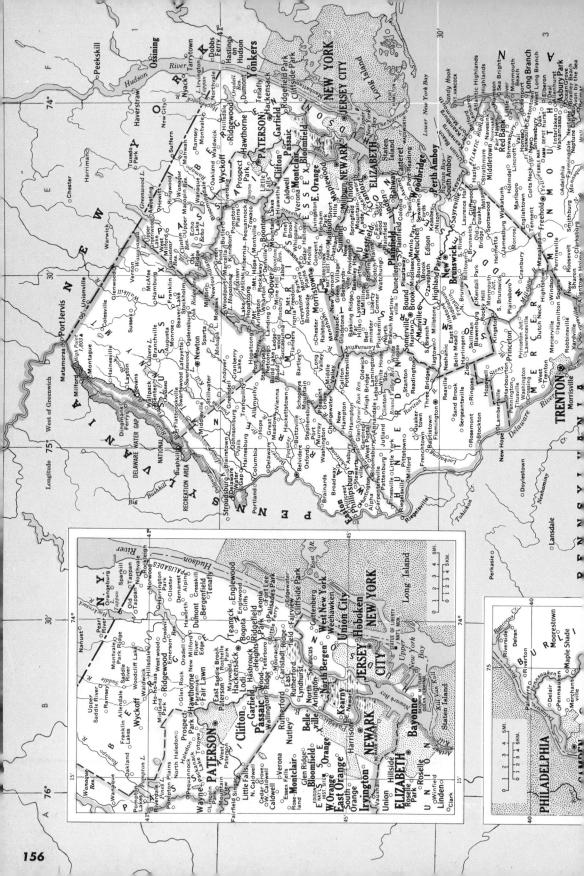

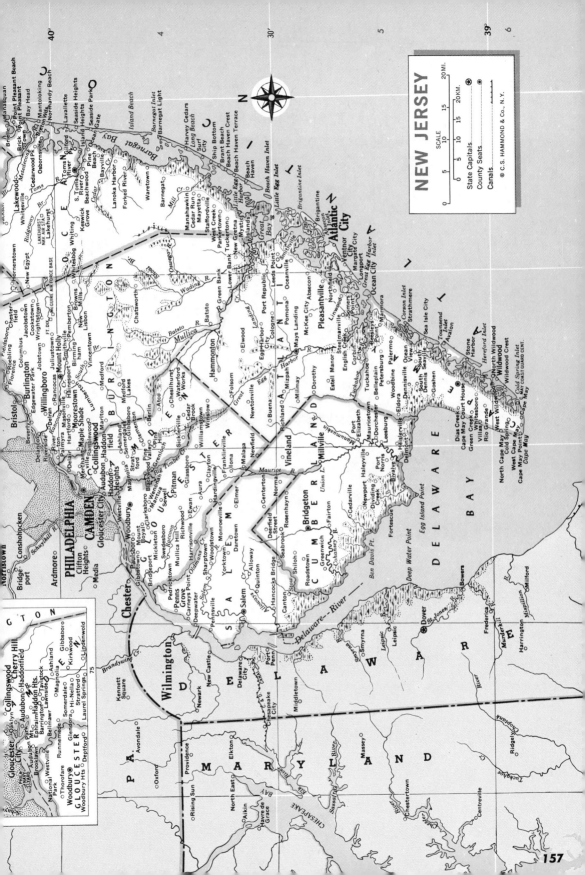

NEW JERSEY

SCALE

0 5 10 15 20 MI.

0 5 10 15 20KM.

State Capitals ⊛
County Seats ◉
Canals

157

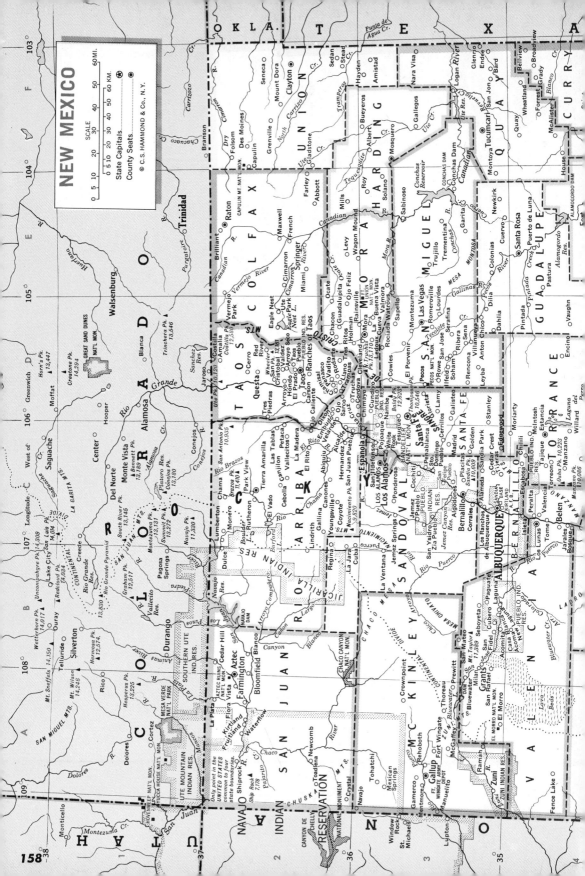

NEW MEXICO

SCALE

State Capitals .... ⊛
County Seats .... ⊙

© C.S. Hammond & Co., N.Y.

158 -38

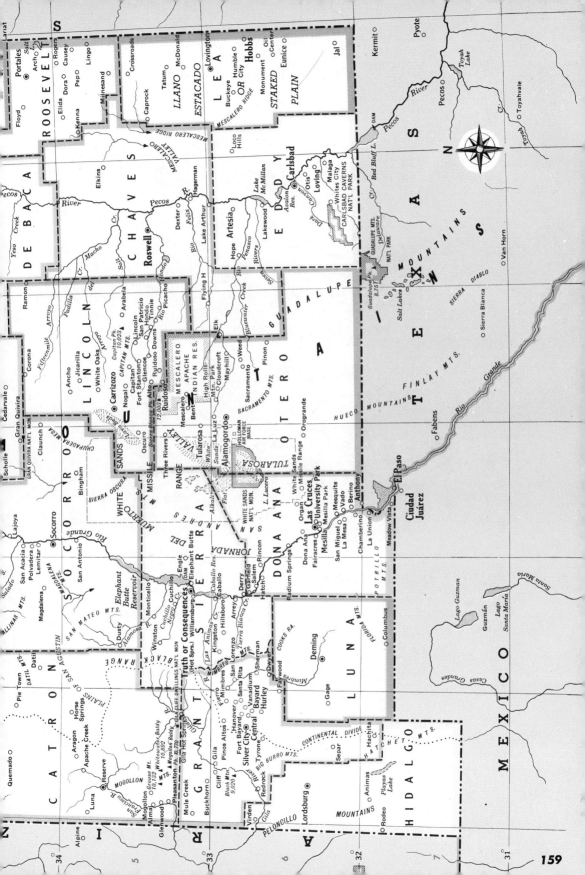

NEW YORK

SCALE
0 5 10   20   30   40 MI.
0 5 10 20   30   40 KM.

State Capitals .... ⊛
County Seats .... ◉
Canals .... —|—|—

© C.S. HAMMOND & Co., N.Y.

SOUTHEASTERN PART OF NEW YORK
Same scale as main map

160

161

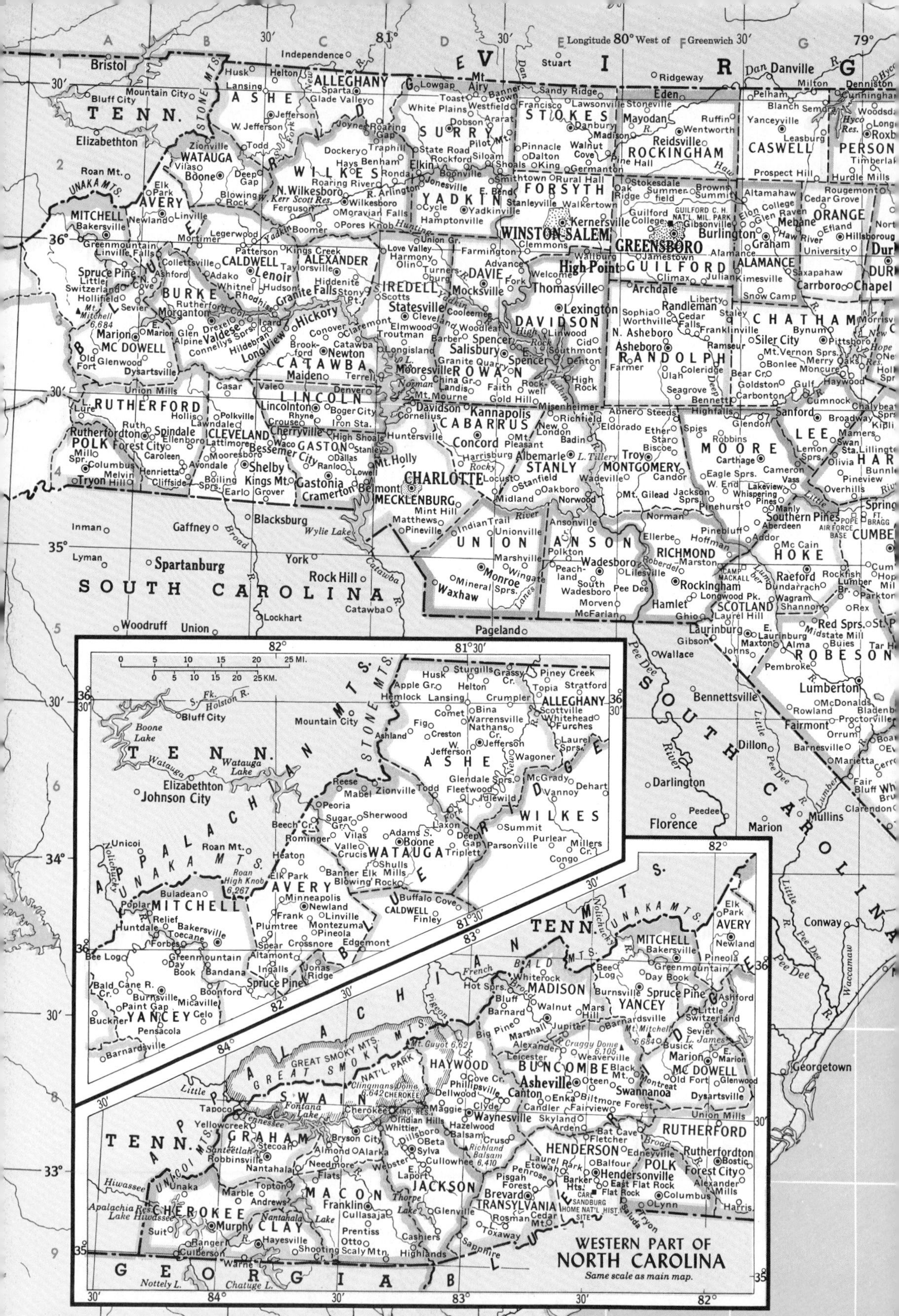
Longitude 80° West of Greenwich
V I R G I N I A
TENN.
SOUTH CAROLINA
GEORGIA
ALLEGHANY
ASHE
SURRY
STOKES
ROCKINGHAM
CASWELL
PERSON
WATAUGA
WILKES
FORSYTH
GUILFORD
ALAMANCE
ORANGE
AVERY
MITCHELL
YADKIN
CALDWELL
ALEXANDER
DAVIE
IREDELL
BURKE
MC DOWELL
CATAWBA
ROWAN
DAVIDSON
RANDOLPH
CHATHAM
RUTHERFORD
LINCOLN
CABARRUS
POLK
CLEVELAND
GASTON
MECKLENBURG
STANLY
MONTGOMERY
MOORE
LEE
UNION
ANSON
RICHMOND
HOKE
SCOTLAND
ROBESON
WINSTON-SALEM
GREENSBORO
High Point
CHARLOTTE
Spartanburg
STONE MTS.
UNAKA MTS.
BLUE RIDGE
WESTERN PART OF
NORTH CAROLINA
Same scale as main map.
APPALACHIAN MTS.
GREAT SMOKY MTS.
NAT'L. PARK
BALD MTS.
YANCEY
MADISON
BUNCOMBE
HAYWOOD
SWAIN
GRAHAM
CHEROKEE
CLAY
MACON
JACKSON
TRANSYLVANIA
HENDERSON
Asheville
0 5 10 15 20 25 MI.
0 5 10 15 20 25 KM.

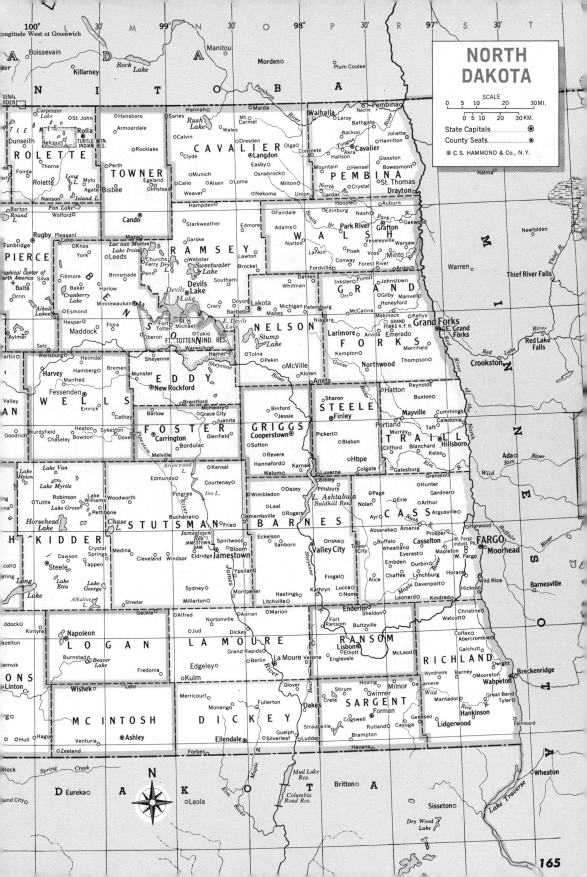

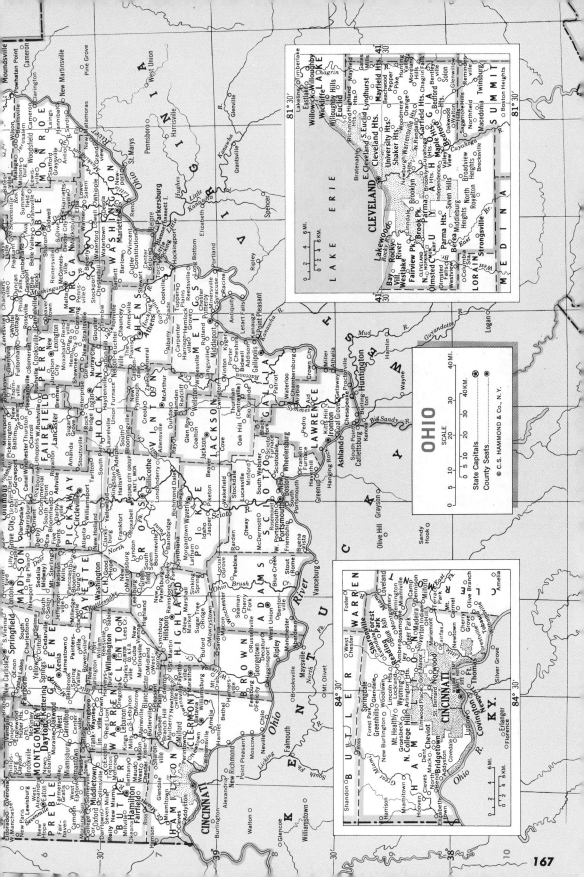

OKLAHOMA

SCALE
0 5 10   20   30   40 MI.
0 5 10   20   30   40 KM.

State Capitals..............⊛
County Seats...............◉

© C.S. HAMMOND & Co., N.Y.

169

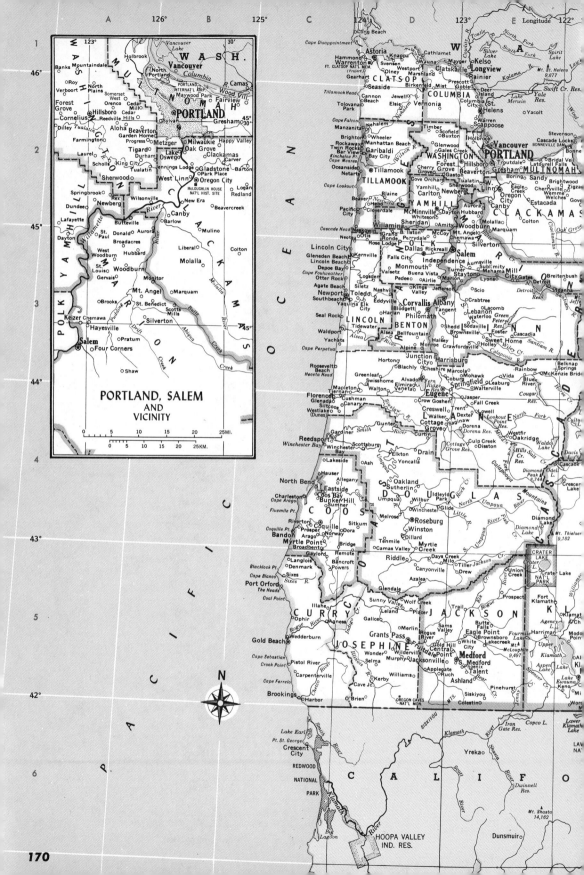

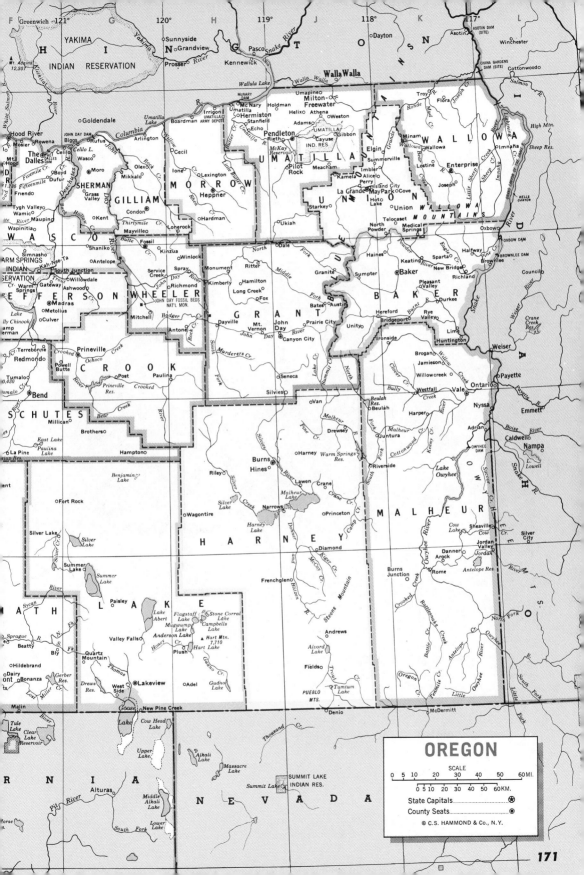

PENNSYLVANIA

SCALE

0 5 10 20 30 40MI.

0 5 10 20 40KM.

State Capitals .... ⊛

County Seats .... ◉

Canals ....

© C.S. HAMMOND & Co., N.Y.

173

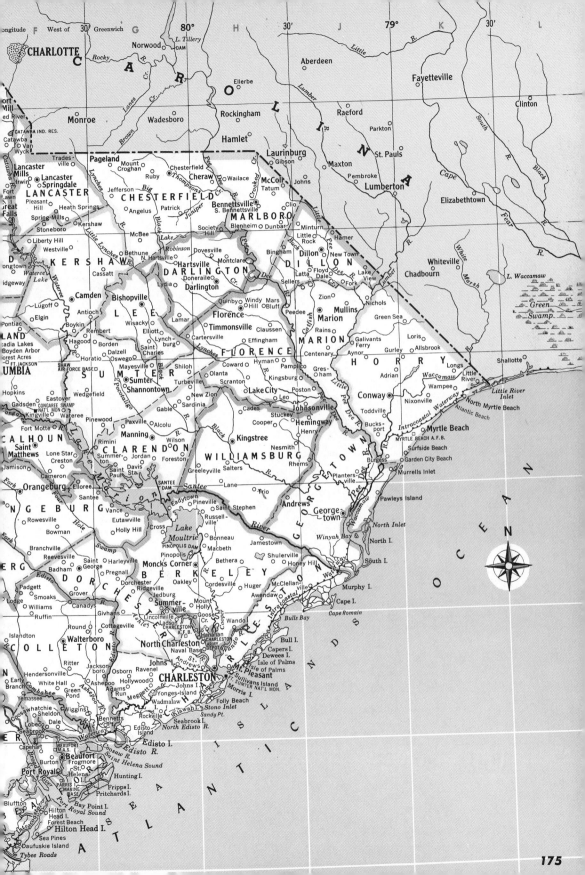

SOUTH DAKOTA

SCALE

0 5 10   20   40   60 MI.

0 5 10 20   40   60 KM.

State Capitals..............⊛
County Seats...............◉

© C.S. HAMMOND & Co., N.Y.

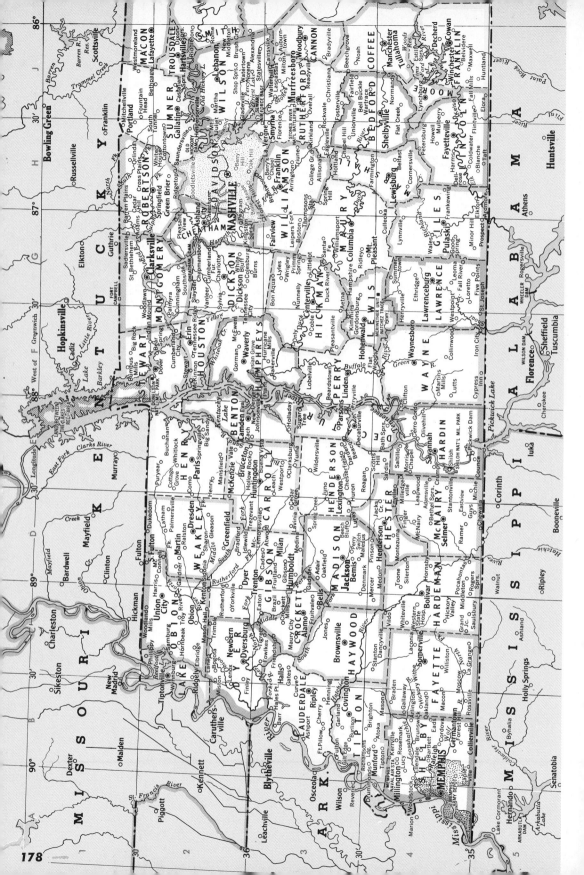

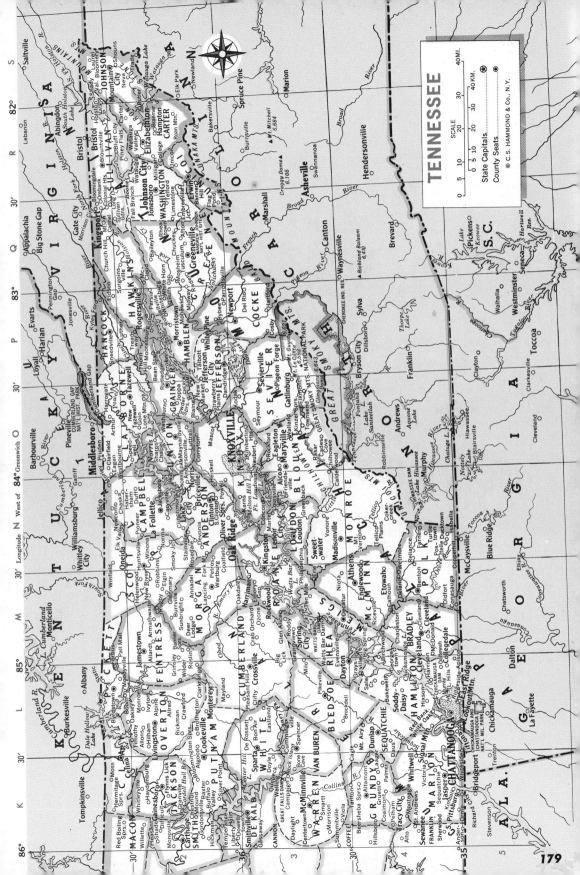

TENNESSEE

SCALE
40MI.
40 KM.

State Capitals ⊛
County Seats ◉

© C.S. HAMMOND & Co., N.Y.

179

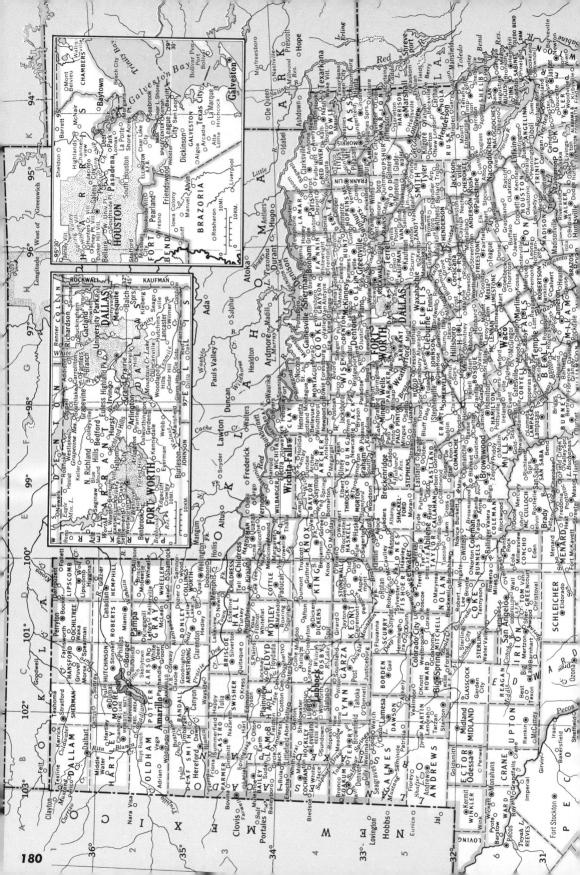

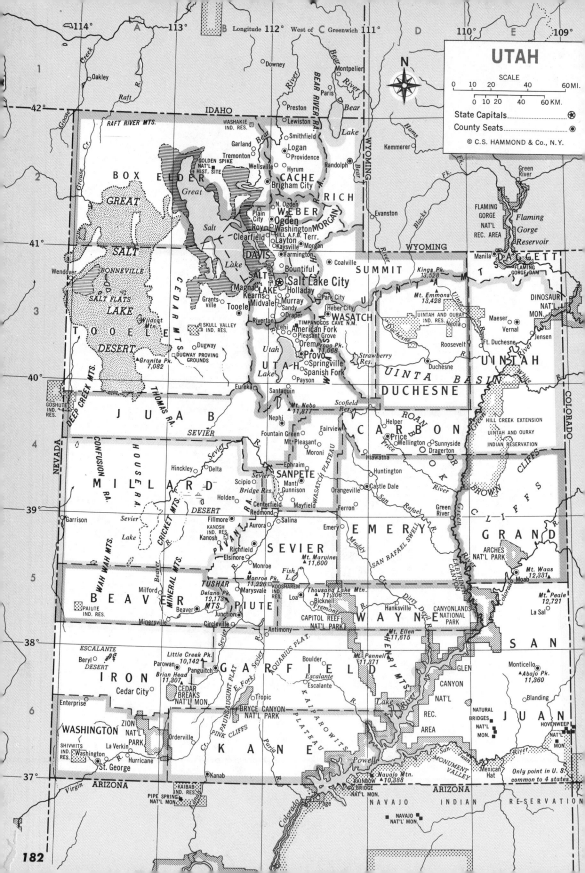

UTAH

SCALE

0 10 20   40   60 MI.

0 10 20 40   60 KM.

State Capitals..................⊛

County Seats..................◉

© C.S. HAMMOND & Co., N.Y.

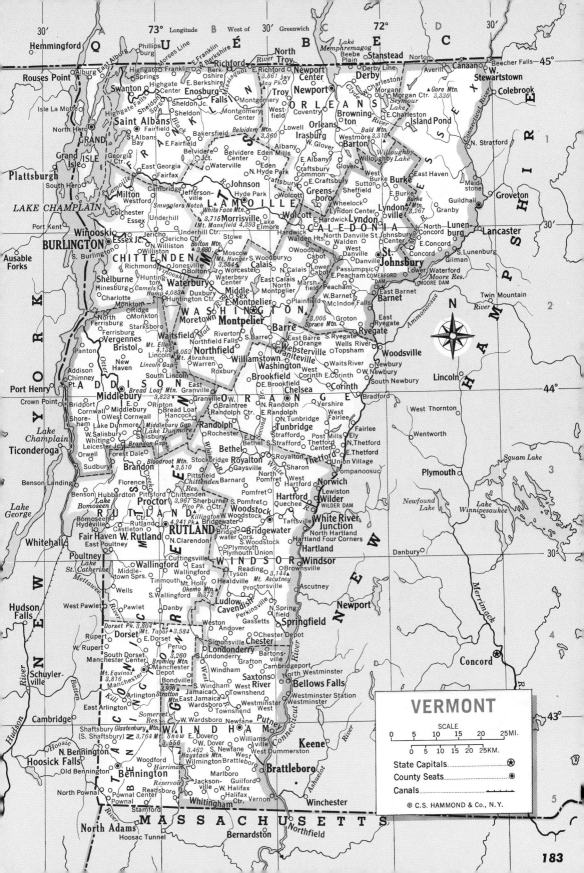

WESTERN PART OF VIRGINIA

Same scale as main map.

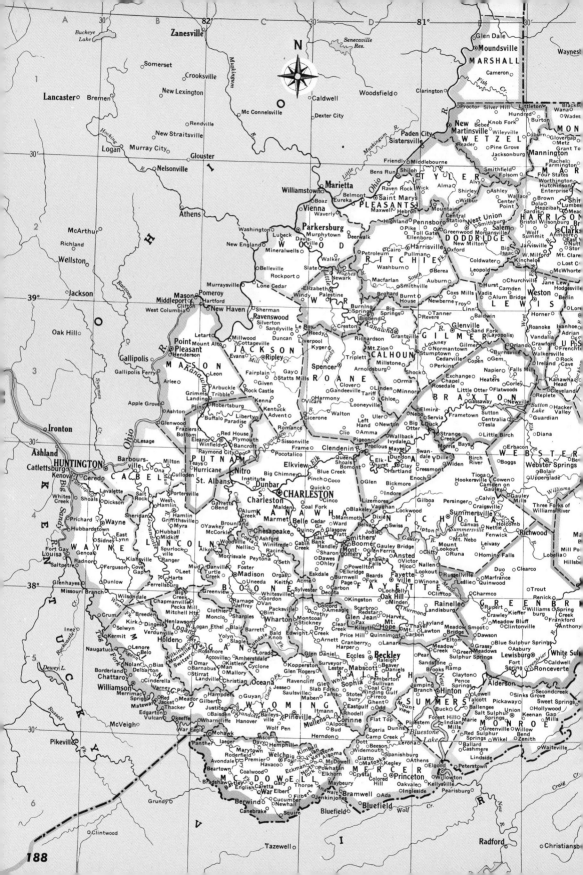

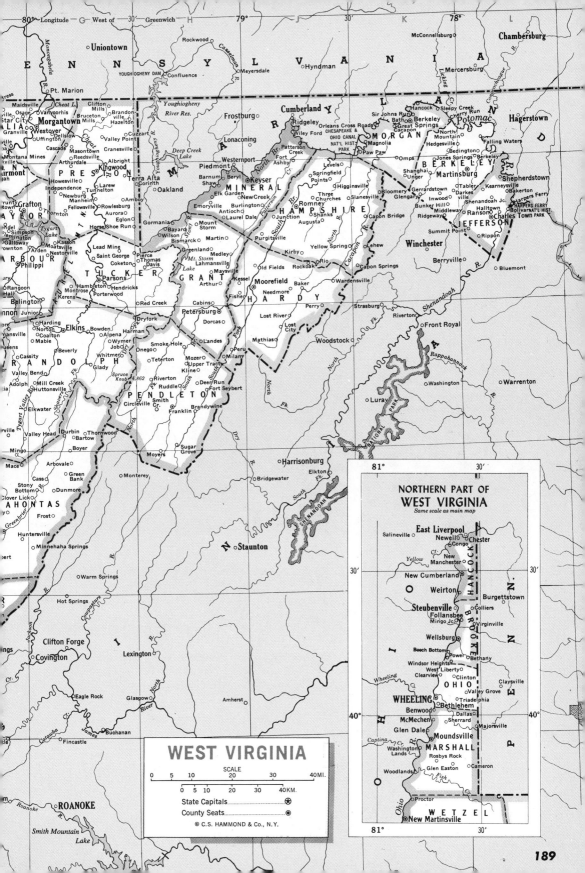

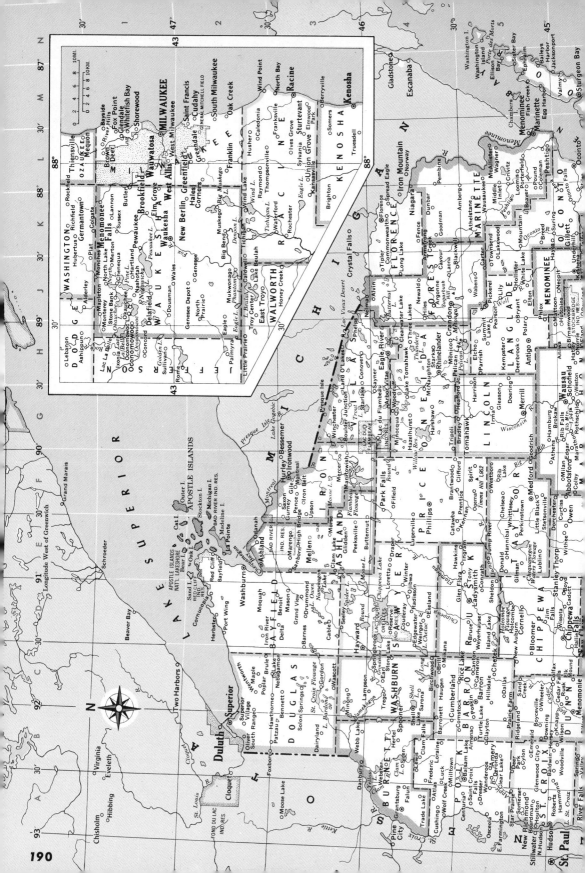

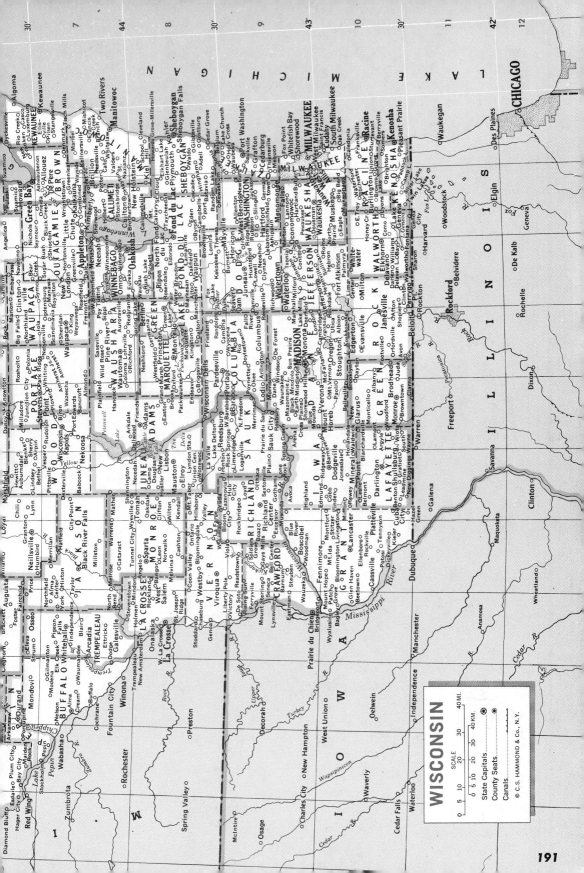

WISCONSIN

SCALE

State Capitals ⊛
County Seats ◉
Canals

⊛ C. S. HAMMOND & CO., N.Y.

SCALE
0   5   10   20   30   40 MI.
0 5 10 20   30   40 KM.

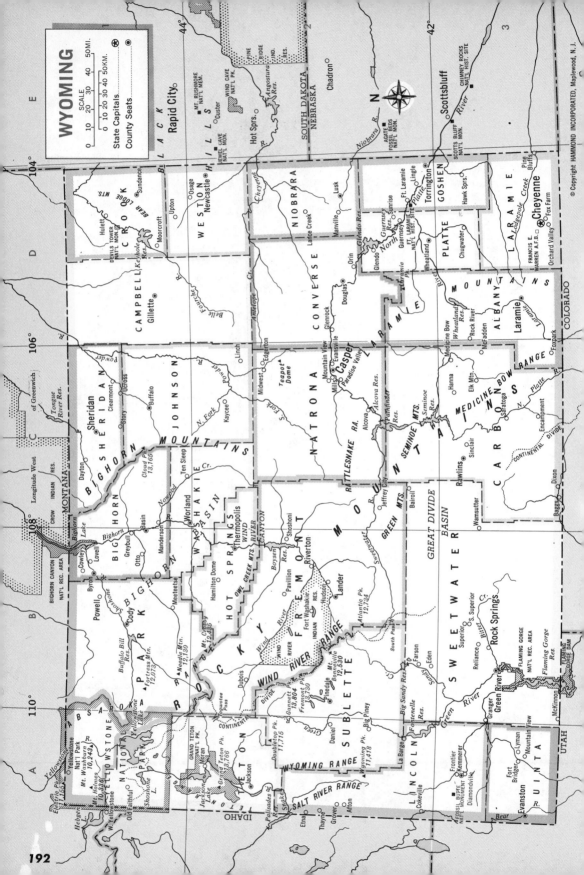

GLOSSARY OF GEOGRAPHICAL TERMS

A. = Arabic Camb. = Cambodian Ch. = Chinese Dan. = Danish Du. = Dutch
Finn. = Finnish Fr. = French Ger. = German Ice. = Icelandic It. = Italian
Jap. = Japanese Mong. = Mongol Nor. = Norwegian Per. = Persian
Port.=Portuguese Russ.=Russian Sp.=Spanish Sw.=Swedish Turk. =Turkish

Å......................	Nor., Sw.	......Stream
Abajo................	Sp.	......Lower
Ada, Adasi.........	Turk.	..........Island
Altiplano............	Sp.	..........Plateau
Älv, Alf, Elf........	Sw.	..........River
Arrecife.............	Sp.	..........Reef
Baai...................	Du.	..........Bay
Bahía................	Sp.	..........Bay
Bahr..................	Arabic...	Marsh, Lake, Sea, River
Baia..................	Port.	..........Bay
Baie..................	Fr.	..........Bay, Gulf
Bañados...........	Sp.	..........Marshes
Barra.................	Sp.	..........Reef
Belt...................	Ger.	..........Strait
Ben...................	Gaelic	...Mountain
Berg..................	Ger., Du.	...Mountain
Bir....................	Arabic	..........Well
Boca..................	Sp.	..........Gulf, Inlet
Bolshoi, Bolshaya..........	Russ.	..................Big
Bolsón..............	Sp.	......Depression
Bong.................	Korean	......Mountain
Bucht................	Ger.	..........Bay
Bugt..................	Dan.	..........Bay
Bukhta..............	Russ.	..........Bay
Burnu, Burun......	Turk.	.....Cape, Point
By.....................	Dan., Nor., Sw.	Town
Cabo.................	Port., Sp.	........Cape
Campos.............	Port.	..........Plains
Canal................	Port., Sp.	....Channel
Cap, Capo........	Fr., It.	..........Cape
Catarátas..........	Sp.	..........Falls
Central, Centrale...........	Fr., It.	..........Middle
Cerrito, Cerro......	Sp.	..........Hill
Ciénaga............	Sp.	..........Swamp
Ciudad..............	Sp.	..........City
Col....................	Fr.	..........Pass
Cordillera..........	Sp.	...Mt. Range
Côte..................	Fr.	..........Coast
Cuchilla............	Sp.	........Mt. Range
Dağ, Dagh........	Turk.	........Mountain
Dağlari.............	Turk.	...Mt. Range
Dal...................	Nor., Sw.	......Valley
Darya................	Per.	........Salt Lake
Dasht................	Per.	.....Desert, Plain
Deniz, Denizi.....	Turk.	.....Sea, Lake
Desierto............	Sp.	..........Desert
Eiland...............	Du.	..........Island
Elv....................	Dan., Nor.	......River
Emi...................	Berber	.....Mountain
Erg...................	Arabic...	Dune, Desert
Est, Este............	Fr., Port., Sp.	...East
Estrecho, Estreito...........	Sp., Port.	......Strait

Étang................	Fr.	....Pond, Lagoon, Lake
Fjørd.................	Dan., Nor.	......Fiord
Fleuve..............	Fr.	..........River
Gebel...............	Arabic	......Mountain
Gebirge............	Ger.	........Mt. Range
Gobi.................	Mongol	..........Desert
Gol....................	Mongol, Turk.	Lake, Stream
Golf..................	Ger., Du.	.........Gulf
Golfe................	Fr.	..........Gulf
Golfo................	Sp., It., Port.	...Gulf
Gölü.................	Turk.	..........Lake
Gora.................	Russ.	......Mountain
Grand, Grande....	Fr., Sp.	..........Big
Groot................	Du.	..........Big
Gross................	Ger.	..........Big
Grosso..............	It., Port.	..........Big
Guba................	Russ.	......Bay, Gulf
Gunto...............	Jap.	.....Archipelago
Gunung............	Malay	......Mountain
Higashi, Higasi....	Jap.	..........East
Ho....................	Ch.	..........River
Hoek.................	Du.	..........Cape
Holm.................	Dan., Nor., Sw.	Island
Hu....................	Ch.	..........Lake
Hwang..............	Ch.	..........Yellow
Île....................	Fr.	..........Island
Insel.................	Ger.	..........Island
Irmak...............	Turk.	..........River
Isla..................	Sp.	..........Island
Isola.................	Sp.	..........Island
Jabal, Jebel........	Arabic	.....Mountains
Järvi................	Finn.	..........Lake
Jaure................	Sw.	..........Lake
Jezira...............	Arabic	..........Island
Jima.................	Jap.	..........Island
Joki..................	Finn.	..........River
Kaap................	Du.	..........Cape
Kabir, Kebir.......	Arabic	..........Big
Kanal...............	Russ., Ger.	...Canal, Channel
Kap, Kapp..........	Nor., Sw., Ice.	..Cape
Kawa................	Jap.	..........River
Khrebet............	Russ.	......Mt. Range
Kiang................	Ch.	..........River
Kita..................	Jap.	..........North
Klein.................	Du., Ger.	.........Small
Kô....................	Jap.	..........Lake
Ko....................	Thai.	..........Island
Koh...................	Camb., Khmer	Island
Köping..............	Sw.	..........Borough
Körfez, Körfezi...	Turk.	..............Gulf
Kuh..................	Per.	.........Mountain

193

Kul	Sinkiang Turki	Lake
Kum	Turk.	Desert
Lac	Fr.	Lake
Lago	Port., Sp., It.	Lake
Lagôa	Port.	Lagoon
Laguna	Sp.	Lagoon
Lagune	Fr.	Lagoon
Llanos	Sp.	Plains
Mar	Sp., Port.	Sea
Mare	It.	Sea
Meer	Du.	Lake
Meer	Ger.	Sea
Mer	Fr.	Sea
Meseta	Sp.	Plateau
Minami	Jap.	Southern
Misaki	Jap.	Cape
Mittel	Ger.	Middle
Mont	Fr.	Mountain
Montagne	Fr.	Mountain
Montaña	Sp.	Mountains
Monte	Sp., It., Port.	Mountain
More	Russ.	Sea
Muong	Siamese	Town
Mys	Russ.	Cape
Nam	Burm., Lao	River
Nevado	Sp.	Snow covered peak
Nieder	Ger.	Lower
Nishi, Nisi	Jap.	West
Nizhni, Nizhnyaya	Russ.	Lower
Nor	Mong.	Lake
Nord	Fr., Ger.	North
Norte	Sp., It., Port.	North
Nos	Russ.	Cape
Novi, Novaya	Russ.	New
Nusa	Malay	Island
O	Jap.	Big
Ö	Nor., Sw	Island
Ober	Ger.	Upper
Occidental, Occidentale	Sp., It.	Western
Oeste	Port.	West
Oriental	Sp., Fr.	Eastern
Orientale	It.	Eastern
Ost	Ger.	East
Ostrov	Russ.	Island
Ouest	Fr.	West
öy	Nor.	Island
Ozero	Russ.	Lake
Pampa	Sp.	Plain
Paso	Sp.	Pass
Passo	It., Port.	Pass
Pequeño	Sp.	Small
Peski	Russ.	Desert
Petit	Fr.	Small
Pic	Fr.	Mountain
Pico	Port., Sp.	Mountain, Peak
Pik	Russ.	Peak
Pointe	Fr.	Point
Poluostrov	Russ.	Peninsula
Ponta	Port.	Point
Presa	Sp.	Reservoir
Proliv	Russ.	Strait
Pulou, Pulo	Malay	Island
Punta	Sp., It., Port.	Point
Ras	Arabic	Cape
Ría	Sp.	Estuary
Río	Sp.	River
Rivier, Rivière	Du., Fr.	River
Rud	Per.	River
Saki	Jap.	Cape
Salto	Sp., Port.	Falls
San	Ch., Jap., Korean	Hill
See	Ger.	Sea, Lake
Selvas	Sp., Port.	Forest
Serra	Port.	Mts.
Serranía	Sp.	Mts.
Severni, Servernaya	Russ.	North
Shan	Ch., Jap.	Hill, Mts.
Shima	Jap.	Island
Shoto	Jap.	Islands
Sierra	Sp.	Mountains
Sjö	Nor., Sw.	Lake, Sea
Spitze	Ger.	Mt. Peak
Sredni, Srednyaya	Russ.	Middle
Stad	Dan., Nor., Sw.	City
Stari, Staraya	Russ.	Old
Su	Turk.	River
Sud, Süd	Sp., Fr., Ger.	South
Sul	Port.	South
Sungei	Malay	River
Sur	Sp.	South
Tagh	Turk.	Mt. Range
Tal	Ger.	Valley
Tandjong, Tanjung	Malay	Cape, Point
Tso	Tibetan	Lake
Val	Fr.	Valley
Velho	Port.	Old
Verkhni	Russ.	Upper
Vesi	Finn.	Lake
Vishni, Vishnyaya	Russ.	High
Vostochni, Vostochnaya	Russ.	East, Eastern
Wadi	Arabic	Dry River
Wald	Ger.	Forest
Wan	Jap.	Bay
Yama	Jap.	Mountain
Yug, Yuzhni, Yuzhnaya	Russ.	South, Southern
Zaliv	Russ.	Bay, Gulf
Zapadni, Zapadnaya	Russ.	Western
Zee	Du.	Sea
Zemlya	Russ.	Land
Zuid	Du.	South

WORLD
STATISTICAL TABLES
and
DISTRIBUTION MAPS

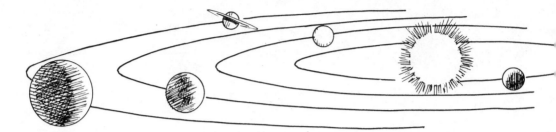

Elements of the Solar System

	Mean Distance From Sun in Miles	Period of Revolution Around Sun	Period of Rotation on Axis	Equatorial Diameter in Miles	Surface Gravity (Earth=1)	Mean Density (Water=1)	Number of Satellites
SUN	....	....	25.4 days	864,000	27.95	1.4	....
MERCURY	36,001,000	87.97 days	59 days	3,100	0.38	5.3	0
VENUS	67,272,000	224.70 days	247 days	7,700	0.88	4.9	0
EARTH	93,003,000	365.26 days	23h 56m	7,927	1.00	5.5	1
MARS	141,708,000	687 days	24h 37m	4,200	0.39	4.0	2
JUPITER	483,880,000	11.86 years	9h 50m	88,698	2.65	1.3	12
SATURN	887,141,000	29.46 years	10h 14m	75,060	1.17	0.7	10
URANUS	1,782,000,000	84.02 years	10h 45m	29,200	1.05	1.3	5
NEPTUNE	2,792,000,000	164.79 years	15h 48m	27,700	1.23	1.6	2
PLUTO	3,664,000,000	248.5 years	6.4 days	8,700?	0.7	?	0

Dimensions of the Earth

Superficial area	192,251,000	sq. miles
Land surface	52,970,000	" "
North America	9,363,000	" "
South America	6,885,700	" "
Europe	4,057,000	" "
Asia	17,128,500	" "
Africa	11,707,000	" "
Australia	2,941,500	" "
Water surface	139,781,000	" "
Atlantic Ocean	31,862,000	" "
Pacific Ocean	64,186,000	" "
Indian Ocean	28,350,000	" "
Arctic Ocean	5,427,000	" "
Equatorial circumference	24,894	miles
Meridional circumference	24,811	"
Equatorial diameter	7,926.677	"
Polar diameter	7,899.988	"
Equatorial radius	3,963.34	"
Polar radius	3,949.99	"
Volume of the Earth	260,000,000,000	cubic miles
Mass, or weight	5,890,000,000,000,000,000,000	tons
Mean distance from the Sun	93,003,000	miles

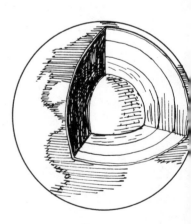

The Moon is the Earth's natural satellite. The mean distance which separates the Earth from the Moon is 237,087 miles. The Moon's true period of revolution (sidereal month) is 27⅓ days. The Moon rotates on its own axis once during this time. The phase period or time between new moons (synodic month) is 29½ days. The Moon's diameter is 2,160 miles, its density is 3.3 and its surface gravity is 0.2.

Principal Lakes and Inland Seas

	AREA IN SQ. MILES		AREA IN SQ. MILES
Caspian Sea	143,243	Lake Peipus	1,400
Lake Superior	31,700	Lake Tana	1,219
Lake Victoria	26,724	Great Salt Lake	1,100
Aral Sea	25,676	Lake Iliamna	1,000
Lake Huron	23,010	Vättern	733
Lake Michigan	22,300	Dead Sea	400
Lake Tanganyika	12,650	Lake Balaton	228
Lake Baykal	12,162	Lake Geneva	224
Great Bear Lake	12,096	Lake of Constance	208
Lake Nyasa	11,555	Lake Tahoe	193
Great Slave Lake	11,269	Lake Garda	143
Lake Erie	9,910	Lake Como	56
Lake Winnipeg	9,417	Lake of Lucerne	44
Lake Ontario	7,340	Lake of Zürich	34
Lake Ladoga	7,104		
Lake Balkhash	7,027		
Lake Chad	5,300		
Lake Onega	3,710		
Lake Titicaca	3,200		
Lake Nicaragua	3,100		
Lake Athabasca	3,064		
Reindeer Lake	2,568		
Lake Turkana (Rudolf)	2,463		
Issyk-Kul'	2,425		
Vanern	2,156		
Lake Winnipegosis	2,075		
Lake Albert	2,075		
Kariba Lake	2,050		
Lake Urmia	1,815		
Lake of the Woods	1,679		

Oceans and Seas of the World

	AREA IN SQ. MILES	GREATEST DEPTH IN FEET	VOLUME IN CUBIC MILES
Pacific Ocean	64,186,000	36,198	167,025,000
Atlantic Ocean	31,862,000	28,374	77,580,000
Indian Ocean	28,350,000	25,344	68,213,000
Arctic Ocean	5,427,000	17,880	3,026,000
Caribbean Sea	970,000	24,720	2,298,400
Mediterranean Sea	969,000	16,896	1,019,400
South China Sea	895,000	15,000	....
Bering Sea	875,000	15,800	788,500
Gulf of Mexico	600,000	12,300	....
Sea of Okhotsk	590,000	11,070	454,700
East China Sea	482,000	9,500	52,700
Japan Sea	389,000	12,280	383,200
Hudson Bay	317,500	846	37,590
North Sea	222,000	2,200	12,890
Black Sea	185,000	7,365	....
Red Sea	169,000	7,200	53,700
Baltic Sea	163,000	1,506	5,360

Longest Rivers of the World

River	LENGTH IN MILES	River	LENGTH IN MILES	River	LENGTH IN MILES
Nile, Africa	4,145	Purus, S.A.	1,995	Kolyma, U.S.S.R.	1,562
Amazon, S.A.	3,915	Yukon, Alaska-Canada	1,979	Ganges, Asia	1,550
Mississippi-Missouri, U.S.A.	3,710	St. Lawrence, Canada-U.S.A.	1,900	Ural, U.S.S.R.	1,509
Yangtze, China	3,434	Rio Grande, U.S.A.-Mexico	1,885	Japurá, S.A.	1,500
Ob-Irtysh, U.S.S.R.	3,362	Syr-Dar'ya, U.S.S.R.	1,859	Arkansas, U.S.A.	1,450
Yenisey-Angara, U.S.S.R.	3,100	São Francisco, Brazil	1,811	Colorado, U.S.A.-Mexico	1,450
Hwang (Yellow), China	2,903	Indus, Asia	1,800	Negro, S.A.	1,400
Amur, Asia	2,744	Danube, Europe	1,775	Dnieper, U.S.S.R.	1,368
Lena, U.S.S.R.	2,734	Salween, Asia	1,770	Irrawaddy, Burma	1,325
Congo, Africa	2,718	Brahmaputra, Asia	1,700	Orange, Africa	1,350
Mackenzie-Peace, Canada	2,635	Euphrates, Asia	1,700	Ohio-Allegheny, U.S.A.	1,306
Mekong, Asia	2,600	Tocantins, Brazil	1,677	Kama, U.S.S.R.	1,262
Niger, Africa	2,585	Si, China	1,650	Columbia, U.S.A.-Canada	1,243
Paraná, S.A.	2,450	Amu-Dar'ya, Asia	1,616	Red, U.S.A.	1,222
Murray-Darling, Australia	2,310	Zambezi, Africa	1,600	Don, U.S.S.R.	1,222
Volga, U.S.S.R.	2,194	Nelson, Canada	1,600	Brazos, U.S.A.	1,210
Madeira, S.A.	2,013	Orinoco, S.A.	1,600	Saskatchewan, Canada	1,205
		Paraguay, S.A.	1,584	Peace-Finlay, Canada	1,195
				Tigris, Asia	1,181
				Darling, Australia	1,160
				Angara, U.S.S.R.	1,135
				Sungari, Asia	1,130
				Pechora, U.S.S.R.	1,124
				Snake, U.S.A.	1,038
				Churchill, Canada	1,000
				Pilcomayo, S.A.	1,000
				Uruguay, S.A.	1,000
				Magdalena, Colombia	1,000
				Platte-N. Platte, U.S.A.	990
				Oka, U.S.S.R.	918
				Canadian, U.S.A.	906
				Tennessee, U.S.A.	900
				Colorado, Texas, U.S.A.	894
				Dniester, U.S.S.R.	876

Great Ship Canals

	LENGTH IN MILES	MIN. DEPTH IN FEET
Volga-Baltic, U.S.S.R.	225	....
Baltic-White Sea, U.S.S.R.	140	16
Suez, Egypt	100.76	42
Albert, Belgium	80	16.5
Moscow-Volga, U.S.S.R.	80	18
Volga-Don, U.S.S.R.	62	....
Göta, Sweden	54	10
Kiel, West Germany	53.2	38
Panama, Canal Zone	50.72	41.6
Houston Ship, U.S.A.	50	36
Amsterdam-Rhine, Netherlands	45	41
Beaumont-Port Arthur, U.S.A.	40	32
Manchester Ship, England	35.5	28
Chicago Sanitary and Ship, U.S.A.	33.8	20
Welland, Canada	27.6	27
Juliana, Netherlands	21	11.8
Chesapeake and Delaware, U.S.A.	19	35
Cape Cod, U.S.A.	17.4	32
Lake Washington, U.S.A.	8	30
Corinth, Greece	3.5	26.25
Sault Ste. Marie, U.S.A.	1.8	27
Sault Ste. Marie, Canada	1.4	27

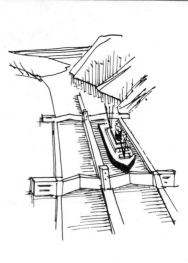

	FEET		FEET
Everest, Nepal-China . . .	29,028	Kazbek, U.S.S.R.	16,512
K2 (Godwin Austen), India .	28,250	Djaja, Indonesia	16,503
Kanchenjunga, Nepal-India .	28,208	Blanc, France	15,771
Lhotse, Nepal-China	27,923	Klyuchevskaya Sopka, U.S.S.R.	15,584
Makalu, Nepal-China . . .	27,824	Rosa (Dufourspitze), Italy-	
Dhaulagiri, Nepal	26,810	Switzerland	15,203
Nanga Parbat, India . . .	26,660	Ras Dashan, Ethiopia . . .	15,157
Annapurna, Nepal	26,504	Matterhorn, Switzerland . .	14,688
Nanda Devi, India	25,645	Whitney, California	14,494
Kamet, India	25,447	Elbert, Colorado	14,433
Tirich Mir, Pakistan	25,230	Rainier, Washington	14,410
Minya Konka, China . . .	24,902	Blanca Peak, Colorado . . .	14,345
Muztagh Ata, China	24,757	Markham, Antarctica . . .	14,272
Communism Peak, U.S.S.R. .	24,599	Shasta, California	14,162
Pobeda Peak, U.S.S.R. . . .	24,406	Pikes Peak, Colorado . . .	14,110
Chomo Lhari, Bhutan-China .	23,997	Finsteraarhorn, Switzerland .	14,022
Muztagh, China	23,891	Tajumulco, Guatemala . . .	13,845
Aconcagua, Argentina . . .	22,831	Mauna Kea, Hawaii	13,796
Ojos del Salado, Chile-Arg. .	22,572	Mauna Loa, Hawaii	13,680
Tupungato, Chile-Argentina .	22,310	Toubkal, Morocco	13,665
Mercedario, Argentina . . .	22,211	Jungfrau, Switzerland . . .	13,642
Huascarán, Peru	22,205	Cameroon, Cameroon . . .	13,350
Llullaillaco, Chile-Arg. . . .	22,057	Gran Paradiso, Italy . . .	13,323
Ancohuma, Bolivia	21,489	Robson, British Columbia . .	12,972
Illampu, Bolivia	21,276	Grossglockner, Austria . . .	12,461
Chimborazo, Ecuador . . .	20,561	Fuji, Japan	12,389
McKinley, Alaska	20,320	Cook, New Zealand	12,349
Logan, Yukon	19,850	Pico de Teide, Canary Is. . .	12,172
Cotopaxi, Ecuador	19,347	Semeru, Java, Indonesia . .	12,060
Kilimanjaro, Tanzania . . .	19,340	Mulhacen, Spain	11,411
El Misti, Peru	19,101	Etna, Italy	11,053
Huila, Colombia	18,865	Lassen Peak, California . .	10,457
Citlaltépetl (Orizaba), Mexico	18,855	Kosciusko, Australia	7,316
El'brus, U.S.S.R.	18,510	Mitchell, North Carolina . .	6,684
Demavend, Iran	18,376		
St. Elias, Alaska-Yukon . . .	18,008		
Popocatépetl, Mexico . . .	17,887		
Dykh-Tau, U.S.S.R.	17,070		
Kenya, Kenya	17,058		
Ararat, Turkey	16,946		
Vinson Massif, Antarctica . .	16,864		
Maraherita (Ruwenzori), Africa	16,795		

Principal Islands of the World

	AREA IN SQ. MILES		AREA IN SQ. MILES		AREA IN SQ. MILES
Greenland	840,000	Sicily	9,926	Oahu	608
New Guinea	305,000	Somerset	9,570	Guadeloupe	584
Borneo	290,000	Sardinia	9,301	Åland Is.	581
Madagascar	226,400	Fiji Islands	7,055	Kauai	553
Baffin	195,928	Shikoku	6,860	Shetland Islands	552
Sumatra	164,000	New Caledonia	6,530	Rhodes	542
Philippines	115,707	Kuril Islands	6,025	Caroline Islands	463
New Zealand	103,736	New Hebrides	5,700	Martinique	425
Great Britain	88,764	Bahama Islands	5,382	Tahiti	402
Honshu	88,000	Falkland Islands	4,618	Pemba	380
Victoria	83,896	Jamaica	4,232	Orkney Islands	372
Ellesmere	75,767	Hawaii	4,038	Madeira Islands	307
Celebes	72,986	Cape Breton	3,981	Dominica	290
Java	48,842	Cyprus	3,572	Tonga	270
Newfoundland	42,031	Puerto Rico	3,435	Molokai	261
Cuba	40,533	Corsica	3,352	St. Lucia	238
Luzon	40,420	New Ireland	3,340	Corfu	229
Iceland	39,768	Crete	3,218	Bornholm	227
Mindanao	36,537	Galápagos Islands	3,075	Isle of Man	227
Molucca Islands	32,307	Wrangel	2,819	Singapore	226
Novaya Zemlya	31,900	Hebrides	2,812	Guam	212
Ireland	31,743	Canary Islands	2,808	Isle Royale	196
Sakhalin	29,500	Kerguélen	2,700	Virgin Islands	192
Hispaniola	29,399	Prince Edward	2,170	Curaçao	182
Hokkaido	28,983	Trinidad and Tobago	1,980	Barbados	166
Banks	27,038	Balearic Islands	1,936	Isle of Wight	145
Tasmania	26,383	Ryukyu Islands	1,767	Lanai	140
Ceylon	25,332	Madura	1,752	St. Vincent	131
Svalbard	23,957	Cape Verde Islands	1,557	Maltese Islands	122
Devon	21,331	South Georgia	1,450	Grenada	120
Bismarck Arch.	18,976	Long I., New York	1,401	Tobago	116
Tierra del Fuego	17,900	Socotra	1,400	Martha's Vineyard	93
Melville	16,274	Samoa	1,209	Seychelles	85
Southampton	15,913	Gotland	1,153	Channel Islands	74
Solomon Islands	15,600	Réunion	969	St. Helena	47
New Britain	14,100	Azores	902	Nantucket	46
Taiwan (Formosa)	13,836	Isle of Pines	849	Ascension	34
Kyushu	13,770	Macías Nguema Biyogo	779	Hong Kong	30
Hainan	13,127	Tenerife	745	Manhattan, New York	22
Prince of Wales	12,872	Maui	729	Bermuda Islands	21
Vancouver	12,079	Mauritius	720		
Timor	11,527	Zanzibar	641		

Eckert Projection (equal-area)

Copyright by C. S. HAMMOND & CO., N. Y.

DENSITY OF POPULATION. One of the most outstanding facts of human geography is the extremely uneven distribution of people over the Earth. One-half of the Earth's surface has less than 3 people per square mile, while in the lowlands of India, China, Java and Japan rural density reaches the incredible congestion of 2000-3000 per square mile. Three-fourths of the Earth's population live in four relatively small areas; Northeastern United States, North-Central Europe, India and the Far East.

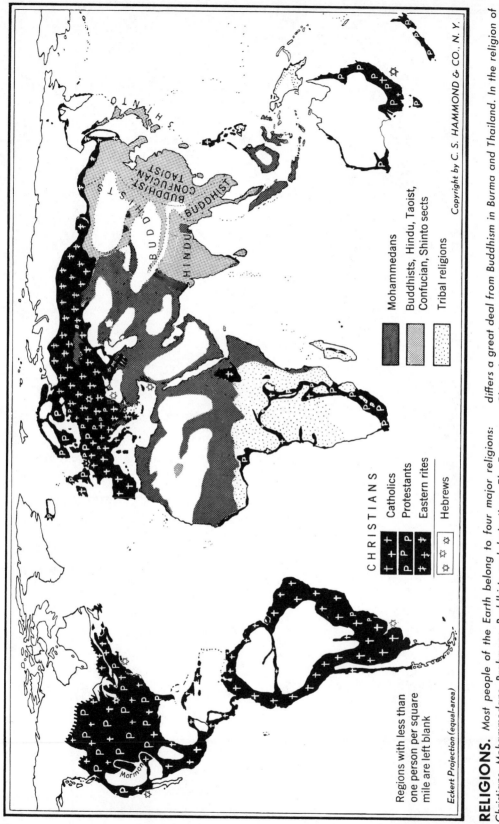

RELIGIONS. Most people of the Earth belong to four major religions: Christians, Mohammedans, Brahmans, Buddhists and derivatives. The Eastern rites of the Christians include the Greek Orthodox, Greek Catholic, Armenian, Syrian, Coptic and more minor churches. The lamaism of Tibet and Mongolia differs a great deal from Buddhism in Burma and Thailand. In the religion of China the teachings of Buddha, Confucius and Tao are mixed, while in Shinto a great deal of ancestor and emperor worship is added. About 11 million Hebrews live scattered over the globe, chiefly in cities and in the state of Israel.

CHRISTIANS

✝ ✝ ✝	Catholics
P P P	Protestants
✝ ✝ ✝	Eastern rites
✡ ✡	Hebrews

Regions with less than one person per square mile are left blank

Eckert Projection (equal-area)

Mohammedans

Buddhists, Hindu, Taoist, Confucian, Shinto sects

Tribal religions

Copyright by C. S. HAMMOND & CO., N. Y.

202

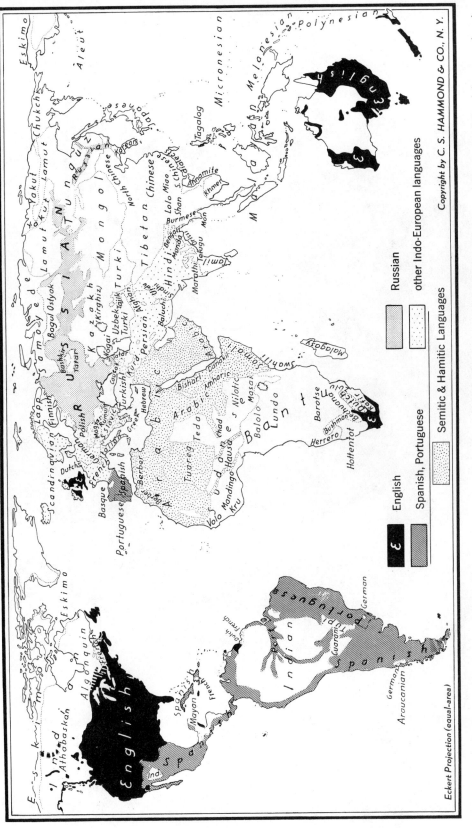

LANGUAGES. Several hundred different languages are spoken in the World, and in many places two or more languages are spoken, sometimes by the same people. The map above shows the dominant languages in each locality. English, French, Spanish, Russian, Arabic and Swahili are spoken by many people as a second language for commerce or travel.

Copyright by C. S. HAMMOND & CO., N. Y.

Eckert Projection (equal-area)

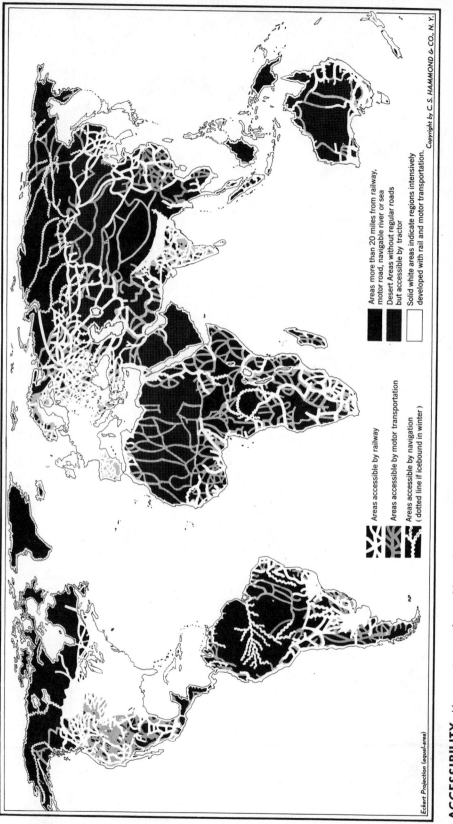

Eckert Projection (equal-area)

Copyright by C. S. HAMMOND & CO., N. Y.

Areas accessible by railway

Areas accessible by motor transportation

Areas accessible by navigation
(dotted line if icebound in winter)

Areas more than 20 miles from railway,
motor road, navigable river or sea

Desert Areas without regular roads
but accessible by tractor

Solid white areas indicate regions intensively
developed with rail and motor transportation.

ACCESSIBILITY. Many regions in the world are far from railways, roads, navigable rivers or the seas. Their economic development is retarded because their products can be brought to the world's markets only at great expense. Such areas are in the tundra (alpine), the boreal forest and in the equatorial rain forest regions. Desert areas, if not too mountainous, can be crossed by tractors. The largest inaccessible area is in Tibet, on account of high mountains, the alpine climate and isolationist attitude of the people. Airplane transportation is helping to bring these inaccessible areas into the orbit of civilization.

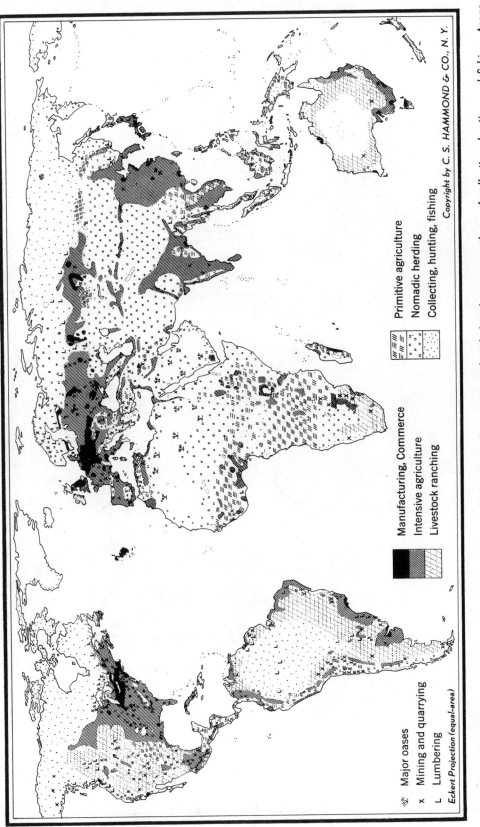

OCCUPATIONS. Correlation with the density of population shows that the most densely populated areas fall into the regions of manufacturing and intensive farming. All other economies require considerable space. The most sparsely inhabited areas are those of collecting, hunting and fishing. Areas with practically no habitation are left blank.

Major oases
x Mining and quarrying
L Lumbering

Eckert Projection (equal-area)

Manufacturing, Commerce
Intensive agriculture
Livestock ranching

Primitive agriculture
Nomadic herding
Collecting, hunting, fishing

Copyright by C. S. HAMMOND & CO., N. Y.

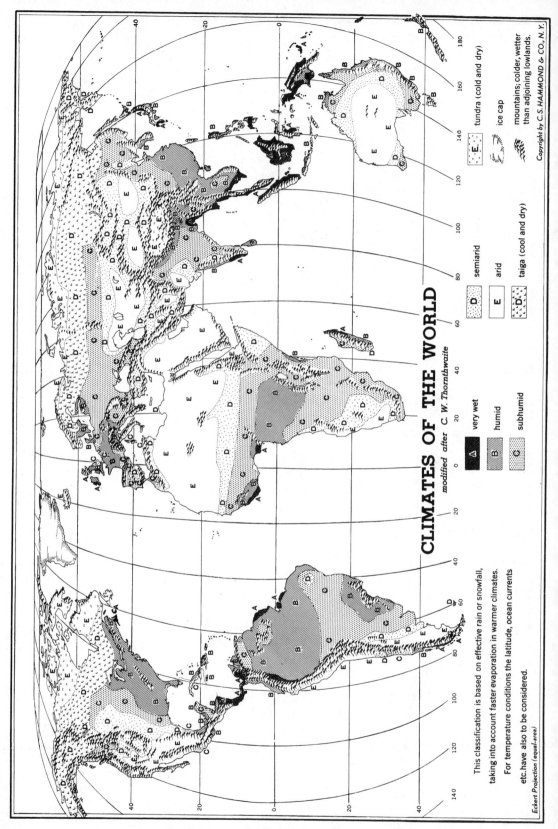

CLIMATES OF THE WORLD

modified after C. W. Thornthwaite

This classification is based on effective rain or snowfall,
taking into account faster evaporation in warmer climates.
For temperature conditions the latitude, ocean currents
etc. have also to be considered.

Eckert Projection (equal-area)

A		very wet
B		humid
C		subhumid
D		semiarid
E		arid
D		taiga (cool and dry)
E		tundra (cold and dry)
		ice cap
		mountains; colder, wetter than adjoining lowlands.

Copyright by C.S. HAMMOND & CO., N.Y.

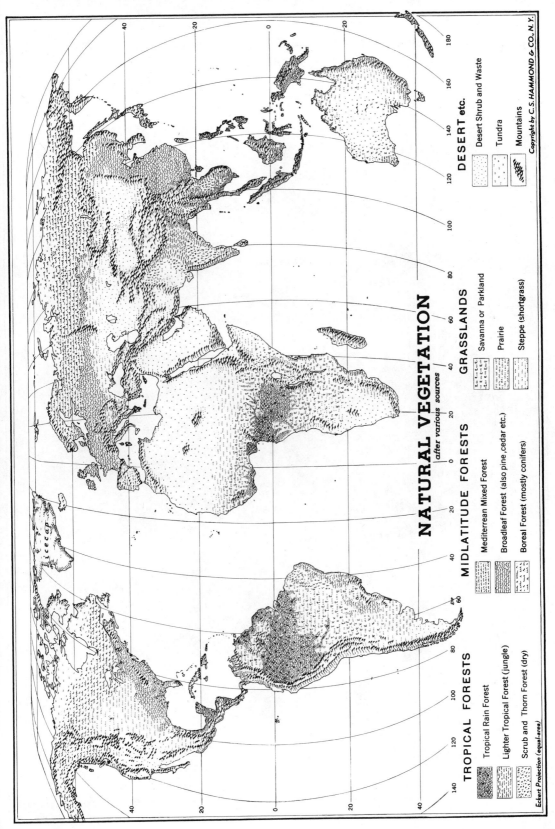

NATURAL VEGETATION
after various sources

TROPICAL FORESTS
Tropical Rain Forest
Lighter Tropical Forest (jungle)
Scrub and Thorn Forest (dry)

MIDLATITUDE FORESTS
Mediterrean Mixed Forest
Broadleaf Forest (also pine, cedar etc.)
Boreal Forest (mostly conifers)

GRASSLANDS
Savanna or Parkland
Prairie
Steppe (shortgrass)

DESERT etc.
Desert Shrub and Waste
Tundra
Mountains

Eckert Projection (equal-area)

Copyright by C.S.HAMMOND & CO., N.Y.

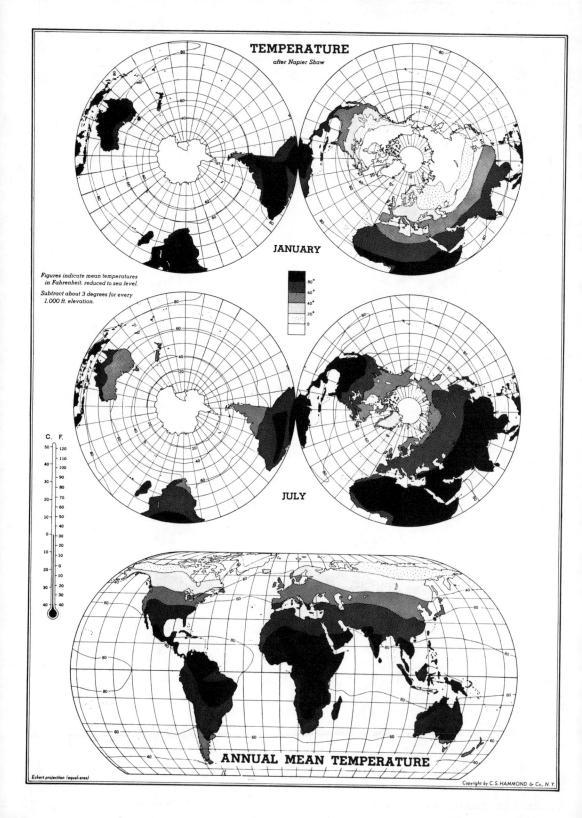

TEMPERATURE
after Napier Shaw

JANUARY

Figures indicate mean temperatures in Fahrenheit, reduced to sea level.

Subtract about 3 degrees for every 1,000 ft. elevation.

JULY

ANNUAL MEAN TEMPERATURE

Eckert projection (equal-area)

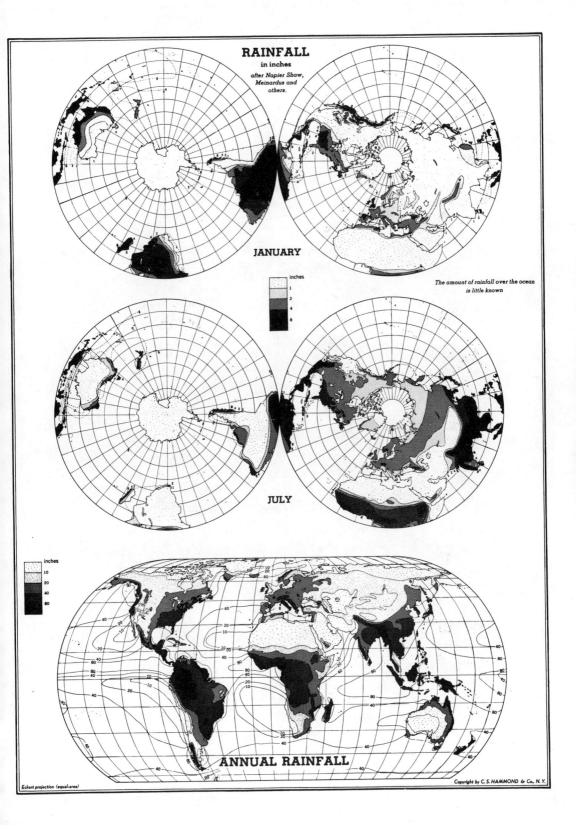

RAINFALL
in inches
after Napier Shaw,
Meinardus and
others.

JANUARY

inches
1
2
4
8

The amount of rainfall over the ocean
is little known

JULY

inches
10
20
40
80

ANNUAL RAINFALL

Eckert projection (equal-area)

Copyright by C. S. HAMMOND & Co., N. Y.

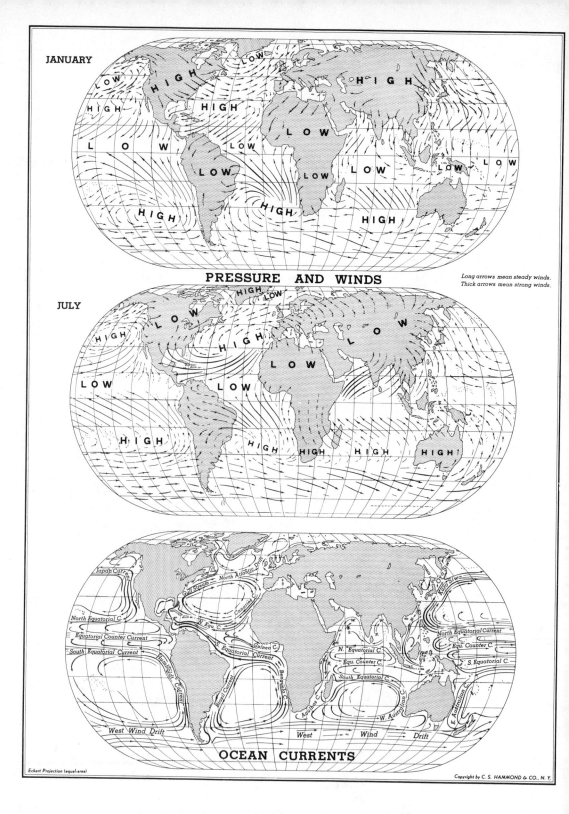

JANUARY

PRESSURE AND WINDS

Long arrows mean steady winds.
Thick arrows mean strong winds.

JULY

OCEAN CURRENTS

Eckert Projection (equal-area)

Copyright by C. S. HAMMOND & CO., N. Y.

210

Illustrated
Social and Economic Tables
of the World

The headline events of the last half-century have made the average person acutely curious of the vast world beyond his country's borders. This new national concern for the external world and its problems is one of the hopeful signs pointing to a better future for mankind. However, no matter how well-intentioned our concern for international relations may be, it is of no value unless it is grounded on an intelligent appreciation of the great diversity of social, economic and political forms extant throughout the globe.

On the following pages the editors have presented information on the world's nations, products, peoples and governments arranged in easily-found tabular form. This arrangement by tables makes comparison between political units a simpler task. These data, used with the maps in this atlas, complete the story of the nations of the world.

Social and Economic Tables

POLITICAL DIVISION	GOVERNMENT	MONETARY UNIT	LANGUAGE	RELIGION
AFGHANISTAN	Independent republic with a president, prime minister and cabinet; under martial law.	afghani	Pushtu (Afghan) Dari (Persian) Turkic languages	Islam
ALBANIA	Soviet-type republic with a head of state, premier, cabinet and unicameral legislature; controlled by the Communist party.	lek	Albanian	Islam Eastern Orthodoxy Roman Catholicism
ALGERIA	Centralized republic under a president, premier, council of ministers, and an elected unicameral legislature.	Algerian dinar	Arabic French Berber	Islam
AMERICAN SAMOA	U.S. territory with an elected governor and bicameral legislature.	U.S. dollar	English Samoan	Protestantism
ANDORRA	Co-principality of the president of France and the Spanish bishop of Seo de Urgel, with an elected Syndic General and a general council.	French franc and Spanish peseta	Catalan Spanish French	Roman Catholicism
ANGOLA	Centralized republic under a president, assisted by a premier, cabinet and revolutionary council.	kwanza	Portuguese Bantu languages	Tribal religions Roman Catholicism
ANTIGUA	Associated British state, with governor, prime minister, cabinet and bicameral legislature.	East Caribbean dollar	English	Protestantism
ARGENTINA	A republic with a president, at present under a military government.	Argentine peso	Spanish	Roman Catholicism
AUSTRALIA	Independent British Commonwealth member with a governor-general, prime minister, cabinet, and a bicameral parliament, composed of a senate and a house of representatives.	Australian dollar	English	Protestantism Roman Catholicism
AUSTRIA	A federal republic with a president, chancellor, cabinet, and a partly elected bicameral parliament.	schilling	German	Roman Catholicism
BAHAMAS	Independent British Commonwealth member, with a governor-general, prime minister, cabinet and bicameral general assembly.	Bahamian dollar	English	Protestantism Roman Catholicism
BAHRAIN	Independent state with an emir, prime minister and cabinet.	Bahraini dinar	Arabic	Islam
BANGLADESH	Independent republic in the British Commonwealth, with a president, prime minister, cabinet and unicameral parliament.	taka	Bengali English Urdu	Islam Hinduism Christianity Buddhism

of the World

MAJOR PRODUCTS

Wheat, barley, corn, rice, sugar beets, nuts & seeds, fruits, cotton, tobacco; livestock; timber; natural gas, salt, copper, lead, talc, coal, lapis lazuli; hides & skins (karakul), wool, textiles, leather, carpets, cement.

Corn, tobacco, wheat, potatoes, cotton, sugar beets, fruits; livestock; fish; timber; petroleum, bitumen, lignite, nickel, copper, iron ore, chromite; textiles, wool, tobacco products, chemicals.

Wheat, barley, oats, corn, grapes, olives, dates, figs, citrus fruits, vegetables, tobacco; fish; livestock; timber; iron ore, petroleum, phosphates, zinc, natural gas, mercury, lead; hides, wine, olive oil, cork, food & tobacco products, leather, textiles, chemicals, machinery, iron & steel, refined petroleum.

Taro, breadfruit, yams, bananas, arrowroot, pineapples, coconuts, oranges; fish; livestock; canned fish, copra, mats.

Tobacco, potatoes, oats, barley; livestock; timber; iron ore, lead; dairy, tobacco, wood & wool products.

Coffee, corn, sugarcane, peanuts, tobacco, rice, palm products, cotton, sisal; iron ore, petroleum, diamonds; fish; livestock; timber; refined petroleum, cement, paper, tires, refined sugar, food products, chemicals.

Sugar, cotton, rice, molasses, fruits, vegetables; fish; processed sugar and cotton, rum.

Wheat, corn, millet, cotton, sugarcane, tobacco, fruits; livestock; timber; petroleum, natural gas, zinc, silver, lead, coal, iron ore, tungsten; wine, vegetable oils, dairy products, meat & meat products, wool, hides, textiles, wood and metal products, iron & steel, machinery, autos, chemicals, leather, petroleum products, cement.

Wheat, oats, barley, fruits, vegetables; livestock; gold, coal, petroleum, copper, iron, lead, silver, bauxite, uranium, zinc; timber, iron & steel, wool, electrical equipment, appliances, chemicals, petroleum products, optical & agricultural implements, machinery, textiles, leather, airplanes, engines, ships, processed meat, sugar, dairy products, building materials, autos, tires.

Rye, wheat, corn, oats, barley, potatoes, sugar beets, hops, flax, tobacco, grapes; livestock; timber; iron ore, copper, lead, graphite, coal, petroleum, salt, magnesite; wine, processed foods, dairy products, iron & steel, aluminum, machinery, tools, chemicals, paper, textiles, cement.

Tomatoes, pineapples, sugarcane, vegetables, sponges, citrus fruits, bananas; fish, crawfish, shells; timber; salt; handcraft products, cement, pulpwood, processed fish, rum, refined petroleum, drugs.

Vegetables, fruits, dates; fish, shellfish; petroleum; refined petroleum, processed aluminum, electrical goods, cement, flour.

Rice, sugarcane, jute, cotton, oilseeds, tobacco, tea, chilies, fruit; timber; cattle, fish; natural gas, coal; textiles, hides & skins, flour, refined petroleum, steel, chemicals, refined sugar, handicrafts, paper, leather goods, jute products.

ALGERIA: A native letter writer in the streets of Constantine, the country's third largest city.

TWA—Trans World Airlines

AUSTRALIA: The country's first oil field at Moonie, Queensland, is in a sheep herding region.

Australian Government

Social and Economic Tables

POLITICAL DIVISION	GOVERNMENT	MONETARY UNIT	LANGUAGE	RELIGION
BARBADOS	Independent British Commonwealth member, with a governor-general, prime minister, cabinet and a bicameral parliament.	Barbadian dollar	English	Protestantism
BELGIUM	Constitutional, hereditary monarchy, with a king, premier, cabinet, and a bicameral parliament.	Belgian franc	French (Walloon) Flemish (Dutch)	Roman Catholicism
BELIZE	Internally self-governing British colony with governor, prime minister, cabinet and bicameral legislature.	Belize dollar	English; Spanish Mayan; Creole	Roman Catholicism Protestantism
BENIN	Republic, at present under a head of state and a committee of the ruling party.	CFA franc	French Sudanese languages	Tribal religions Islam Christianity
BERMUDA	Partly self-governing British colony with a governor, prime minister, cabinet and a bicameral legislature.	Bermuda dollar	English	Protestantism
BHUTAN	Monarchy with a king, councils, and a unicameral assembly.	Indian rupee; ngultrum	Dzongka Nepali	Buddhism Hinduism
BOLIVIA	Centralized constitutional republic, with a president and cabinet, presently ruled by decree.	Bolivian peso	Spanish Quechua Aymará	Roman Catholicism
BOTSWANA	Constitutional republic within the British Commonwealth, with a president, cabinet, a unicameral parliament and an advisory house of chiefs.	pula	English Setswana Sindebele Bushman Afrikaans	Tribal religions Protestantism
BRAZIL	Federal republic with a president, vice-president, appointive cabinet and a bicameral legislature, at present ruled by decree.	cruzeiro	Portuguese Italian German Japanese	Roman Catholicism
BRUNEI	Internally self-governing British protected sultanate, with a chief minister, cabinet, and councils.	Brunei dollar	Malay English	Islam
BULGARIA	Soviet-type republic with a cabinet, state council and unicameral parliament, which elects a presidium whose chairman is chief of state. Actual control is by the Communist party.	lev	Bulgarian Turkish Greek	Eastern Orthodoxy Islam
BURMA	One-party socialist republic with a unicameral assembly, prime minister and cabinet, and a state council with its chairman the president.	kyat	Burmese Karen; Kachin Shan; Chin English Hindi; Tamil Chinese	Buddhism Tribal religions
BURUNDI	One-party republic with a president, premier, and revolutionary council.	Burundi franc	French; Kirundi Kiswahili	Tribal religions Roman Catholicism
CAMBODIA (KAMPUCHEA)	Communist state with a president, vice-president and a revolutionary council.	—	Khmer French	Buddhism

of the World

MAJOR PRODUCTS

Sugarcane, vegetables, cotton; fish; manjak (asphalt); sugar, molasses, rum, edible oils, margarine.

Wheat, rye, oats, barley, potatoes, sugar beets, tobacco, vegetables, fruit, hops; livestock, poultry; fish; coal, iron, zinc, lead, dolomite; coke, iron & steel, machinery, metal products, textiles, lace, glass, chemicals, petroleum & uranium refining, sugar, beer, paper, wine, wool, cut diamonds, dairy products, aircraft, cement, autos.

Rice, corn, bananas, vegetables, citrus fruits, cocoa, sugarcane; cattle; hard and softwoods; fish, shellfish; rum, meat, fruit & fish products.

Palm products, tobacco, peanuts, cotton, corn, copra, coffee, castor oil, kapok, millet; livestock; fish; gold, diamonds, bauxite, iron ore; oil seed milling, textiles.

Lily bulbs, onions, bananas, citrus fruits, vegetables, potatoes; coral; poultry, fish; limestone; perfume, pharmaceuticals, concrete.

Rice, wheat, barley, millet, corn, fruits; timber; cattle, yaks; handicrafts, dairy products.

Potatoes, corn, wheat, barley, rice, cassava, sugarcane, cotton, coffee, fruits; timber; livestock; tin, zinc, lead, silver, antimony, copper, natural gas, petroleum, tungsten, gold, sulphur; hides & skins, textiles, chemicals, cement, beer, tobacco products.

Kaffir cotton, sorghum, millet, corn, wheat, beans, fruits & nuts; livestock; diamonds, nickel, copper, coal, salt, talc, manganese ore; hides & skins, meat & dairy products, leather goods, brewing.

Coffee, corn, rice, wheat, cotton, cocoa, sugarcane, soybeans, cassava, rubber, fibers, carnauba wax, medicinal plants, fruits & nuts, tobacco; livestock; timber; iron & manganese ore, diamonds, lead & zinc, bauxite, gold & silver, mica, asbestos, chromite, tungsten, petroleum, quartz, beryllium, copper, coal; meat products, hides, textiles, chemicals, petrochemicals, drugs, paper, lumber, machinery, autos, metal products, iron & steel, sugar, aluminum, tires, cement.

Rice, sago, rubber, jelutong, cutch, tapioca, bananas; timber; livestock; petroleum, natural gas; boat building, cloth, brass and silverware, refined petroleum.

Wheat, corn, barley, cotton, tobacco, sugar beets, potatoes, seeds, fruits, vegetables; timber; livestock; fish; iron ore, copper, lead, coal, manganese, petroleum, zinc; food, leather & tobacco products, sugar, refined minerals & petroleum, textiles, wine, iron & steel, machinery, cement.

Rice, corn, cotton, pulses, sugarcane, tobacco, fruits & nuts, jute, rubber, sesame; livestock; timber (teak); petroleum, lead, zinc, tungsten, nickel, silver, copper, precious stones; sugar, food, tobacco & wood products, drugs, chemicals, textiles, cement, refined petroleum, steel.

Coffee, tea, cotton, corn, beans, fruits & nuts, sweet potatoes, sorghum; cattle; fish; timber; nickel; hides & skins, textiles, cement, beer, soap, shoes, food products.

Rice, tobacco, corn, beans, sugarcane, rubber, cotton; cattle; fish; timber; phosphates, gold, precious stones; food products, textiles, sugar, glass, drugs.

BELGIUM: The Grand' Place in Brussels, with its flower market surrounded by Gothic and Renaissance architecture.

Belgian Gov't Info. Ctr.

BRAZIL: Baling cotton for export by rail and sea in the state of São Paulo.

Pan American Union

Social and Economic Tables

POLITICAL DIVISION	GOVERNMENT	MONETARY UNIT	LANGUAGE	RELIGION
CAMEROON	One-party republic, with a president, prime minister, cabinet, and unicameral elected assembly.	CFA franc	French; English Sudanese and Bantu languages	Tribal religions Christianity Islam
CANADA	Independent confederation of the British Commonwealth, with a governor-general, prime minister, cabinet and a bicameral parliament, composed of an appointed senate and an elected house of commons.	Canadian dollar	English French	Protestantism Roman Catholicism
CAPE VERDE	Republic, ruled by the president as chairman of the only political party; prime minister and cabinet.	Cape Verdean escudo	Portuguese	Roman Catholicism
CENTRAL AFRICAN EMPIRE	Constitutional monarchy, with an emperor, premier and cabinet.	CFA franc	French; Sangho Sudanese and Bantu languages	Tribal religions Christianity Islam
CHAD	Republic with a head of state and a cabinet.	CFA franc	French, Arabic Bantu and Sudanese languages	Tribal religions Islam Roman Catholicism
CHILE	Republic ruled by a president and an advisory council of state.	Chilean peso	Spanish	Roman Catholicism
CHINA (PEOPLE'S REPUBLIC)	Nominal republic, ruled by a prime minister & cabinet (state council); controlled by Communist party's politburo, headed by the standing committee and its chairman.	yuan	Chinese Mongol Turkic languages Tibetan	Confucianism Buddhism Taoism Islam
CHINA (REPUBLIC OF): TAIWAN	Republic with a president, prime minister, cabinet, a legislative yuan and a national assembly, the latter electing the president.	new Taiwan dollar (yuan)	Chinese	Confucianism Buddhism Taoism Christianity Tribal religions
COLOMBIA	A centralized federal republic with a president, vice-president, appointive cabinet, and elective bicameral congress.	Colombian peso	Spanish	Roman Catholicism
COMOROS	Republic with a president, premier, cabinet and unicameral legislature.	CFA franc	Arabic French Kiswahili	Islam
CONGO	Republic of the French Community, with a president, premier and a presidium.	CFA franc	French Sudanese and Bantu languages	Tribal religions Roman Catholicism
COOK ISLANDS	Internally self-governing state associated with New Zealand with a commissioner, prime minister, cabinet and legislative assembly.	New Zealand dollar	Polynesian dialects English	Protestantism
COSTA RICA	Constitutional republic with president, cabinet and elected unicameral assembly.	colón	Spanish	Roman Catholicism

of the World

Cocoa, coffee, rubber, nuts, tea, rice, tobacco, palm products, cotton; livestock; fish; timber; bauxite, gold, petroleum; hides & skins, wood, rubber & tobacco products, textiles, beer, food products, palm oil.

Wheat, oats, barley, corn, potatoes, vegetables, sugar beets, tobacco, fruits, oilseeds; livestock; poultry; fish, shellfish; timber; furs; gold, copper, nickel, zinc, lead, silver, potash, molybdenum, platinum, iron ore, titanium, cobalt, radium, uranium, petroleum, natural gas, coal, asbestos, salt, gypsum, sulphur; hydroelectric power; foods, apparel, meat & dairy products, transportation equipment, iron & steel, aluminum, metal products, lumber, pulp, paper & wood products, textiles, electric goods, chemicals, autos, cement, processed minerals, refined petroleum, machinery.

Coffee, bananas, nuts, oilseeds, corn; livestock; salt, lime; hides & skins, preserved fish, sugar, cement.

Coffee, cotton, peanuts, tobacco, corn, rice, sorghum; timber; livestock; gold, diamonds, uranium; wood & palm products, textiles, flour, soap, beer.

Millet, sorghum, rice, cotton, vegetables, dates, cassava, peanuts, gum arabic, ivory, ostrich feathers; livestock; fish; natron (salt); hides, cloth, meat products.

Cereal grains, seeds, sugar beets, potatoes, vegetables, fruits, tobacco; livestock; fish; timber; copper, nitrates, iron ore, manganese, silver, gold, molybdenum, zinc, coal, petroleum; chemicals, petrochemicals, wood & metal products, textiles, paper, pulp, drugs, wine, iron & steel, food & leather products, cement.

Rice & cereal grains, soybeans, fruits, vegetables, nuts, oilseeds, tea, silk, cotton, sugarcane, tobacco; livestock, poultry; fish; timber; iron ore, petroleum, coal, tungsten, tin, antimony, magnetite, manganese, molybdenum, natural gas, mercury, bauxite, lead, zinc; meat & food products, textiles, apparel, ceramics, cement, iron & steel, machinery, metal products, aluminum, chemicals, vehicles, armaments.

Rice, sugarcane, tea, sweet potatoes, bananas, pineapples, mushrooms, soybeans, tobacco; livestock; fish; timber; coal, natural gas; food & wood products, cement, glass, chemicals, petrochemicals, steel, bicycles, sugar, electric & electronic goods, machinery, metal products, textiles, apparel.

Coffee, rice, cotton, sugarcane, bananas, cacao, wheat, corn, tobacco, rubber, fibers; livestock; fish; timber; petroleum, gold, platinum, emeralds, silver, salt; sugar, food & tobacco products, beer, textiles, cement, iron & steel, machinery, metal & leather products, chemicals, meat.

Sugarcane, vanilla, rice, root vegetables, copra, sisal, coffee, essential oils (ylang, citronella), cloves, cacao, perfume plants; timber; rum distilling.

Palm products, coffee, cocoa, bananas, tobacco, sugarcane, rice, corn, peanuts, fruits; livestock; timber; petroleum, potash, lead, zinc, gold; hardwoods & wood products, textiles, beer, cement, sugar, food products.

Citrus fruits, coconuts, copra, oilseeds, tomatoes, arrowroot, pineapples, breadfruit, taro, kumaras, plantains, yams; mother-of-pearl, textiles, processed fruits.

Coffee, bananas, cocoa, corn, sugarcane, rice, potatoes, tobacco; cattle; tuna; timber; gold, salt, bauxite; dairy, tobacco & food products; electrical goods, beef, sugar, textiles, furniture, cement, apparel.

CHILE: Bathers and cabanas on the Pacific sands of Las Salinas, a popular beach at Viña del Mar.

Hamilton Wright

COLOMBIA: One of the country's principal products, coffee, drying under the tropical sun.

Pan American Union

Social and Economic Tables

POLITICAL DIVISION	GOVERNMENT	MONETARY UNIT	LANGUAGE	RELIGION
CUBA	Communist republic with a president, cabinet and an elected legislature, but with dictatorial powers held by the president and council of state.	Cuban peso	Spanish	Roman Catholicism
CYPRUS	British Commonwealth republic, at present divided into Greek and Turkish states, each with a president and unicameral legislature.	Cyprus pound	Greek Turkish English	Greek Orthodoxy Islam
CZECHOSLOVAKIA	Soviet-type republic with a president, premier, cabinet, bicameral legislature, and Czech and Slovak National Councils, with actual power residing in the Communist party presidium.	koruna	Czech and Slovak	Roman Catholicism Protestantism
DENMARK	Constitutional, hereditary monarchy with a queen, a unicameral elective legislature and an appointed cabinet and premier.	krone	Danish	Protestantism
DJIBOUTI	Independent republic with a president, premier and a unicameral assembly.	Djibouti franc	Hamitic languages French Arabic	Islam
DOMINICA	Independent British Commonwealth republic, with a president, prime minister, cabinet and a unicameral parliament.	East Caribbean dollar	English French patois	Roman Catholicism Protestantism
DOMINICAN REPUBLIC	Republic with a president, vice-president, appointed cabinet, and bicameral legislature.	Dominican peso	Spanish	Roman Catholicism
ECUADOR	Constitutional republic with a president, cabinet and unicameral legislature.	sucre	Spanish Indian languages (Quechua, etc.)	Roman Catholicism
EGYPT	Arab republic with a president, appointed prime minister, cabinet, and a partly elected unicameral assembly.	Egyptian pound	Arabic	Islam Christianity
EL SALVADOR	Republic with a president, cabinet, and unicameral legislature.	colón	Spanish	Roman Catholicism
ENGLAND AND WALES	Integral part of the United Kingdom, with executive power nominally residing in the Crown, but actually exercised by the prime minister, cabinet and bicameral parliament, composed of a house of lords and a house of commons.	pound sterling	English Welsh	Protestantism Roman Catholicism
EQUATORIAL GUINEA	One-party centralized republic with a president and a unicameral national assembly.	ekuele	Spanish Fang; Bubi	Tribal religions Roman Catholicism
ETHIOPIA	Military state, with the chairman of the military council as head of state, and a cabinet.	birr	Amharic Hamitic languages	Coptic Christianity Islam Tribal religions
FALKLAND ISLANDS	British colony with a governor, executive & legislative councils.	pound sterling	English	Protestantism Roman Catholicism
FIJI	Independent British Commonwealth member with a governor-general, prime minister, cabinet, and a bicameral parliament.	Fiji dollar	English; Fijian Hindi; Chinese Polynesian dialects	Protestantism Roman Catholicism Hinduism Islam

of the World

MAJOR PRODUCTS

Sugarcane, tobacco, coffee, rice, fruits; cattle; timber; fish; nickel, iron ore, chromite, manganese, copper; sugar, tobacco, meat & food products, textiles, cement, chemicals, steel, refined petroleum & metals, electrical goods, rum.

Wheat, barley, grapes, raisins, olives, potatoes, carobs, nuts, citrus fruits, tobacco, vegetables; fish; livestock; copper & concentrates, iron pyrites, asbestos, chromite, gypsum, marble; tobacco, leather & food products, cement, wine, textiles, refined petroleum.

Wheat, rye, oats, barley, corn, sugar beets, potatoes; livestock; timber; coal, iron ore, magnesite, uranium, lead, salt; munitions, machinery, metal, rubber, leather & wood products, cement, iron & steel, textiles, shoes, porcelain, paper, chemicals, aircraft, autos, glass & glassware, beer, apparel, sugar, food products.

Barley, oats, rye, wheat, potatoes, sugar beets, vegetables; poultry, livestock; stone, clay, iron ore; meat & meat products, dairy products, canned foods, beverages, machinery, transportation equipment, metal & rubber products, chemicals, apparel, shoes, furniture, glassware, earthenware, electrical goods, ships, cement, paper, tobacco products.

Salt; hides & skins; livestock; boats.

Bananas, citrus fruits, timber, pumice, edible and essential oils, copra.

Sugarcane, cacao, coffee, tobacco, bananas, rice, fruits, corn; cattle; lumber; nickel, bauxite; nickel & petroleum refining, chocolate, sugar, meat, cigars, textiles, cement, beer, flour, peanut oil, leather goods, rum.

Rice, cocoa, coffee, sugarcane, corn, bananas, cotton, cinchona; livestock; fish & shellfish; timber; petroleum, gold, silver; food, rubber, leather & wood products, textiles, toquilla (panama) hats, sugar, beer, cement, chemicals & petrochemicals, drugs, glass.

Cotton, cereal grains, sugarcane, fruits, vegetables; livestock; fish; petroleum, phosphates, salt, iron ore, manganese, limestone; cotton ginning, iron & steel, refined petroleum, food processing, textiles, chemicals, cement, petrochemicals, sugar.

Coffee, cotton, cereal grains, cacao, tobacco, henequén, sugarcane; fish, shellfish; livestock; timber; silver; sugar, textiles, food products, drugs, chemicals, electric goods.

Potatoes, vegetables, cereal grains, hay, hops, fruits; livestock, poultry; fish; coal, petroleum, natural gas, iron ore, copper, lead, nickel, tin; dairy products, wool, cotton & linen textiles, electrical goods, vehicles, steel, scientific instruments, cutlery, foods & beverages, leather & tobacco products, apparel, chemicals, petrochemicals, pottery, china, machinery, locomotives, knitwear, drugs.

Cocoa, coffee, bananas, sugarcane, palm oil & kernels; timber, cabinet woods; fish; copra, beverages, soap.

Coffee, wheat, corn, barley, durra, teff, pulses, oilseeds, chat, civet, fruits, vegetables, sugarcane, spices; poultry, livestock; gold, platinum; hides & skins, meat & food products, textiles, cement, sugar, refined petroleum, drugs.

Oats, vegetables, hay; sheep; wool, hides & skins, tallow, animal & vegetable oil.

Sugarcane, coconuts, rice, fruits, cotton, rubber, ginger, oilseeds, vegetables, bananas, cocoa, corn, tobacco; livestock; timber; fish; gold, silver, manganese; sugar, copra, coconut oil, molasses, candlenut oil, cement, beer, meat products, flour, shipbuilding.

DENMARK: Amalienborg Palace in Copenhagen, the queen's residence, and the statue of King Frederik V.

Danish Nat'l Travel Office

FRANCE: Fresh fruits and vegetables occupy a market in Paris, near the right bank of the Seine.

TWA—Trans World Airlines

Social and Economic Tables

POLITICAL DIVISION	GOVERNMENT	MONETARY UNIT	LANGUAGE	RELIGION
FINLAND	Constitutional republic with a president, premier, cabinet, and a unicameral parliament.	markka	Finnish Swedish	Protestantism
FRANCE	A constitutional republic with a president, premier, bicameral elective legislature and appointive council of ministers.	franc	French	Roman Catholicism
FRENCH GUIANA	Overseas department of France governed by a prefect with an elective general council.	French franc	French	Roman Catholicism
FRENCH POLYNESIA	Overseas territory of France, with a governor, government council, and an elected territorial assembly.	CFP franc	Polynesian dialects French	Protestantism Roman Catholicism
GABON	One-party republic of the French Community with a president, appointed prime minister, and unicameral national assembly.	CFA franc	French Bantu languages	Roman Catholicism Tribal religions Islam
GAMBIA	Republic of the British Commonwealth, with a president, vice-president, cabinet and unicameral legislature.	dalasi	English Sudanese languages	Islam Tribal religions Protestantism
GERMANY	Divided country with two governments. The western democratic Federal Republic has a president, chancellor, cabinet & bicameral parliament. The eastern Democratic Republic is ruled by the chairman of the state council, a prime minister & cabinet, & a unicameral legislature; actual power resides in the head of the Communist party.	West German Deutsche mark East German Ostmark (GDR mark)	German	Protestantism Roman Catholicism
GHANA	Republic of the British Commonwealth, with a military council and appointed cabinet.	cedi	English Sudanese languages	Tribal religions Protestantism Islam
GIBRALTAR	Partly self-governing British colony, with governor, cabinet, house of assembly and local council.	pound sterling	English Spanish	Roman Catholicism
GILBERT ISLANDS (KIRIBATI)	Self-governing British colony, with a governor and local councils.	Australian dollar	English Gilbertese	Protestantism Roman Catholicism
GREAT BRITAIN	See: England and Wales, Northern Ireland, Scotland.			
GREECE	Constitutional republic, with a president, premier, and unicameral parliament.	drachma	Greek	Greek Orthodoxy
GREENLAND (KALÂTDLIT-NUNÂT)	Self-governing community of Denmark with a premier and elected legislature.	Danish krone	Danish Greenlandic Eskimo	Protestantism
GRENADA	Independent British Commonwealth member with a governor-general, premier and revolutionary council.	East Caribbean dollar	English French patois	Roman Catholicism Protestantism
GUADELOUPE	Overseas department of France with a prefect and elected general council.	French franc	French French patois (Creole)	Roman Catholicism
GUAM	Unincorporated U.S. territory, with an elected governor, advisory staff, and a unicameral legislature.	American dollar	English Chamorro Spanish	Roman Catholicism

of the World

MAJOR PRODUCTS

Hay, potatoes, cereal grains; livestock, poultry, reindeer; timber; fish; copper, iron ore, titanium, zinc, nickel; lumber, plywood, furniture, pulp, paper, wood products, textiles, food & dairy products, meat, chemicals, china, glass, machinery, ships, transportation equipment, electrical & metal products, vehicles, apparel, iron & steel.

Sugar beets, potatoes, cereal grains, turnips, fruits, nuts, grapes, buckwheat; livestock; fish; coal, iron ore, bauxite, pyrites, potash, salt, sulphur, natural gas; iron & steel, chemicals, machinery, metal & leather goods, autos, aircraft, ships, aluminum, porcelain, food & dairy products, apparel, cosmetics, perfumes, sugar, wines & spirits, electric & electronic goods, lace, silk, cotton, rayon, wool & linen textiles.

Rice, bananas, sugarcane, corn, manioc; timber; livestock; shrimp; bauxite, gold; hides, shoes, rum, fish glue.

Coconuts, bananas, pineapples, oranges, vanilla, sugarcane, coffee, bamboo; fish; mother-of-pearl, sugar, rum, copra.

Coffee, cocoa, rubber, corn, rice, bananas, cassava; timber; fish; manganese, uranium, petroleum, iron ore, gold, natural gas, lead, zinc, copper, diamonds, phosphates; refined petroleum, processed metals, textiles, plywood.

Peanuts, rice, millet, sorghum, fruits, palm kernels; livestock; fish; textiles, peanut oil refining, fish processing, palm products, beverages.

Cereal grains, potatoes, sugar beets, fruits, hops; livestock; fish; timber; coal, lignite, iron ore, potash, salt, uranium, lead, zinc, natural gas, fluorspar; iron & steel, autos, bicycles, machinery, aluminum, cement, electrical & transportation equipment, ships, metal & electronic products, cotton & woolen textiles & yarn, rayon fiber, precision & optical instruments, shoes, apparel, food products, sugar, beer, wine, chemicals, sulphuric acid, soda, ammonia, synthetic rubber, drugs, petrochemicals.

Cocoa, coconuts, kola nuts, fruits, tobacco, coffee, peanuts, rubber; livestock; fish; timber; gold, diamonds, manganese, bauxite; aluminum, refined petroleum, textiles.

Fish; ship repairing, beer, local food processing.

Coconuts, breadfruit; phosphate of lime; pearl shell, fish; pigs, poultry; copra, palm products.

Cereal grains, tobacco, sugar beets, cotton, fruits, olives; livestock; sponges, fish; iron ore, emery, manganese, magnesite, marble, silver, nickel, bauxite, salt, chromite; textiles, olive oil, processed meat, fruit & vegetables, dairy, wood & leather products, steel, machinery, refined aluminum & petroleum, chemicals, wine, olive oil, cement, drugs.

Grass for fodder; cod and other fish; sheep, furs; cryolite, lead, zinc; processed fish, skins.

Cocoa, nutmeg, coffee, mace, limes, bananas, sugarcane, coconuts, vegetables, cotton; fish; livestock; timber; sugar, cotton ginning, copra, lime oil, rum, beer, cigarettes.

Sugarcane, bananas, pineapples, mangoes, avocados, coffee, cotton, sisal, cocoa, vanilla, cassava; fish; rum, sugar.

Coconuts, corn, bananas, citrus fruits, mangoes, papayas, breadfruit, sweet potatoes, cassava, vegetables, sugarcane, pineapples; livestock, poultry; fish; dairy & coconut products.

GREECE: An "evzone," one of the uniquely uniformed guards at the palace in Athens.

J. Walter Thompson

GUATEMALA: Removing the nuts from the pods at a cacao "finca," or plantation, is the first stage of processing chocolate.

I.I.A.A.

Social and Economic Tables

POLITICAL DIVISION	GOVERNMENT	MONETARY UNIT	LANGUAGE	RELIGION
GUATEMALA	Republic with a president, cabinet and an elected unicameral congress.	quetzal	Spanish Maya-Quiché dialects	Roman Catholicism
GUINEA	One party republic with a president, cabinet, premier and unicameral national assembly.	syli	French Sudanese languages	Islam Tribal religions Roman Catholicism
GUINEA-BISSAU	Independent republic, with a state council under the president, and a one-party unicameral assembly.	Guinea-Bissau escudo	Portuguese Sudanese languages	Tribal religions Islam Roman Catholicism
GUYANA	Republic within the British Commonwealth, with president, prime minister, cabinet, and unicameral assembly.	Guyana dollar	English	Christianity Hinduism Islam
HAITI	Nominal republic with president (for life), cabinet, and a unicameral legislature.	gourde	French Creole	Roman Catholicism
HONDURAS	Republic, at present with a president, advisory cabinet and military council.	lempira	Spanish	Roman Catholicism
HONG KONG	British colony ruled by a governor assisted by executive and legislative councils.	Hong Kong dollar	English Chinese (Cantonese)	Confucianism Buddhism Taoism Christianity
HUNGARY	Soviet-type republic with a president, council, premier and unicameral assembly. Actual power is in the hands of the politburo of the Communist party.	forint	Hungarian	Roman Catholicism Protestantism
ICELAND	A republic with a president, premier, an elective bicameral parliament, and an appointive cabinet.	króna	Icelandic	Protestantism
INDIA	An independent republic within the British Commonwealth with a president, vice-president, prime minister, cabinet and a bicameral parliament.	Indian rupee	Hindi; English Assamese, Bengali, Gujarati, Kannada, Kashmiri, Malayalam, Marathi, Oriya, Panjabi, Sanskrit, Tamil, Telugu, Urdu	Hinduism; Islam Buddhism Animism Christianity Sikhism Jainism Zoroastrianism Lamaism
INDONESIA	Republic headed by a president, appointed cabinet, and consultative assembly (containing a unicameral parliament).	rupiah	Bahasa Indonesia (Indonesian Malay) Papuan	Islam Christianity Hinduism Buddhism Tribal religions
IRAN	Republic, provisionally governed by a premier and a secret revolutionary council.	Iranian rial	Persian (Farsi) Kurdish Arabic Turkic languages	Islam Zoroastrianism Christianity Judaism
IRAQ	Nominal republic headed by a president and a revolutionary council, and an appointed cabinet.	Iraqi dinar	Arabic Kurdish	Islam Christianity Judaism
IRELAND	Republic with a president, prime minister, cabinet, and a partly-elected bicameral parliament.	Irish pound	Irish English	Roman Catholicism Protestantism

MAJOR PRODUCTS

Coffee, bananas, sugarcane, tobacco, rubber, cotton, chicle, abacá; fish; cattle; mahogany; nickel, zinc, lead; textiles, chemicals, essential oils, wood, metal & electric goods, processed meat & foods, sugar, hides & skins, apparel.

Rice, millet, coffee, kola nuts, peanuts, palm oil & kernels, quinine, pineapples, cassava, bananas; livestock; bauxite, iron ore, diamonds, gold; timber; hides & skins, textiles, wood & food products, cigarettes, aluminum.

Rice, palm kernels, palm oil, wax, peanuts, coconuts; hides and skins; fish; timber.

Sugarcane, corn, rice, coconuts, coffee, citrus & tropical fruits, cacao, balata, rubber; timber; livestock; shrimp; bauxite, diamonds, manganese, gemstones, gold; textiles, milled rice, beer, rum, lime oil, sugar, wood & pulp, molasses, aluminum.

Coffee, sugarcane, sisal, cotton, fruits, rice, corn, cocoa; livestock; shellfish; bauxite; fiber, cement, essential oils, handicrafts, molasses, textiles, cement, sugar, soap, rum.

Bananas, coffee, coconuts, tobacco, corn, beans, sugarcane, cotton, rice, henequén, mahogany; cattle; lead, zinc, gold, silver; meat & food products, sugar, lumber, vegetable oils.

Rice, sugarcane, vegetables; fish; poultry, pigs; iron ore, wolfram, graphite; iron & steel, ships, enamel ware, apparel, textiles, cotton & plastic goods, toys, cameras, radios, electric & electronic goods.

Cereal grains, sugar beets, tobacco, grapes, fruits, potatoes; livestock, poultry; fish; timber; coal, petroleum, natural gas, iron ore, bauxite; flour, sugar, iron & steel, wines, textiles, chemicals, cotton & woolen goods, dairy, food, wood & paper products, machinery, tools & metal products, transportation equipment, drugs, aluminum, bicycles, cement.

Hay, potatoes, turnips, fruits, vegetables; livestock; fish; diatomite; dairy products, processed fish & fish products, meat, hides & skins, textiles, apparel, chemicals, cement, motors, vegetable oils.

Cereal grains, peanuts, seeds, tea, tobacco, opium, jute, cotton, rubber, coffee, sugarcane; fish; livestock; timber; coal, manganese, iron ore, petroleum, salt, mica, chromite, ilmenite, clay, copper, bauxite, gypsum; textiles, silk, cotton & jute fabrics, carpets, wood & metalwork, leather, cement, ships, refined petroleum, sugar, iron & steel, machinery, typewriters, aluminum, autos, transportation equipment, aircraft, chemicals.

Rice, sugarcane, corn, coconuts, cassava, sweet potatoes, spices, tea, coffee, fruits, rubber, tobacco, cotton, kapok; livestock; fish; timber; tin, petroleum, iron ore, natural gas, salt, bauxite, nickel, copper; refined petroleum & products, sugar, cement, copra, textiles, paper, ships, chemicals, palm oil, food products, glass, rubber goods, autos.

Cereal grains, cotton, dates, raisins, fruits, opium, sugar beets, nuts, tea, tobacco; livestock; fish; timber; petroleum, natural gas, copper, lead, coal, iron ore, salt; hides, wool, textiles, carpets, leather & tobacco products, caviar, sugar, glass, tools, vehicles, iron & steel, cement, aluminum, refined petroleum, metal products, chemicals & petrochemicals, vehicles, flour, processed foods.

Dates, fruits, barley, wheat, rice, tobacco, cotton, vegetables, sorghum; livestock; petroleum, sulphur, salt; refined petroleum, cement, chemicals, drugs, hides & skins, wool, glass, textiles, processed foods, electrical equipment.

Hay, potatoes, turnips, sugar beets, cereal grains; fish; livestock; lead, zinc, silver; tobacco, textiles, apparel, wood, clay, paper & metal products, machinery, dairy products, meat, processed foods, beer, malt, chemicals, vehicles.

INDIA: A typical scene in one of the busy streets of the native section in Bombay.
TWA–Trans World Airlines

INDONESIA: Educational progress—a mother and daughter attending school together.
Indonesian Info. Office

Social and Economic Tables

POLITICAL DIVISION	GOVERNMENT	MONETARY UNIT	LANGUAGE	RELIGION
ISRAEL	Republic with a president, prime minister, cabinet and elected unicameral parliament.	Israeli **pound**	Hebrew Arabic English	Judaism Islam Christianity
ITALY	Constitutional republic with a president, premier, a bicameral elective parliament and an appointive cabinet.	lira	Italian	Roman Catholicism
IVORY COAST	One-party republic with a president, cabinet, and a unicameral legislature.	CFA franc	French Sudanese languages	Tribal religions Islam Christianity
JAMAICA	Independent member of the British Commonwealth, with a governor-general, prime minister, cabinet, and bicameral parliament.	Jamaican dollar	English Jamaican Creole	Protestantism Roman Catholicism
JAPAN	Constitutional monarchy, with a prime minister, cabinet, and a bicameral diet. The duties of the emperor are merely ceremonial.	yen	Japanese	Buddhism Shintoism Christianity
JORDAN	Constitutional monarchy, with a king, prime minister and cabinet.	Jordanian dinar	Arabic English	Islam
KENYA	One-party republic of the British Commonwealth, with a president, vice-president, cabinet, and unicameral national assembly.	Kenyan shilling	English; Kiswahili Bantu, Hamitic and Sudanese languages	Christianity Tribal religions Islam
KOREA	Divided country with two governments. South Korea is a republic with a president, prime minister, cabinet & unicameral assembly. North Korea is ruled by the politburo of the Communist party, and has a president, prime minister & unicameral assembly.	won	Korean	Buddhism Confucianism Christianity
KUWAIT	Constitutional state with an emir, prime minister and cabinet, at present ruled by decree.	Kuwaiti dinar	Arabic	Islam
LAOS	Communist republic with a president, premier and appointed assembly, controlled by the party.	kip	Lao French	Buddhism Tribal religions
LEBANON	Republic with a president, an appointed premier and cabinet, and an elected unicameral assembly.	Lebanese pound	Arabic French	Islam Christianity
LESOTHO	Monarchy presently ruled by a prime minister (by decree), cabinet and assembly.	South African rand	Sesotho English	Christianity Tribal religions
LIBERIA	One-party republic, with a president, cabinet, and an elective bicameral Congress.	U.S. (Liberian) dollar	English Sudanese languages	Tribal religions Christianity Islam
LIBYA	Arab republic ruled by a council under its president, with an appointed premier and cabinet.	Libyan dinar	Arabic; Berber English Italian	Islam

MAJOR PRODUCTS

Wheat, cotton, tobacco, vegetables, fruits; livestock, poultry; fish; potash, salt, petroleum; textiles, apparel, processed foods, dairy products, glass, drugs, instruments, paper, metal, wood, rubber & leather products, polished diamonds, electric & electronic products, chemicals, wine, vehicles, refined petroleum, transportation equipment.

Cereal grains, sugar beets, potatoes, tomatoes, olives, grapes, citrus fruits, tobacco; timber; fish; livestock; natural gas, sulphur iron ore, coal, zinc, bauxite, mercury, marble; textiles, chemicals, wine, autos, machinery, electrical goods, sugar, olive oil, apparel, processed foods, petrochemicals, typewriters, iron & steel, aluminum, shoes, transportation equipment.

Coffee, cocoa, sugarcane, bananas, pineapples, nuts, rubber, cotton; tropical woods; livestock; fish; diamonds, iron ore; textiles, processed foods, lumber & wood products, refined petroleum, metal products, palm oil.

Sugarcane, bananas, tobacco, coconuts, coffee, citrus fruits, pimento, spices; fish; timber; bauxite, gypsum; rum, molasses, textiles, aluminum, copra, apparel, chemicals, processed foods, sugar, cement, metal, paper & rubber products.

Rice, wheat, barley, potatoes, fruits, vegetables, sugarcane, hemp, tobacco, soybeans, tea; livestock; fish; timber; petroleum, iron ore, manganese, gold, silver, copper, coal, natural gas; textiles, silk, iron & steel, machinery, autos, ships, instruments, electric & electronic goods, paper, pulp, porcelain & earthenware, toys, sugar, chemicals, apparel, aluminum, fish products, metal products.

Wheat, barley, grapes, vegetables, fruits, olives; livestock; phosphates, potash, marble; wool, tobacco & leather products, cement, soap, olive oil, beverages, refined petroleum.

Sisal, wheat, tea, coffee, pyrethrum, cotton, sugarcane, corn, peanuts, coconuts, wattle bark; livestock; timber; gold, silver, fluorspar, salt; sisal, meat & dairy products, sugar, cement, soda ash, hides & skins, petroleum products.

Rice, barley, wheat, soybeans, tobacco, corn, cotton, fruits; timber; livestock; fish; tungsten, gold, silver, iron ore, copper, coal, petroleum, lead, graphite, kaolin; textiles, silk, apparel, electric & electronic goods, metal, rubber, paper, wood & petroleum products, chemicals, cement, machinery, iron & steel.

Fruits, vegetables; pearls; fish; petroleum, natural gas; refined petroleum & petroleum products, ammonia, chemicals, fertilizer, cement, fish products, wool.

Rice, coffee, tea, citrus fruits, corn, cinchona, opium, potatoes, tobacco, cardamon, stick-lac; livestock; timber; tin; textiles, cigarettes, beverages, lumber, milled rice.

Wheat, barley, corn, potatoes, fruits, onions, vegetables, olives, tobacco; livestock; iron ore; textiles, metal & tobacco products, refined petroleum, chemicals, processed foods, cement, olive oil.

Cereal grains, beans, peas; livestock; diamonds; wool, mohair, hides & skins, carpets, textiles, shoes, candles, chemicals, jewelry, processed foods.

Rubber, rice, coffee, sugarcane, cocoa, palm oil & kernels, piassava; timber; fish, shrimp; iron ore, diamonds; petroleum products, cement, processed foods & rubber, lumber.

Barley, wheat, olives, grapes, dates, vegetables, figs, peanuts, citrus fruits, almonds, esparto; livestock, sponge & tuna fishing; hides & skins; petroleum, natural gas; textiles, crude petroleum, processed foods, leather, olive oil.

ITALY: A gondolier and his craft on one of the many waterways in Venice.

TWA—Trans World Airlines

LUXEMBOURG: La Place Guillaume, in the heart of the grand duchy's picturesque capital city.

Office Nat'l du Tourisme

Social and Economic Tables

POLITICAL DIVISION	GOVERNMENT	MONETARY UNIT	LANGUAGE	RELIGION
LIECHTENSTEIN	Constitutional hereditary monarchy, with a prince, prime minister, and unicameral parliament.	Swiss franc	German Alemannic dialect	Roman Catholicism
LUXEMBOURG	Constitutional monarchy with a grand duke, premier, cabinet, and a bicameral parliament.	Luxembourg franc	Letzeburgisch (German dialect) French; German	Roman Catholicism
MACAO	Partly autonomous Portuguese overseas province, under a governor, cabinet, and a legislative assembly.	pataca	Chinese (Cantonese) Portuguese	Buddhism; Taoism Confucianism Christianity
MADAGASCAR	Republic of the French Community with a head of government, premier and legislature. Rule is by a military council.	Malagasy franc	Malagasy French Bantu languages	Tribal religions Christianity Islam
MALAWI	One-party republic of the British Commonwealth, with president (for life), cabinet, and unicameral assembly.	Malawi kwacha	Chichewa English Bantu languages	Christianity Islam Tribal religions
MALAYSIA	Constitutional monarchy of the British Commonwealth, with a paramount ruler, prime minister, cabinet and bicameral parliament.	ringgit	Malay English Chinese Hindi, Tamil	Islam; Buddhism Confucianism Hinduism; Taoism Christianity
MALDIVES	Republic with a president and unicameral legislature.	Maldivian rupee	Divehi	Islam
MALI	Republic ruled by a president and a military committee.	Malian franc	French Sudanese and Hamitic languages	Islam Tribal religions
MALTA	An independent member of the British Commonwealth, with a president, prime minister, a cabinet and a unicameral parliament.	Maltese pound	Maltese English	Roman Catholicism
MARTINIQUE	Overseas department of France, with a prefect and an elected general council.	French franc	French Creole	Roman Catholicism
MAURITANIA	One-party republic, with a president, premier, appointed cabinet, and a unicameral assembly.	ouguiya	French; Arabic Sudanese and Hamitic languages	Islam
MAURITIUS	Independent member of the British Commonwealth, with a governor-general, prime minister, cabinet, and unicameral parliament.	Mauritian rupee	English; French Creole; Tamil Hindi; Urdu Chinese	Hinduism Christianity Islam Buddhism
MAYOTTE	French territorial collectivity.	CFA franc	Arabic; French Kiswahili	Islam
MEXICO	Constitutional federative republic with a president, council of ministers and a bicameral congress.	Mexican peso	Spanish	Roman Catholicism
MONACO	Constitutional hereditary principality, with a prince and a unicameral council.	French franc	French	Roman Catholicism
MONGOLIA	Soviet-type republic, with a president (chairman of Communist party politburo) & unicameral legislature.	tughrik	Mongolian Turkic languages	Lamaism

226

of the World

MAJOR PRODUCTS

Corn, wheat, potatoes, grapes; livestock; textiles, wine, leather, dairy products, ceramics, precision instruments, drugs, canned foods, postage stamps.

Oats, potatoes, wheat, rye, grapes; livestock; timber; iron ore, slate, salt, gypsum; iron & steel, metal products, chemicals, tobacco, leather, wine, dairy products, rubber products, fertilizers, plastic goods.

Rice, vegetables; fish; cement, metal work, lumber, processed tobacco, matches, wine, textiles, fireworks.

Cassava, rice, corn, sweet potatoes, vanilla, cloves, sugarcane, coffee, bananas, beans, manioc, sisal, tobacco, raffia; timber; livestock; fish; graphite, mica, chromite; textiles, processed meat & foods, refined petroleum & petroleum products, cement, paper, sugar, beer, leather.

Tobacco, tea, cotton, sugarcane, tung nuts, pulses, sisal, corn, fruits, sorghum, rice, millet, peanuts, rubber; timber; livestock; bauxite, stone, gold; hides & skins, tung oil, meat, transportation equipment, machinery, ghee, sugar.

Rubber, rice, coconuts, sugarcane, coffee, cocoa, pineapples, pepper, tea, tobacco, vegetables; livestock; fish; timber; tin, petroleum, copper, gold, antimony, bauxite, iron ore, manganese; rubber & wood products, steel, autos, refined petroleum, textiles, electric goods, sugar, fibers.

Coconuts, corn, millet, pumpkins, sweet potatoes, fruits, nuts; fish, cowries; mats, boats, dried fish & fish products, handicrafts, copra, coir, ambergris, lace.

Millet, rice, sorghum, peanuts, corn, cotton, tobacco, nuts, sisal; livestock; fish; salt, gold, bauxite, iron ore, uranium; hides & skins, ceramics, jewelry, leather, rice mills, soap, processed fish & foods, textiles, sugar, cement, meat, fibers.

Wheat, barley, potatoes, onions, grapes, vegetables, fruits, cumin seed, cotton; livestock; fish; lace, wine, beer, cigarettes, buttons, pipes, gloves, textiles & yarn, flowers, ceramics, rubber & electronic goods, apparel.

Sugarcane, cocoa, mangoes, avocados, pineapples, bananas, coffee; fish; rum, sugar.

Cereal grains, beans, peanuts, melons, dates, gum arabic, henna, sweet potatoes; livestock; lobsters, fish; manganese, gypsum, iron ore, copper, salt; hides & skins, fish products.

Sugarcane, aloe fiber, corn, coffee, vanilla beans, hemp, potatoes, sisal, peanuts, tea, yams, manioc, pineapples, tobacco, coconuts; molasses, rum, copra, sugar, dairy, tea & tobacco products, processed foods, textiles, fibers.

Vanilla, sisal, sugarcane, essential oils, rum; fish.

Grains, coffee, cotton, tomatoes, sugarcane, bananas, chicle, beans, oranges, henequén; timber; fish; shrimp; livestock; silver, gold, lead, zinc, petroleum, coal, sulphur, manganese, natural gas, iron ore, copper; sugar, hides, textiles, fibers, chemicals, aluminum, machinery, autos, refined petroleum, petrochemicals, cement, paper, drugs, metal products.

Principal revenue from gambling casino and tourism. Postage stamps, perfume, liqueurs, olive oil, oranges, chemicals, instruments, glass, processed foods, ceramics.

Grains; livestock; coal, petroleum, lead, gold; dairy products, wool, hides & skins, processed foods, machinery, furs, meat & dairy products, textiles, leather, cement.

MEXICO: The Pyramid of the Sun at San Juan Teotihuacan, not far from Mexico City.

J. Walter Thompson

MOROCCO: Downtown Casablanca, the chief port, with the Place Lyautey in the foreground.

French Gov't Tourist Office

Social and Economic Tables

POLITICAL DIVISION	GOVERNMENT	MONETARY UNIT	LANGUAGE	RELIGION
MOROCCO	Constitutional monarchy, with a king, an appointed prime minister, cabinet, and a unicameral parliament.	dirham	Arabic Berber French Spanish	Islam Judaism Christianity
MOZAMBIQUE	One-party republic with a president, cabinet and a unicameral assembly.	Mozambique escudo	Portuguese Bantu languages	Tribal religions Islam Roman Catholicism
NAURU	Republic with a president, cabinet, and unicameral assembly.	Australian dollar	English Nauruan	Protestantism
NEPAL	Constitutional monarchy, with king, prime minister, cabinet, and a unicameral parliament.	Nepalese rupee	Nepali; Newari Hindi English	Hinduism Buddhism Christianity
NETHERLANDS	A constitutional, hereditary monarchy governed by the queen, a premier and cabinet, and a bicameral partly elected states general.	guilder (florin)	Dutch	Roman Catholicism Protestantism
NETHERLANDS ANTILLES	Self-governing part of Netherlands Union with governor, minister-president, cabinet & unicameral legislature (staten).	Dutch guilder	Dutch Papiamento Spanish	Roman Catholicism Protestantism

NEW CALEDONIA	French overseas territory with a governor, government council & an elected territorial assembly.	CFP franc	Melanesian and
			  Polynesian
			  dialects
			French
				Roman Catholicism
				Tribal religions

NEW HEBRIDES	British and French condominium administered by British and French high commissioners, with a partly elected assembly.	Australian dollar New Hebrides franc	Melanesian dialects Pidgin English English; French	Tribal religions Protestantism Roman Catholicism
NEW ZEALAND	An independent member of the British Commonwealth governed by a governor-general, a prime minister, a cabinet and a unicameral parliament.	New Zealand dollar	English Maori	Protestantism Roman Catholicism
NICARAGUA	Constitutional republic with a president, cabinet, and elective bicameral congress.	córdoba	Spanish	Roman Catholicism
NIGER	One-party republic, with a president, the head of a military government.	CFA franc	French Sudanese and Hamitic languages Arabic; Berber	Islam Tribal religions
NIGERIA	Federal republic of the British Commonwealth, now under the chairman of a supreme military council, with an advisory federal executive council.	naira	English Sudanese languages	Islam Tribal religions Christianity

NIUE	Self-governing New Zealand dependency, with a prime minister and an assembly.	New Zealand dollar	Melanesian
			  and Polynesian
			  dialects; English
				Protestantism

NORTHERN IRELAND	Integral part of the United Kingdom with local government presently being reorganized.	pound sterling	English	Protestantism Roman Catholicism

of the World

MAJOR PRODUCTS

Wheat, barley, legumes, olives, nuts, citrus fruits, sugar beets, grapes; vegetables; cork, timber; livestock; fish; phosphates, iron ore, fluorite, coal, lead, zinc, manganese, petroleum, cobalt; textiles, carpets, pulp, wine, essential oils, olive oil, food & fish products, perfumes, wool.

Sugarcane, cereal grains, coconuts, cotton, cashew nuts, peanuts, sisal, beans, tea, tobacco; timber; livestock; fish, shellfish; gold, coal, iron ore, bauxite; sugar, textiles, milled rice, cement, vegetable oils, processed foods & fish, copra.

Phosphates.

Rice, wheat, corn, millet, jute, sugarcane, potatoes, tea, oilseeds, medicinal herbs; timber; livestock; iron ore, copper; processed rice, tobacco, leather & wood products, textiles, sugar, chemicals, ghee, hides & skins.

Potatoes, sugar beets, cereal grains, flax, legumes, flower bulbs, seeds, vegetables, fruits; livestock; fish; coal, petroleum, natural gas, salt; metal products, textiles, paper, chemicals, processed foods, apparel, ships, ceramics, cement, dairy, wood & tobacco products, petroleum products, machinery, electric & electronic products, transportation equipment, flowers, glass, processed diamonds.

Fish; salt, phosphates; refined petroleum, petrochemicals, electronic equipment, textiles, beer.

Coconuts, coffee, cotton, corn, tobacco, bananas, pineapples, vegetables, rice; timber; livestock; nickel, chrome, manganese, iron ore, cobalt, copper, lead, silver, gold; canned meat, nickel & coffee processing, copra.

Coconuts, cocoa, coffee, bananas, yams, taro, manioc, fruits; timber; cattle; fish, trochus shell; manganese; meat and fish products, copra, lumber.

Cereal grains; livestock; timber; fish; gold, coal, mineral sands, limestone, petroleum, natural gas; meat, wool, hides & skins, apparel, timber & wood products, dairy products, food & tobacco products, autos, chemicals, fertilizers, beer, bricks, cement, electrical goods, machinery, paper, rubber & petroleum products.

Coffee, sugarcane, sesame, corn, bananas, rice, cocoa, tobacco, cotton, beans; cattle; fish; hardwoods; gold, copper, silver; sugar, wood products, meat products, textiles, cottonseed, chemicals, petroleum products, paper, food products.

Millet, rice, manioc, peanuts, cotton, gum arabic, beans, sorghum; livestock; uranium, cassiterite, limestone, salt, natron; hides & skins, meat, food & leather products, textiles, cement, peanut oil.

Palm oil and kernels, cocoa, spices, tobacco, peanuts, cotton, rubber, soybeans, corn, rice, millet, coffee; livestock; fish, shrimp; timber; tin, coal, limestone, natural gas, petroleum, marble; metal products, cement, timber & wood products, textiles, beer, refined petroleum, hides & skins, processed foods & oils.

Limes, kumaras, passion fruit, bananas; copra, woven handicrafts.

Potatoes, oats, fruits, vegetables, barley, hay; poultry, livestock; limestone, basalt & igneous rocks, sand & gravel; linen, apparel, wool textiles, dairy products, meat & meat products, aircraft, machinery, tobacco, whiskey, electronic & transportation equipment, ships.

NEW ZEALAND: Mt. Cook, the country's highest peak, and the Southern Alps are seen across Lake Matheson, on the South Island.

Nat'l Publicity Studios

NORWAY: The popular resort of Balestrand, on the Sogne Fjord in western Norway.

Scandinavian Travel Comm'n

Social and Economic Tables

POLITICAL DIVISION	GOVERNMENT	MONETARY UNIT	LANGUAGE	RELIGION
NORWAY	Constitutional hereditary monarchy, with a king, premier, cabinet, and unicamerally elected but bicamerally operating parliament.	Norwegian krone	Norwegian	Protestantism
OMAN	An independent sultanate and an absolute monarchy, with an advisory cabinet.	Omani rial	Arabic Hindi; English	Islam Hinduism
PACIFIC ISLANDS, TRUST TERR.	United States U. N. trusteeship, with a high commissioner. Northern Marianas are to become a U.S. commonwealth.	U.S. dollar	English Micronesian dialects	Roman Catholicism Protestantism
PAKISTAN	Federal republic with a president, presently ruled by a military council and an administrator.	Pakistani rupee	Urdu English Punjabi, Pushtu Sindhi, Baluchi	Islam
PANAMA	Nominal republic with a president and unicameral legislature.	balboa	Spanish	Roman Catholicism
PAPUA NEW GUINEA	Independent British Commonwealth member, with a governor-general, prime minister, cabinet, and unicameral parliament.	kina	English Pidgin English Hiri Motu	Tribal religions Protestantism Roman Catholicism
PARAGUAY	Centralized republic with a president, an appointed cabinet and a bicameral congress.	guaraní	Spanish Indian (Guaraní)	Roman Catholicism
PERU	Nominal republic, presently ruled by a military junta, with a president, prime minister and cabinet.	sol	Spanish Indian (Quechua, Aymará)	Roman Catholicism
PHILIPPINES	Republic governed by a president and an assembly.	piso	Pilipino (Tagalog) English; Spanish	Roman Catholicism Protestantism Islam Tribal religions
PITCAIRN ISLANDS	British colony, with a governor, an island magistrate & council.	New Zealand dollar	English	Seventh Day Adventist
POLAND	Soviet-type republic with a chief of (council of) state, premier, & unicameral parliament; actual power lies with the politburo of the Communist party.	zloty	Polish	Roman Catholicism
PORTUGAL	Constitutional republic with a president, premier, cabinet and unicameral parliament.	escudo	Portuguese	Roman Catholicism
PUERTO RICO	Self-governing commonwealth associated with the United States, with a governor, advisory council, and bicameral congress.	U.S. dollar	Spanish English	Roman Catholicism
QATAR	Independent state with an emir and advisory council.	Qatari riyal	Arabic	Islam
RÉUNION	French overseas department, with a prefect and general council.	French franc	French	Roman Catholicism

MAJOR PRODUCTS

Hay, oats, barley, wheat, rye, potatoes, fruits; livestock; fish; timber; iron ore, petroleum, nickel, zinc, natural gas, coal; pulp, paper, cellulose, ships, aluminum, machinery, chemicals, metal & electro-chemical products, transportation equipment, iron & steel, processed & canned fish & foods, textiles, wool, dairy products, leather, furs.

Wheat, alfalfa, dates, limes, frankincense, coconuts, tobacco; livestock; fish; petroleum; dried fish & limes, ghee.

Vegetables, tropical fruits, coconuts; fish, trochus shell; poultry, livestock; copra, meat, handicrafts.

Cereal grains, cotton, sugarcane, citrus fruits, dates, tobacco; livestock; fish; petroleum, salt, chromite, natural gas, gypsum, limestone; textiles, rugs, apparel, leather, wool, hides & skins, handicrafts, surgical instruments, sporting goods, sugar, chemicals, cement, iron & steel, refined petroleum, electric goods, tires.

Bananas, cocoa, abacá, coconuts, rice, sugarcane, coffee, fruits; fish, shrimp; livestock; timber; beer, sugar, wood & leather products, textiles, refined petroleum, processed foods, cement, apparel, drugs, fishmeal.

Coconuts, coffee, copra, cocoa, rubber, sago, rice, kapok, sisal, bamboo, bananas; dairying, livestock, poultry, fish; timber; gold, silver, copper; tobacco products, boats, brewing.

Cotton, tobacco, sugarcane, cereal grains, yerba maté, soybeans, coffee, citrus fruits; livestock; timber, quebracho; beef, meat products, flour, refined petroleum products, oil-cake & essential oils, hides, textiles, cement.

Cotton, sugarcane, potatoes, cereal grains, beans, potatoes, vegetables, fruits, coffee, guano; fish; livestock; petroleum, lead, zinc, copper, silver, gold, salt, iron ore; textiles, foodstuffs, fishmeal, sugar, cement, apparel, chemicals, refined metals, iron & steel, tires, hides & skins.

Rice, sugarcane, abacá, corn, tobacco, cocoa, coffee, nuts, kapok, peanuts, vegetables, maguey, rubber, fruits; livestock; fish; timber, gum resins; gold, iron ore, copper, chromite, silver, manganese, salt, coal, petroleum; sugar, textiles, rubber & tobacco products; lumber & wood products, autos, handicrafts, milled coconut oil & rice, fruit canning, copra, steel, cement, glass, chemicals, paper.

Fruits, vegetables; goats, poultry; handicrafts, postage stamps.

Potatoes, cereal grains, sugar beets; livestock; fish; timber; coal, lead, zinc, sulphur, iron ore, petroleum, copper, natural gas; iron & steel, chemicals & petrochemicals, coke, electric & electronic equipment, autos, ships, aluminum, metal, food & dairy products, sugar, glass, transportation equipment, cement, machinery, paper.

Cereal grains, potatoes, tomatoes, citrus fruits, grapes, olives; livestock; fish; timber; coal, wolfram, iron ore, sulphur, tungsten; wine, olive oil, cork, canned fish, food products, pulp, refined petroleum, ships, autos, textiles, electronic equipment, machinery, cement, steel.

Sugarcane, tobacco, fruits, coconuts, coffee, cotton, vegetables; livestock; stone, sand & gravel; rum, molasses, sugar, canned fish & fruit, tobacco products, cement, leather, textiles, apparel, petrochemicals, metal & electronic products.

Dates, fruit, vegetables; shrimp, fish; livestock; natural gas, limestone, petroleum; fish products, cement, refined petroleum, petrochemicals.

Sugarcane, tea, tobacco, vanilla, corn, manioc; livestock; essential oils, fruit & vegetable products, rum, sugar, molasses.

PERU: The beginning of festivities in the bull ring in Lima, the capital city.

Pan American World Airways

PORTUGAL: The Praça dos Restauradores in Lisbon, with the monument dedicated to the seventeenth century restorers of Portuguese independence.

Photo "Sni-Yan"

Social and Economic Tables

POLITICAL DIVISION	GOVERNMENT	MONETARY UNIT	LANGUAGE	RELIGION
RUMANIA	A Soviet-type republic with a president, a state council, a cabinet, and a unicameral assembly; actual power resides in Communist party politburo.	leu	Rumanian Hungarian	Rumanian Orthodoxy Roman Catholicism
RWANDA	Nominal republic, at present under military rule by a president and advisory committee.	Rwanda franc	Kinyarwanda French Kiswahili	Roman Catholicism Tribal religions Islam
ST. CHRISTOPHER-NEVIS-ANGUILLA	Associated British state with a governor, prime minister, cabinet & unicameral assembly.	East Caribbean dollar	English	Protestantism
ST. HELENA	British colony with a governor, legislative and executive councils.	pound sterling	English	Protestantism
ST. LUCIA	Independent British Commonwealth state with a governor, prime minister, cabinet & unicameral assembly.	East Caribbean dollar	English French patois	Roman Catholicism Protestantism
ST. PIERRE AND MIQUELON	French overseas department, with a prefect and general council.	CFA franc	French	Roman Catholicism
ST. VINCENT	Associated British state with a governor, prime minister, cabinet & unicameral assembly.	East Caribbean dollar	English	Protestantism Roman Catholicism
SAN MARINO	Republic with two regents, a cabinet, and unicameral council.	Italian lira	Italian	Roman Catholicism
SÃO TOMÉ AND PRÍNCIPE	One-party republic with a president, appointed premier and cabinet, and a unicameral assembly.	São Tomean escudo	Bantu languages Portuguese	Tribal religions Roman Catholicism
SAUDI ARABIA	Absolute monarchy under a king and advisory council of ministers; the king exercises all authority.	Saudi riyal	Arabic	Islam
SCOTLAND	Integral part of United Kingdom, with secretary of state for Scotland in the U.K. cabinet, controlling local agriculture & fisheries, home & health, education, development, & economic planning.	pound sterling	English Gaelic	Protestantism Roman Catholicism
SENEGAL	One-party republic of the French Community, with a president, a prime minister, cabinet and unicameral assembly.	CFA franc	French Sudanese languages	Islam Tribal religions Roman Catholicism
SEYCHELLES	British Commonwealth republic with a president, appointed cabinet and unicameral assembly.	Seychellois rupee	French Creole English; French	Roman Catholicism
SIERRA LEONE	One-party republic of the British Commonwealth, with a president, cabinet and unicameral parliament.	leone	English Sudanese languages Pidgin (Krio)	Tribal religions Islam Christianity
SINGAPORE	Republic of the British Commonwealth, with a president, prime minister, cabinet & unicameral parliament.	Singapore dollar	Chinese (Mandarin) Malay Tamil; Hindi English	Confucianism Buddhism Taoism; Hinduism Islam Christianity
SOLOMON ISLANDS	Independent member of the British Commonwealth with a governor-general, prime minister, cabinet and a unicameral parliament.	Solomon Islands dollar	English Pidgin English Melanesian dialects	Tribal religions Protestantism Roman Catholicism
SOMALIA	One-party republic with a president and advisory cabinet, all power being held by the party's central committee.	Somali shilling	Somali; Arabic English Italian	Islam

MAJOR PRODUCTS

Wheat, barley, corn, potatoes, sugar beets, tobacco, fruits; livestock; timber; petroleum, natural gas, coal, lignite, salt, iron ore, copper, bauxite, manganese, uranium; iron & steel, machinery, chemicals, lumber, wood & paper products, electric goods, refined petroleum, ships, cement, sugar, food products, textiles, metal products.

Coffee, cotton, rice, tea, corn, peanuts, pyrethrum, vegetables; livestock; cassiterite, tungsten, tantalite, beryl, wolfram; textiles, handicrafts, processed foods, beer, hides.

Sugarcane, cotton, rice, vegetables, tropical fruits, corn, yams, coconuts, livestock; fish, shellfish; salt; molasses.

Fruit, vegetables, lily bulbs, flax, sweet potatoes, potatoes; livestock, poultry; cordage, fibers, lace.

Bananas, coconuts, cocoa, tropical & citrus fruits, nutmeg, mace; fish; rum, copra, coconut oil, soap, cigarettes.

Codfish; cattle; sienna earth, yellow ocher; fish products, furs.

Bananas, arrowroot, coconuts, rice, tropical fruits, cotton, corn, spices, peanuts, cocoa; fish; livestock; copra, rum, processed foods, cigarettes.

Wheat, fruits, grapes, vegetables; stone; livestock; textiles, postage stamps, wine, pottery, hides, cement, paper, leather.

Cacao, coffee, coconuts, cinchona, bananas; livestock; palm oil, copra.

Dates, corn, wheat, coffee, fruits, henna, vegetables; fish; livestock; petroleum, gold, silver, gypsum, lead, copper; refined petroleum, petrochemicals, fertilizers, iron & steel, cement, meat & dairy products, hides, wool.

Potatoes, sugar beets, wheat, barley, vegetables, fruits; livestock; fish, shellfish; petroleum, coal, iron ore, lead, stone; iron & steel, machinery, metal, dairy, tobacco & food products, textiles & yarn, watches, transportation equipment, electric & electronic goods, autos, ships, paper, whiskey, refined petroleum, aluminum, chemicals.

Millet, sorghum, rice, corn, peanuts, cotton, fruits, vegetables, sweet potatoes; livestock; fish; phosphates, titanium, limestone; textiles, processed fish & foods, cement, peanut oil & cakes, refined petroleum, chemicals.

Coconuts, cinnamon, patchouli, vanilla, tea; fish, tortoise shell, guano; copra, coconut oil, dried fish, coir, essential oils.

Palm oil & kernels, rice, coffee, kola nuts, ginger, vegetables, cassava, piassava, peanuts, cocoa; livestock; fish, shrimp; diamonds, iron ore, bauxite, rutile; palm products, rice & oil milling.

Rubber, coconuts, fruits, vegetables, rice, coffee, tapioca, tobacco; livestock; fish; tin, rubber & petroleum processing, rice & coconut milling, steel, chemicals, cement, lumber & wood products, textiles, bricks, palm & food products, paper, refined petroleum, drugs, ships, electric goods.

Copra; livestock; fish; timber; copper, bauxite, nickel.

Sugarcane, cotton, cereal grains, peanuts, sesame, tobacco, bananas, beans; livestock; fish, shellfish; salt; fish, food & meat products, sugar, textiles, hides & skins.

PUERTO RICO: One of the island's chief products, pineapples, on their way to the cannery.

Hamilton Wright

SCOTLAND: Loch Garten, a highland lake in the eastern part of Inverness.

British Travel Ass'n

Social and Economic Tables

POLITICAL DIVISION	GOVERNMENT	MONETARY UNIT	LANGUAGE	RELIGION
SOUTH AFRICA	Constitutional republic, with a state president, prime minister, cabinet & bicameral parliament. Transkei was granted independence in 1976; Bophuthatswana in 1977.	rand	Afrikaans English Bantu languages Bushman Tamil; Hindi	Protestantism Roman Catholicism Islam Hinduism Buddhism Judaism
SOUTH-WEST AFRICA (NAMIBIA)	South African controlled territory with an administrator-general.	South African rand	Afrikaans English; German Bantu languages Bushman	Tribal religions Protestantism
SPAIN	Monarchy with a king, premier and cabinet, and a bicameral parliament.	peseta	Spanish (Castilian) Catalan; Valencian Basque Galician	Roman Catholicism
SRI LANKA (CEYLON)	Independent republic of the British Commonwealth, with a president, a prime minister, a cabinet and a unicameral assembly.	Sri Lanka rupee	Sinhala Tamil English	Buddhism Hinduism Christianity Islam
SUDAN	Republic with a president, cabinet and unicameral assembly. Local autonomy has been granted the southern provinces.	Sudanese pound	Arabic English Sudanese and Hamitic languages	Islam Tribal religions Christianity
SURINAME	Independent republic with a president, premier, cabinet, and elective unicameral parliament.	Suriname guilder	Dutch Creole English	Christianity Hinduism Islam
SWAZILAND	British Commonwealth monarchy, with a titular king, prime minister (who rules by decree) and cabinet.	lilangeni	English siSwati Afrikaans	Tribal religions Christianity
SWEDEN	A constitutional hereditary monarchy with a titular king, prime minister, cabinet and a unicameral parliament.	krona	Swedish	Protestantism
SWITZERLAND	Federal republic with a president, vice-president & executive federal council, & a bicameral elected federal assembly.	Swiss franc	German French Italian Romansch	Protestantism Roman Catholicism
SYRIA	Arab republic with a president, premier, and unicameral legislative people's council, appointed by presidential decree.	Syrian pound	Arabic; Armenian Turkish; Kurdish French; English	Islam Christianity
TANZANIA	One-party united republic of the British Commonwealth, with a president, vice-president, prime minister, cabinet and unicameral parlament proportionately representing Tanganyika and Zanzibar.	Tanzanian shilling	Kiswahili English Bantu languages Arabic Gujarati	Tribal religions Islam Christianity Hinduism
THAILAND (SIAM)	Constitutional monarchy, at present under a prime minister and a bicameral assembly.	baht	Thai Khmer; Malay Chinese; Lao	Buddhism Islam Confucianism

of the World

MAJOR PRODUCTS

Cereal grains, tobacco, sugarcane; fruits, peanuts; livestock; fish, lobsters; gold, coal, diamonds, copper, asbestos, manganese, limestone, platinum, chromite, iron ore, vanadium, tin, antimony, uranium; timber; chemicals, wool, iron & steel, machinery, apparel, textiles, fish & food products, sugar, aluminum, metal products, hides, autos, cement, transportation equipment, dairy products.

Livestock; fish, shellfish; diamonds, copper, lead, zinc, salt, tin, manganese, vanadium, iron ore, cadmium, silver, fluorspar, tantalite, phosphate, sulfur, germanium; karakul wool & hides, fish processing, dairy products.

Cereal grains, potatoes, legumes, citrus fruits, vegetables, olives, grapes, sugar beets, esparto, flax, hemp, pulses, nuts, sugarcane; livestock, poultry; fish; timber; coal, lignite, iron ore & pyrites, lead, zinc, mercury, copper, uranium, gypsum; textiles, paper, cement, hides, wine, olive oil, processed foods, cork, machinery, chemicals, leather, autos, refined petroleum, apparel, silk, shoes, processed foods & fruit, iron & steel.

Tea, coconuts, rubber, rice, cotton, spices, cocoa, nuts, sugarcane, fruits; fish; livestock; graphite, mineral sands, ilmenite, gem stones, limestone, salt, pearls; copra, plywood, leather, shoes, glass, steel, acetic acid, ceramics, quinine, strychnine, chemicals, drugs, textiles, cement, beer, refined petroleum, coconut & tobacco products, paper, apparel.

Cotton, cereal grains, gum arabic, oilseeds, senna, castor beans, resins, peanuts, sesame, dom & shea nuts, dates; livestock; ivory, trochus shell, mother-of-pearl; iron ore, manganese, chromite, salt, gold; textiles, cement, hides & skins, cottonseed, oilcake, sugar, leather, paint, soap.

Rice, citrus fruits, coconuts, coffee, bananas, sugarcane, cacao, balata, corn, tobacco; livestock; shrimp; timber; balata; gold, bauxite; sugar, rum, lumber & plywood, molasses, aluminum, food & dairy products.

Tobacco, corn, peanuts, sugarcane, sorghum, cotton, rice, pineapples, citrus fruits; livestock; timber; asbestos, iron ore, coal; meat & dairy products, sugar, pulp, canned fruits, textiles, hides & skins, wood & tobacco products.

Hay, sugar beets, potatoes, oilseeds, oats, wheat, rye, barley; timber; livestock; fish; iron ore, zinc, copper, lead; lumber, paper & wood products, machinery, textiles, iron & steel, metal & electric goods, chemicals, dairy, food & tobacco products, porcelain, glass, ships, furs, transportation equipment, matches, autos, munitions, liquor, instruments.

Cereal grains, sugar beets, potatoes, vegetables, fruits, tobacco; livestock; timber; salt, iron ore, manganese; dairy & tobacco products, watches & clocks, electric & glass products, instruments, jewelry, machinery, metal products, chocolate, wine, drugs, textiles & yarn, chemicals, aluminum, iron & steel, cement, sugar, meat, apparel, dyes, foods.

Cereal grains, cotton, vegetables, olives, grapes, sugar beets, tobacco; livestock; petroleum, natural gas, phosphates, gypsum; leather, textiles, cement, refined petroleum, wool, hides & skins, sugar, processed foods & oils, apparel, glass, tobacco goods.

Sisal, fruits, cocoa, coconuts, cotton, cloves, pyrethrum, spices, coffee, tobacco, nuts, tea, oilseeds, sugarcane; livestock; hides & skins; diamonds, gold, phosphates, mica, salt, tin, gem stones; processed foods, cement, textiles, refined petroleum, copra, hides & skins, sugar, dairy & wood products, cordage, rolled iron & aluminum.

Rice, coconuts, sugarcane, rubber, peanuts, tobacco, tapioca, jute, kenaf, cotton, corn; teak & other timber; livestock; fish; tin, wolfram, lead; lac, sugar, cement, textiles, tobacco & petroleum products, paper.

SOUTH AFRICA: Commissioner Street, in the downtown part of Johannesburg, the country's largest city.
South African Gov't Info. Office

SWITZERLAND: Milk still being delivered by dog cart in a rural section of the republic.
TWA–Trans World Airlines

235

Social and Economic Tables

POLITICAL DIVISION	GOVERNMENT	MONETARY UNIT	LANGUAGE	RELIGION
TOGO	One-party republic with a president and an appointed civilian-military cabinet.	CFA franc	French Sudanese languages	Tribal religions Roman Catholicism Islam
TOKELAU	An island territory of New Zealand governed by an administrator.	New Zealand dollar	Samoan	Protestantism Roman Catholicism
TONGA	Constitutional British Commonwealth monarchy, with a king, appointed prime minister, and unicameral assembly.	pa'anga	Tongan English	Protestantism Roman Catholicism
TRINIDAD AND TOBAGO	Independent British Commonwealth republic with a president, prime minister, cabinet and bicameral parliament.	Trinidad and Tobago dollar	English Hindi	Protestantism Roman Catholicism Hinduism; Islam
TUNISIA	Republic with a president (for life), an appointed premier and cabinet, and an elective unicameral assembly.	Tunisian dinar	Arabic French Berber	Islam
TURKEY	Constitutional republic with a president, premier, cabinet, and a bicameral parliament.	Turkish lira	Turkish Kurdish Arabic	Islam
TUVALU	Independent member of the British Commonwealth with a governor-general, prime minister and a unicameral parliament.	Australian dollar	English Samoan	Protestantism
UGANDA	Republic of the British Commonwealth with a provisional government, president and cabinet.	Ugandan shilling	English; Kiswahili Sudanese, Bantu, and Hamitic languages	Christianity Tribal religions Islam
U.S.S.R.	Federation of 15 union republics with a bicameral Supreme Soviet, which elects the presidium & council of ministers. Real power is largely exercised by the politburo & secretariat (under its general secretary) of the central committee of the Communist party.	ruble	Russian, Ukrainian, White Russian, Uzbek, Tatar, Azerbaidzhani, Georgian, Lithuanian, Latvian, Mordvinian, Chuvash, Tadzhik, Estonian, Kazakh, etc.	Russian Orthodoxy Islam Roman Catholicism Judaism
UNITED ARAB EMIRATES	Constitutional Arab federation of seven sheikhdoms, with a president, vice-president, premier and cabinet and a unicameral assembly.	U.A.E. dirham	Arabic	Islam
UNITED KINGDOM	See: England and Wales, Northern Ireland, Scotland.			
UNITED STATES	Federal republic with a president, vice-president, an appointed cabinet, and a bicameral congress (senate and house of representatives). It consists of 50 states, each with a governor and a state legislature (all except Nebraska being bicameral).	U.S. dollar	English	Protestantism Roman Catholicism Judaism
UPPER VOLTA	Republic with a president, premier and a unicameral assembly.	CFA franc	French Sudanese languages	Tribal religions Islam Roman Catholicism

of the World

MAJOR PRODUCTS

Palm oil & kernels, manioc, kapok, cocoa, coconuts, yams, cereal grains, coffee, cotton, peanuts, nuts, cassava; livestock; timber; phosphates, limestone; textiles, copra, cement.

Coconuts, fiber, taro; pigs, chickens; fish; hats, mats, copra.

Coconuts, bananas, yams, breadfruit, taro, cassava, papayas, pineapples, melons, tobacco, corn, peanuts, candlenuts; fish; livestock, poultry; copra, processed fruits.

Coffee, cocoa, coconuts, sugarcane, citrus fruits; cattle; timber; petroleum, natural gas, asphalt, coal, clay; rum, textiles, sugar, chemicals, plastic, glass, clay, wood & food products, cement, electric goods, refined petroleum.

Cereal grains, grapes, esparto, olives, vegetables, nuts, fruits, dates; cork, timber; livestock; fish; phosphates, petroleum, iron ore, lead, zinc; flour, wine, olive oil, sugar, wool, pottery, leather, textiles, food processing, chemicals, iron & steel, paper, refined petroleum, metal & electric goods.

Tobacco, cereal grains, cotton, fruits, opium, seeds, olives, nuts, sugar beets; livestock; fish; timber; chromite, iron ore, petroleum, copper, coal, lignite; textiles, iron & steel, chemicals, refined petroleum, rugs, paper, olive oil, wool, furs, sugar, mohair, silk, cement, skins.

Copra, fish, handicrafts, postage stamps.

Cotton, coffee, tea, plaintains, sisal, peanuts, millet, corn, tobacco, sugarcane; livestock; salt, copper, gold, phosphates, tin; cement, beverages, sugar, chemicals, smelted copper, processed foods, textiles, hides & skins, steel.

Cereal grains, sugar beets, cotton, flax, potatoes, seeds, vegetables, tobacco; livestock; fish; timber; petroleum, natural gas, bauxite, uranium, platinum, iron ore, lead, zinc, copper, phosphates, mercury, gold, manganese, nickel, chromite, asbestos, potash; iron & steel, machinery, chemicals, refined petroleum, petrochemicals, ships, autos, aircraft, lumber & wood products, meat & dairy products, textiles, wool, sugar, tools & metal products, aluminum, furs, cement, paper, electric goods, instruments, transportation equipment, foods & beverages.

Dates, cereal grains, vegetables; livestock; fish, pearl fishing; petroleum; cement, refined petroleum, petrochemicals, postage stamps, dried fish.

Cereal grains, hay, soybeans, potatoes, peanuts, sugar beets, sugarcane, vegetables, nuts, fruits, cotton, tobacco, flax; livestock, poultry; fish, shellfish; timber; petroleum, natural gas, coal, iron ore, copper, lead, zinc, gold, silver, molybdenum, bauxite, gypsum, phosphates, sulphur, stone, sand & gravel; iron & steel, machinery, transportation equipment, metal products, electric & electronic goods, autos, ships, aircraft, munitions, chemicals, tobacco, leather, rubber & plastic products, glass, wool, textiles, cement, food & dairy products, lumber & wood products, paper, refined petroleum, petrochemicals.

Cereal grains, sweet potatoes, peanuts, cassava, karite (shea nuts), vegetables, cotton, sisal, sesame, tea; livestock; gold, manganese, copper; hides & skins, meat products, sugar, flour, textiles, processed foods & oils, soap, cigarettes.

THAILAND: The heroine and hero in costume for a classical dance in the Asian kingdom.

Gov't of Thailand

TURKEY: The Galata Bridge, spanning the Golden Horn in Istanbul, one of the most heavily traveled bridges in the world.

Turkish Info. Office

Social and Economic Tables

POLITICAL DIVISION	GOVERNMENT	MONETARY UNIT	LANGUAGE	RELIGION
URUGUAY	A republic governed by a president, cabinet and a council of state.	Uruguayan **peso**	Spanish	Roman Catholicism
VATICAN CITY	The Pope exercises absolute legislative, executive & judicial power.	Italian lira	Italian Latin	Roman Catholicism
VENEZUELA	Constitutional federal republic with a president, appointive cabinet, and an elected bicameral congress.	bolívar	Spanish	Roman Catholicism
VIETNAM	Communist republic with a president, premier and unicameral assembly; actual rule is by the party's central committee and politburo.	dong	Vietnamese Khmer; Cham Lao French; Chinese Montagnard	Buddhism Taoism Confucianism Roman Catholicism Tribal religions
VIRGIN ISLANDS (BR.)	British colony with an administrator, chief minister and councils.	B. W. I. dollar; U.S. dollar	English Creole	Protestantism
VIRGIN ISLANDS (U.S.)	Unincorporated U.S. territory with an elected governor & unicameral legislature.	U.S. dollar	English Creole	Roman Catholicism Protestantism
WALLIS & FUTUNA	French overseas territory with an administrator, & a local council and assembly.	CFP franc	French Polynesian dialects	Roman Catholicism
WESTERN SAMOA	Independent member of the British Commonwealth, with a head of state, prime minister, cabinet and unicameral legislative assembly.	tala	Samoan English	Protestantism Roman Catholicism
YEMEN ARAB REP.	Arab republic with a president, premier and cabinet, and an advisory military council.	Yemeni riyal	Arabic	Islam
YEMEN, PEOPLES DEM. REP. OF	One-party Arab republic with a presidential council.	South Yemeni dinar	Arabic	Islam
YUGOSLAVIA	A Soviet-type federal republic with a president (for life), premier and federal executive council, and a bicameral assembly. Actually ruled by the Communist party.	Yugoslav dinar	Serbian-Croatian Slovenian Macedonian Montenegrin	Eastern Orthodoxy Roman Catholicism Islam
ZAIRE	One-party republic with a president, premier, executive council and unicameral legislative council; rule is by decree.	zaire	Bantu languages French	Tribal religions Roman Catholicism
ZAMBIA	One-party republic of the British Commonwealth, with a president, prime minister, cabinet, and a unicameral assembly.	Zambian kwacha	Bantu languages English	Tribal religions Christianity Hinduism Islam
ZIMBABWE RHODESIA	Self-proclaimed independent state with a president, premier, council of state, cabinet and parliament.	Zimbabwe Rhodesian dollar	English Bantu languages	Tribal religions Protestantism Islam

of the World

MAJOR PRODUCTS

Cereal grains, seeds, peanuts, fruits, hops, sugar beets, grapes, tobacco; livestock, meat & meat products, hides, wool, textiles, leather, wines, chemicals, refined petroleum, aluminum, steel, cement, sugar, metal products.

Postage stamps, religious articles.

Coffee, cotton, cocoa, sugarcane, cereal grains, tobacco, beans, sisal, balata, rubber, bananas; livestock; fish, shrimp; petroleum, natural gas, iron ore, gold, coal, phosphates, nickel, salt, diamonds; leather, rubber, metal & wood products, sugar, food, dairy & meat products, vehicles, chemicals, refined petroleum, petrochemicals, paper, steel, transportation equipment, apparel.

Rice, corn, sugarcane, coffee, fruits, nuts, vegetables, tea, manioc, peanuts, sweet potatoes, tobacco, cotton, rubber, silk; livestock, poultry; fish, shellfish; timber; coal, iron ore, chromite, uranium, phosphates, gold, tin; paper, textiles, chemicals, machinery, tobacco, lumber & wood products, sugar, processed foods, glass, beer, handicrafts, steel.

Bananas, tropical fruits, coconuts, vegetables; livestock, poultry; fish, turtles; handicrafts, rum, petroleum refining.

Vegetables, sugarcane, citrus fruits, coconuts; cattle; fish; rum, bay rum & oil, molasses, handicrafts, sugar, lime juice, hides, bitters.

Coconuts, bananas, taro, yams, cassava, arrowroot, vegetables; livestock, poultry; fish, trochus shell; copra, handicrafts.

Breadfruit, coconuts, coffee, fruits, seeds, yams, pawpaws, cocoa, bananas, taro; fish; timber; livestock; copra, handicrafts, hides, lumber, processed foods, apparel, beverages, soap.

Coffee, cereal grains, cotton, grapes, fruits, qat, sesame; cattle; fish; rock salt; textiles, hides, leather, handicrafts.

Dates, cereal grains; coffee, qat, gums, tobacco, cotton, fruit, sesame; livestock; fish; salt; ship bunkering, refined petroleum, hides & skins, textiles, fish products.

Cereal grains, sugar beets, tobacco, potatoes, seeds, hemp, nuts, fruits; livestock; fish; timber; coal, gold, iron ore, manganese, petroleum, bauxite, chromite, mercury, antimony, copper, lead, zinc, salt; textiles, lumber & wood products, cement, sugar, food & metal products, machinery, chemicals, iron & steel, ships, wine.

Palm oil & kernels, cotton, coffee, tea, cocoa, rice, sugarcane, rubber; livestock; ivory, timber; copper, diamonds, gold, cobalt, tantalite, petroleum, zinc, manganese, bauxite, cassiterite; textiles, processed foods, sugar, rubber products.

Cereal grains, tobacco, peanuts, cassava, sugarcane, fruits, cotton; timber; fish; livestock; copper, lead, coal, manganese, zinc, cobalt; iron & steel, metal & tobacco products, textiles, chemicals, refined petroleum & copper, processed foods & beverages, sugar, drugs, tires.

Corn, tobacco, peanuts, wheat, cotton, tea, sugarcane, citrus fruits; livestock; fish; copper, gold, asbestos, chromite, coal; textiles, apparel, cigarettes, wood, food, dairy & rubber products, meat & meat products, sugar, iron & steel, vehicles, electrical goods, metal products, chemicals, hides.

UNITED STATES: The American Falls at Niagara Falls, New York, a major tourist attraction.

N.Y. State Dep't of Commerce

VENEZUELA: Avenida Bolívar and the thirty story office buildings of downtown Caracas.

Hamilton Wright

ECUADOR: Independence Plaza in Quito, with the Cathedral, the center of tourist activity in the country.

Hamilton Wright

ENGLAND: Trafalgar Square and the famous pillar dedicated to Lord Nelson, in London.

British Info. Services

AUSTRALIA: A view of Sydney Harbour, with the botanical gardens at Farm Cove in the foreground.

Qantas

INDIA: The Hawa Mahal at Jaipur, in the state of Rajasthan, with old and new forms of transportation.

Gov't of India Info. Bur.

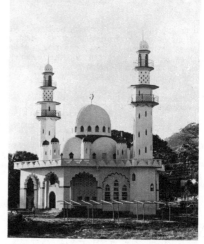

TRINIDAD & TOBAGO: A typical mosque in Port of Spain.

Trinidad & Tobago Tourist Board

INDEX OF PRINCIPAL CITIES OF THE WORLD

This alphabetical list of cities and towns gives statistics of population based on the latest official census reports or most recent reliable estimates. Each line begins with the name of a place, followed by the name of the country or state, the population, the index reference and plate number. This index reference gives the location of the city or town name on ,the accompanying map plates. The name is found within the square formed by the two lines of latitude or longitude which enclose each of the co-ordinates—i.e. the marginal letters and numbers. In the case of maps consisting entirely of insets, the name is found near the intersection point of imaginary lines' connecting the co-ordinates.

Where space on the map has not permitted giving the complete form of a name, the extended form is shown in the index. Where a place may be known under different names or by various spellings of the same name, the different forms have been included, to a large extent, in the index. Where an alternative spelling in parentheses is shown on the map itself, the first name gives the local official form, the conventional form following in parentheses.

* Capitals of countries, states and provinces. † Population figure includes suburbs or subdivision.